Whispers of Truth

Whispers of Truth

Rosemary Burgo

2007

Whispers of Truth

JOURNEY BACK

Tentatively, I hand you over little one
And shine the light into those dark corners that surrounded
you
It is your voice that will speak now, and it is safe you can show
your tears today, and forget to be brave

I tried to keep you from harm but it's time now to tell your
story
You were the best of me, always
I'm sorry I didn't know how to cherish you, or nurture you
But I knew enough to keep you close in the hopes that the day
would come I could set you free

I hope you're met with love and bring the joys to others you
have brought to me
For the darkest days were made lighter thinking of you

You who only wanted love and deserved to be cherished
I know you will never belong solely to me again for I have
untied your wings and pray that you have not forgotten how
to fly
Forgive me, little one- it took so long and sometimes I forgot
you were there
As I wore the apparel of mature success, I forgot to remember
the purity of your laugh and the way joy really felt

They didn't destroy you because the hiding place I chose was
very deep. But it's safe now
So tentatively, I hand you over knowing you are even more
beautiful because of your uncertainty.

ACKNOWLEDGEMENTS

Thanks to Heather Quirke for her expert technical assistance and to Claire Szostak who, having typed this book, was the first to read it. Thanks Claire for your exceptional skills and gentleness. Thanks also to Lorraine DeNinno for her artistic skills and to Scott Daily for his graphic design.

Thanks also to Mary Anne Dooley whose life-long friendship and unadulterated support and encouragement mean everything. And to Carole Kunicki, whose innocence and kindness gave me pause to remember and so to write.

Thanks to Betty Ann Forte for her insistence that this book be published and published it is due to that insistence. Thanks also to Diane Gervasi who supports me in all things and has borne the brunt of listening to so many details of this book's publication with grace. Thanks to Marianne Crisafulli, the first "non-involved" party to read this book, for her encouragement and understanding.

Thanks to Matt Parks, my mentor, who despite his pragmatic nature, always encouraged my fanciful bent and writing.

Thanks to my family—those who have passed and those who remain. From each of you, I have received a gift. Thanks especially to Aunt Jo and Rosetta for your sustained kindness and love during my losses.

But I must extend special thanks to my mother, Millie Burgo, who in giving me a sense of humor about myself and a belief in God, is responsible for my joyful and productive life. You were everything mom. Thank you.

For my Grandmother, Rose Burgo, who saved me.

<u>*September 16th, 1954*</u>

Today is my ninth birthday. My mother says I'm not having a party because my father's in the hospital, but she's probably only joking. I've never not had a party since I was born and she'll be home from the hospital early enough for me to have one, so I must remember to act surprised. My birthdays have always been very important. My mother says my father went AWOL from the Army when I was born, refusing to go to war until he saw me. My grandmother even hid him from the FBI. That makes me feel really special. My mother also says I weighed 7 pounds, 11 ounces when I was born and that, she says, is a very, very lucky number. I was born on a Sunday, which is also good because it's God's day of rest.

My name is Milissa Maroni and they call me Missy. My friends always say Missy Maroni like it's one word. At school, they call me Macaroni, but my grandmother says that's because my teeth don't stick out or because I don't have a big nose. She says all kids tease you when they like you. Well, I wish they'd liked me less or something. That Macaroni joke is getting old.

I am the oldest of three children. I have a brother two years younger, Vince, and a sister, Catherine, six years younger. My brother, Vince, is retarded. Once I was ashamed of him and felt so bad that every time people ask me now if I have sisters or brothers, I always say I have a sister and a brother, who's retarded. I figure I'll do this as penance for being ashamed, probably until I die.

We're Italian and we're Catholic. And being ashamed of your family is probably the worst thing you could ever do. I try to help Vince and all. I'm not a monster, but sometimes he gets on my nerves. My sister gets on my nerves too. Everyone says I'm a poor eater, eat too much junk food, and am too skinny. I think to be skinny to Italians is both an original and mortal sin, especially to my grandmother. But I do like candy and potato chips. So one day, I decided that my mother wouldn't give me any chips, so I asked my sister to ask her for a bag. I figured she'd get it because she eats very well, and also because she's the baby and very cute. So, she goes up to my mother and says, "Missy wants a bag of potato chips." Boy, did I want to kill her. I figure it was the least she could do for me since she's going through this phase where she can't fall asleep unless someone sits with her. Every night at 7 o'clock, I have to sit with her until she falls asleep, and miss my TV shows. So one night I asked her if she was asleep, and she said, "Yes." That's how stupid she is. So I pinched her. Sometimes I get frustrated. I hate being the oldest, but for the most part I'm nice to them. If you ask me, they get away with murder. Vince is sick, Cathy's a baby, you should know better. I often wonder if it ever occurred to them that I'm only nine.

I hear my mother coming in from the hospital and she has no cake. She goes upstairs and brings down a box, unwrapped, there it is, my birthday gift - a car coat, an ugly beige car coat with buttons that look like those candy barrels. I hate it.

She wasn't kidding. There's no cake, nothing. She told me I was lucky to get the car coat. I can't understand how she doesn't know how important today is. Birthdays only come once a year. A cake wouldn't have made a difference to anybody. After all, my father's not dying. But she's saying I have to understand that sometimes there are more important things in the world than me, and that I shouldn't be so selfish. I tune her out. And now I'm going to have to go to confession again because apparently with one disappointed look, I committed the sins of not caring for anybody but myself, not loving my father, and being ungrateful. They're three big sins around here, and in the Catholic Church too. As penance, I'll probably have to go to 10 masses and maybe even have to say the Stations of the Cross a few times. There's another sin I committed that she didn't pick up on. I was very mad, so mad that I could have spit. She sent me to my room anyway. Some birthday. No one even kissed me. I think I'm adopted. When I say this to my mother, she usually answers, "Yeah, just what I needed, a baby at 17." I guess that means I'm not, but I'll tell you the truth, I'm not like anybody around here, and if I didn't look a little like my father, I would be sure I was adopted.

September 18th, 1954

Today is Saturday, the day Confessions are heard, and I have to go. I attend Catholic school and am in the fourth grade. Every Sunday we have to go to Mass with our class, and the nuns watch us like hawks to see who goes to Communion and who doesn't. "Bless me, Father, for I have sinned, it's been one week since my last Confession. I was selfish on one occasion. I was ungrateful once. I was disrespectful to my parents two times. I lied three times. I got angry once." Then I tell Father Romano how sorry I am and he says, "For your penance, say five Hail Marys and five Our Fathers." And I float out of the confessional because he didn't give me any Stations of the Cross or Masses. Ten prayers are a cinch. I bless myself; and as I'm leaving the confessional, I feel that probably being glad that I got such a small penance is a sin too. But I can't go back in and tell Father that I was happy because I wasn't given a long penance; then he would probably give me a different one which, as I see it, could either make me happy again or angry, which is a sin too. I don't think Father Romano wants to hear my confession all day so I just tell God I'm sorry if my reaction is not holy. I really hope he hears me because I don't want to receive Communion tomorrow with a mortal sin on my soul. That is a biggie, I'm sure you go to hell for that. We're told in school that if you die with a mortal sin (serious offenses) on your soul, you go to hell, a venial sin (lesser offenses) sends you to Purgatory, and if you are without sin then, and only then, do you go to heaven. I always wish that when I die I can make a Confession at the very second before I die because that's the only way I'm going up to heaven. You see, thoughts can be sins too. If you think it, you've done it. That's what the nuns and priests say. So I've killed about five people so far, my sister twice.

October 13th, 1954

I won a spelling bee today. Everybody tells me I'm smart. I changed schools this year. I used to go to Saints Peter and Paul, and now I go to Our Lady of Mount Carmel. They seem the same to me, but I'm happy we moved because I was starting to get a reputation in Saints Peter and Paul for always being late. Sometimes my mother worked and wasn't home to get me up, so I had to get up myself and didn't always get up on time. Sister Cabrini told me when I was in the third grade that if I was late one more time, I would be in big, big trouble. The very next day I was late, so I decided I'd play hooky from school. I hid in the bushes behind our house and waited for the kids to walk home for lunch. When they passed by, I strolled into my house, pretending to be home for lunch. But my mother knew I played hooky because this old guy next door told her. I don't remember if I had lunch, but I do remember my mother marching me to school. Seriously, we marched. She was going to teach me a lesson I didn't really want to learn. She explained to Sister Cabrini the huge sin I had committed and they smiled at each other, these two lovers of children, and then she left. Sister slapped me right in the face in the hallway and I peed my pants, which made the trouble I was already in much worse. I could always count on my bladder giving in to pressure. I didn't like Sister Cabrini because once she called me to the front of the class and told everyone that my uniform was too short. I wanted to die right there. I had a crush on Bobby Lagis and I couldn't even look at him because I was so embarrassed. At least, no one laughed. But I felt poor. I had never felt poor until that day. My mother said she couldn't afford a new uniform. Maybe that's why we moved.

November 12th, 1954

My mother is going to have another baby, just what I need. I don't want her to have any more. She doesn't have enough time for anything now. Everybody's really happy and saying that maybe it will be a boy. That the great Lawrence Maroni should have a son, and that makes me really mad. What am I, nothing? And what about Vince? He's a boy. He's a son. I don't understand why they are making such a big deal. My mother's stomach is sticking out just a little, and she says the baby's inside. That's too stupid for words. My cousin, Rosalie Maroni, is nine months older than me and she said that the man sticks his privates into a woman's thing and that's how they get a baby. First, I thought she was making it up but after a while, I knew it was true. And I told her I'm never, ever going to do that because it sounded awful and like it would hurt. She says that it feels good. I'm not sure where she's getting her information. She also told me that blood will someday come from down there and then I will know I'm a woman. This is too much so I call her on it. And my aunt, her mother, says it's true. I don't think I'll ever grow up. They're both smiling at one another. Probably they're teasing me like when my Aunt Estelle gave me liver for dinner and told me it was steak. Probably they're only making a joke because that can't be true.

November 26th, 1954

It's Thanksgiving and I hate it. All this food and I'll be in trouble before the first course is over. The first course is escarole soup which I eat because I like the meatballs. So far, so good. The next course is ravioli which I love but I'm already stuffed from the meatballs. I eat one ravioli. I look around at the many happy faces eating and I realize I just don't get it. I can't figure out why they make such a big deal about eating. You chew for one minute and then it's gone. Now bubblegum, that is good. It lasts for 10 to 15 minutes, at which time you can put in another piece. The first burst of flavor isn't always the best. It has to be chewed about six times before you get the full flavor. Uh oh, here it comes, "Soda's going down but not the food, right Missy? Take that soda away from her. Eat. Why aren't you eating? She's nothing but a *lick-a-lick*." This happens every time we have a big dinner, my grandmother then starts talking quietly in Italian. This is becoming a huge problem. They're always saying I'm too skinny, I'm going to die if I don't eat. My father says that it's disgusting to watch me eat. I wait for the words "Leave the table," but they never come. Instead, my mother says I am not leaving the table until I eat everything on my plate. This is going to be a long night. I often wonder why they can't figure out that if I don't eat it when it's hot, I surely won't eat it when it's cold. But they never do. That's another reason why I think I'm adopted. Everybody in this family loves to eat and they're big. I hate to eat and I'm a "toothpick." That's what they call me. They also call me "skinny" and "speed." Speed is for a different reason though. They say I move too slowly, so they call me "Speedy." They're funny people. My father bought a movie camera and a film starring StepandFetchIt because he said it reminded him of me. He always makes it run backwards, and that's really funny.

After dinner, I thought I'd be helpful (they like that) so I carried the pie dish into the shed where all the women are washing the dishes. I ask, since I thought you were supposed to if you didn't know, where to put the dish. My Aunt Stell says, "On the floor." So I put the plate on the floor and leave. Everyone is laughing hysterically. I still don't know why. They always laugh at me. My grandmother says I have "no sense, no feeling." My mother says, "As smart as she is, that's as dumb as she is." Sometimes I'm not really there when they're talking because I like to daydream. I'm also told a lot that I have no common sense. What is common sense, I wonder, and I hope I get some. I really don't like it when they laugh at me. I pretend to laugh, but I don't like it. Most of the time I just don't even understand. Like the other day I was cutting my toenails and I cut the index finger on my left hand. I ran to my mother and she started to laugh until tears rolled down her face. I could tell she couldn't wait to tell everybody. Then, they'd all laugh. When you cut your toenails, your left hand holds your foot. So, why is it so funny? I don't get it.

Sometimes, I look at these people and wonder what they're talking about, why they yell and carry on. And it's then that I think that I'm adopted. Maybe I really don't look like my father that much at all.

December 17th, 1954

It's almost Christmas. My mother left four stupid board games on the chair in my room. I guess that's what I'm getting.

The top one is a presidents game. Yuck. This "smart" thing is being carried much too far. I wanted a bike, but my mother says it's too dangerous, I'll get hurt. But I ride pretty good. My cousin, Rosalie, said that all I had to do was get on her two-wheeler, say a prayer to the Blessed Mother, and I would be able to ride. And that's just what I did, but Rosalie wasn't too happy about that. Now I have to beg her to let me ride her bike. Once a week, she might let me, but she'll only allow me to go up one block and then I have to get off. She's so selfish. She has a whole shed full of toys, but she won't let me play with them unless I beg; and even then, only sometimes. When I was about seven, she was given a beautiful—and I mean beautiful—doll from a friend of her father's she said liked her a lot. So I went to church and prayed to God that this friend would like me too and give me a doll just like hers. It never happened though. I don't like dolls any more, so it doesn't matter. They are ever so boring. My last doll was a Betsy Wetsy and you fed her water and she peed. Big whoop. After the first time, it was really boring.

My father told me that there was no Santa Claus when I was about seven. My cousin had already told me, but I figured I'd pretend I still believed because if I didn't, I wouldn't get what I wanted. I remember when he told me, we were walking down Spruce Street, going to my grandmother's, and he was holding my hand. I knew it was coming so I tried to will him not to tell me, but he did, and then he said the words I dreaded hearing, "You must understand that Mommy and Daddy don't have a lot of money, so remember that when you ask for what you want." Bummer, drummer. This "you must understand" crap is really getting to me. Since the games are on my chair, there won't be any surprises Christmas morning. I can't even complain about it because my mother will say she only got an apple when she was small, and my father will say I'm ungrateful. And then they'll say that toys are a waste, just like kids. They don't feel like a waste when I play with my cousin's on the rare occasions I'm allowed. My cousin and I have $10 each to spend for Christmas. There is a small store around the corner on Third Street which sells everything. I buy my father a key chain; my mother a bottle of really good perfume ($3); my grandmother a handkerchief; and my brother a Yo-Yo. My sister's only three, so I buy her a coloring book and crayons. Then I need to buy wrapping paper so I can try to wrap my gifts. I find it really hard to wrap, and my mother always says I'm not too good with my hands. She is very good.

<u>December 25th, 1954</u>

It's Christmas morning and I haven't slept since 4 a.m. I can't wait to go down and see what I got. I wait until it's light so I can tiptoe down the stairs. There they are—four games, unwrapped. Surprise! Nothing else. I try to make a fuss over the games but it's really hard when you're trying to hold back tears. I did get some clothes and pajamas too.

Now all I have to look forward to is the family dinner. I won't think about it now because it will be just like Thanksgiving. That's guaranteed.

<u>January 15th, 1955</u>

My mother's stomach is really getting big like a watermelon. I guess the new addition will be coming soon. She says it's due in March. I hope she stops having kids because all my friends have older brothers and sisters or none, except me. I'm ashamed that my parents still have sex. My friends' parents don't, I think. One time I went into my parents' bedroom and they were naked. I was embarrassed all day. All my friends have mothers and fathers who are old-fashioned and old but me. I wonder if it's a sin to have sex when you're married. My mother says that no one should see me naked. They're probably both going to hell. I hope they don't leave 25 kids before they do. Because being the oldest, no doubt, I'll be expected to take care of them. I also wonder why parents only say, "You're the oldest," and never, "You're the youngest," or, "You're in the middle." Like I don't know I'm the oldest. They say it all the time. And it's usually followed by what I have to do or should have done, need to learn or didn't learn. Every time they say it, I feel bad about myself. I wish I didn't have any brothers and sisters. They're nothing but problems for me. I have one question that I always ask God: if I should know better, like they say all the time, and I'm so smart, like they say all the time, how come I don't know better (like they say all the time)?

February 10th, 1955

Valentine's Day is on the 14th and I got this huge box of really cute cards. I'll send them to everyone in my class, even the boys I don't like, because I don't want to hurt anybody's feelings. I have lots of friends, but my best friend is Mary Lou Carl, and she is a "medigan." That's what they say, so I ask what a "medigan" is and I'm told that's anybody who isn't Italian. It seems the world is divided into Italians and "medigans," but also colored people and Jews. They call my Aunt Stell a Polack. So I guess the world is divided five ways. I ask my mother what a Polack is and she says that's a person who's Polish. Polish and polish are spelled the same, I found out. Since that didn't satisfy me, I ask what Polish means and she says that my aunt's parents were from Poland and ours were from Italy. I ask her then if my aunt was a "medigan." This seemed to be too much for her because she then said I ask too many questions. Even though Mary Lou is a "medigan," everybody likes her anyway. She's really pretty and nice. Everybody in our class has dark hair and eyes, and she has blonde hair and hazel eyes, so she is exotic. She said she's Yugoslavian. Wow! I told her she probably shouldn't tell anybody that, especially those silly boys, or they'll make fun of her by saying, you———go, something or other. I shudder at the possibilities. Mary Lou is an only child and her mother worries about her all the time. I don't think my mother worries about me since I'm the oldest and all.

I'm in the choir now and I have to get up really early because we sing at dead masses, masses said when people die. We took over my grandmother's store this year and I like it because we have a shower. We didn't have any tub where we lived before and I used to get washed in a big tin tub or come to my grandmother's. I would rather have a tub, but the shower's pretty good. We also have a dining room and four bedrooms instead of two, and the house is really pretty. Anyway, I have to get up real early to make my lunch. All the kids at school wonder what their mothers made them for lunch, and then they look disgusted because all they got was an apple instead of cookies or a Tastykake. I get to make what I want, but I still tell them my mother makes it because I don't want them to think that my mother doesn't love me or worry that I eat right. When I open my lunch bag, I even act surprised and I have to confess this every week. I told my mother that I felt bad about her not making my lunch and she started to make it, and now she's even leaving notes in it like "You better eat all of this." That makes me very happy and I show everybody, and they all laugh, and I feel like everybody else whose mother loves and worries about them.

My cousin told me once when I was seven that the reason I could do so many dangerous physical things was because my mother didn't watch me. That she didn't care what I did because probably she didn't love me, having all those other kids and all.

I got really mad at my cousin, but she was right about the part that my mother didn't worry about what I was doing. I would hang by the back of my legs on a rail and jump from high steps. I didn't know it was dangerous or anything. I hope she isn't right about my mother not loving me because of the others and all. Maybe some people don't have a lot of love to give. My mother never kisses me, my father either. I never sit on my mother's lap because she has all these other kids and she doesn't want to be bothered most of the time. Once I took a trip with my Uncle Carmen and his family, and I was sitting in the back of the car with his sister-in-law, Ann, and she told me if I wanted, I could lay my head on her shoulder. I wanted to do that a whole lot, but I couldn't because I thought I would be bothering her, and maybe she was just being nice. I sit on my grandmother's lap all the time. She is very big and smells like Chantilly perfume. I feel like I'm on a bed when I sit on her. I feel happy, though, really happy and safe.

When I stayed with my aunt and uncle, I pretended I had a stomach ache. I knew I was pretending too. I remember they gave me a bubble bath and warm milk with honey, and that was the first time I had either. My Aunt Jo is the most beautiful person I ever saw, and she has a voice that reminds me of bells because it always sounds happy. I like it even if she just says my name, my uncle too. And they talk real quietly and smile all the time. When I stayed over, it was Christmas time, and they took me to this large department store in Philadelphia where there was a big Christmas display with a chute which delivered a gift to me. Everything seemed real and large and beautiful. I still believed in Santa then, so it was all like a wonderful dream. I don't remember lots of kisses, but they would always hold my hand and motion for me to sit on their laps. And sometimes when we were walking, my uncle would just pick me up, just like that, on the street.

We played all kinds of games. My aunt has a niece, Lucy, who's my age and she's very nice. I went to her house one afternoon and she got mad at her mother and wouldn't talk to her. I couldn't believe it. Her mother was tickling her and trying to make her laugh. I never saw anything like it. I wondered what my mother would do if I got mad, so when I got home, I tried it. I scrunched my face up into a pout, just like Lucy had done, and my mother never even noticed.

I remember crying when I got home, and that made my mother mad. She asked me why I was crying, but I didn't know. It had been so nice and I was going to miss them, I think. Our house always seemed very empty after that.

Lucy and I both were flower girls in my aunt and uncle's wedding. We were both 6. And I got to wear this beautiful green gown with green ballet slippers to match. They got married in May; and about two weeks before, I got the chicken pox. We didn't know if I'd be able to even be in the wedding, but I was. I only had two remaining pocks, one in the middle of my forehead, and one on my right foot. "No one will notice," my mother said. But I thought they would. My mother fixed up my hair in curls and I felt like a princess.

It's been a lot better since we moved here. My grandmother moved down the street with her daughter, my Aunt Boot, but she comes every day. So does my aunt. My parents are in the store and my Aunt Boot cooks and cleans for us. My aunt's name really is Rose, but we call her Aunt Bootie. I don't know why, but we do. My father doesn't hit my mother anymore because he probably knows his mother will kill him. When we lived in the other place, he hit her a lot. He even broke her nose once. I came home from my cousin, Rosalie's, and my mother was lying on the sofa with this big bandage on her nose, and I asked her what happened. She said, "Your father broke my nose." That was two years ago. I tried to stop him when he hit her. They would wake me up because they were talking real loud, and then I'd hear the hits and her crying. I'd go to the steps and tell my father to stop, and he'd tell me if I didn't go to bed, he was going to come up and hit me too. I would get really scared and go to bed. I would lay on my right side and put my hands between my knees and pray that he would stop. When he did, then I would go to sleep. But in the morning, I was always afraid to go downstairs to see what he did to my mother. My mother used to say my father doesn't love anybody but himself. I guess that includes me. She said he's nothing but a lazy bum who spends his money on whores and doesn't worry about whether his kids have anything to eat. She told me that when he was driving a cab, instead of getting paid a fare, he screwed women for payment. I didn't know what this meant, but by the way she said it, I think it was really bad.

Now that we moved here, I hear them at night talking downstairs in quiet voices, and I know she's safe and I can go to sleep. That's why I like it here.

February 14th, 1955

I got lots of valentines. I'm one of the most popular girls in my class. Everybody says I'm funny and they laugh at the things I say, but not at me. Life's pretty good right now.

February 15th, 1955

My mother's not talking to me. She said I didn't even give her a birthday card. Her birthday is Valentine's Day and I was so busy with my Valentine's cards for school, I forgot. I told her I was sorry, but she won't talk to me which means no money for movies, no friends over, nothing, until she talks to me again.

February 22nd, 1955

My mother talked to me today. You can bet I'll never forget her birthday again. I couldn't go to the movies with Mary Lou because I didn't have any money. Whenever I displease my mother, she says, "You're just like your father." But she says it in a tone of voice like, of all the things I could ever be, this was the worst.

March 9th, 1955

I got up to go to school today and my father says, "You have a brother." I ask if he's cute and he says he'll get cuter. Now, I'm worried. It's bad enough having all these brothers and sisters when nobody else does, but what if he's ugly too! All day I can't get it out of my mind. Suppose he looks like a monster. I'll still have to walk him in the coach and everybody will look in and maybe they'll even throw up or something. The nuns at school say it's wrong to be concerned with the way people look, that it is a sin. Sometimes, I think they should have Confession every day because there is no way, at the rate I'm going, I'm ever going to get into heaven. We recently learned about a place called Limbo which is where unbaptized babies go because they can't go to heaven since they have not been baptized, and they can't go to hell since they haven't committed any sins. Of course, we're all born with original sin. These babies just float in this place called Limbo, and I hate it. Every time I close my eyes now, I see all those babies floating with this dumb look on their faces because they don't know what they're doing or where they're going. I hope my parents baptize my brother, Larry, real soon. They named him Lawrence after my father, but my mother says my father's real name is Joseph Lawrence. So I don't understand how my brother is named after him, but they do call my father Larry, so I guess that's it. I have an uncle Joe, and we call him Uncle Joe. So my grandmother had two sons with the same name. I may be only nine, but this doesn't make any sense to me. I can't ask my mother right now with the new baby and all.

We're all sitting waiting for my mother to come home with the new baby, and my Aunt Bootie says that we shouldn't all be so happy because our noses have been cut off. I feel my face to see if I still have a nose, and I do, so I don't really understand. Everybody's laughing so it's probably a joke. My mother is home and her stomach doesn't stick out so far any more. I'm afraid to look at my new brother. What if he's so ugly he could make you throw up? The nuns say we should love everybody, no matter what they look like. So I pray a little and look at him with my eyes half closed so I won't get sick or anything. He's a little wrinkled, but he looks okay, at least, human.

March 31st, 1955

Everybody's really happy my mother had a boy. I think boys are awful. I can't hold him because my mother says she doesn't trust me. He smells good though and he is getting cuter. I wonder if you can send babies back if you don't like them like returning a dress to a store. I never heard of people doing that, but I learned about adoption in school. So some people must give them back I guess.

We are adopting a pagan child in school because, as Christians, it is the right thing to do. But I don't want a potential Limbo person sending me pictures because then when I have nightmares about it, I'll recognize the face of my own pagan baby. They taught us in Religion class how to baptize people in case of an emergency. It's something everyone is allowed to do, so I sit by my brother's crib all the time with some water in case he begins to die, and if he does, I'll baptize him and he can go to heaven and won't have to fly around Limbo for eternity.

He doesn't do very much. He eats, poops and sleeps, yet everyone is always fussing around him. If he opens his eyes, that's a major thing. I don't know who he looks like, but I guess they're not going to adopt him out.

Sometimes I wish they would have adopted me out so I wouldn't be the oldest, and maybe my new parents would worry about me because they'd die if something happened to me. I don't think my parents would die if something happened to me. They'd just have another girl. At least I'm baptized. Probably I won't go to hell because I never killed anybody or ate meat on Friday, or failed to go to Mass on Sunday, but I'll never get to heaven unless, like I said before, I can say a good Act of Contrition one second before I die. I'll probably go to Purgatory. I think I've gotten two people out of Purgatory so far, so maybe when I die, someone will pray for me and I'll get out fast. I wasn't baptized until I was one year old because my father was in the service. And they talk about how I weighed 30 pounds. They think that was wonderful because, I guess, although I'm nine, I don't weigh much more now. But it keeps me up at night to know that for one year I had the potential of going to Limbo.

May 5th, 1955

I love spring. In the afternoons, the nuns open the windows and I can smell the air of hopscotch and jump rope. We'll all get out of school and play for two hours before we have to eat dinner. I really like jump rope because it's so much fun, and I'm also learning Double Dutch and, not to brag, but I'm pretty good. The nuns say we shouldn't brag because that's a sin of pride and pride is a deadly sin. Sometimes I want to brag that I won a spelling bee or that I got an A in math or was voted most popular, but I stop myself because that would be showing off. Sister said it's okay if someone else does it, then you can feel good, but not too good. Sometimes I get compliments and I find myself feeling too good and having to go back to Confession. But sometimes they don't compliment me and I'm tempted to brag and I give in to the temptation sometimes, but sometimes I don't.

Even though we live in the city, we have lots of fun. We play jacks, charades, and Monopoly. We roller-skate and we dance. I'm taking tap dancing and jazz from Mrs. Bowman, and it's my most favorite thing to do. Unfortunately, my father knows this and every time I don't toe the line, I'm not allowed to go to my lesson. I love being on stage with everyone looking at me. I'm a natural, Mrs. Bowman says. I feel beautiful and special when I'm dancing. My mother came to a recital and she said I was a show-off just like my father. But she said I'm a good dancer too.

It's really so much better living here. I remember at the old place, one of the eighth graders came up to me in the schoolyard and said I was cute and she wanted me to be her flower girl, or something like that. She asked my mother and my mother said it was okay. At least I'd get to wear my Communion dress again. But she couldn't come to see me then because she had my brother and sister. I remember when I walked down the aisle, I pretended she was there and I walked tall and proud. But I felt sad she wasn't. Sometimes I think she and my uncle, her brother, were looking at me through the church door. I'm not sure whether I was pretending or it was true. But now with everybody in our house, she can come to my recitals. When I'm dancing, I pretend I'm a major movie star and everybody has come to see me and me alone. My father says if I like to dance, I need to do it solo because that's the only way I'll make any money. Our jazz class did this dance routine to "Sixteen Tons" and the record player broke, so we sang. We wore black slacks, shirt, a derby hat and white gloves. The hat was used in the routine. It was the best of the best. Jazz is a lot different from tap. My friend, Angela, takes ballet, but that's too hard, I think, and I hate those tutus because I look stupid in them being so skinny. I love tap dancing. The shoes are really neat. Once we even got to spray them silver. We danced to "In the Good Old Summertime, " and "Zippity Doo Da." Every year we perform and next year, a few of us have been chosen to be in Mrs. Bowman's private show. It's so hard not to feel good and special, but when I do feel like this, I also feel a lot of guilt for a long time.

I decided I want to be an actress. I love the feeling I get when I'm on stage, and I express all types of feelings that I can't around here. If I cry, I'm a baby. I'm not allowed to get mad ever, not even at my sister and especially not at my brother, Vince, who is retarded. It's funny, everybody else gets mad all the time. They yell and scream at each other. I stay out of their way most of the time because I start crying when they yell at me, and then I can't breathe and that makes my mother really, really mad, because she says I'm pretending. I'm not though. Sometimes my mother even gets mad if I laugh too much. She says I'm silly and I don't have any problems. She tells me I should have had a life like hers, then I wouldn't laugh so much. My mother sings us a song and it goes like this:

> Where is my mommy?
> Where did she go?
> I miss my mommy.
> I love her so.
>
> Daddy is so unhappy.
> He misses mommy too.
> So if you see my mommy
> Tell her to come back home.

When she sings this, I'm expected to cry. If I don't cry, she says my problem is I'm heartless and I don't care about anybody but myself. It does make me cry because she is so unhappy when she sings it and because she has this deep, low voice and also because it doesn't really rhyme. She sings it a lot.

My mother's name is Marie Maroni. Her mother went to a hospital for the insane when my mother was small, and we're never, ever allowed to use the word "crazy." Once I did, and my mother didn't talk to me for two weeks. She says they used to tell her, when she was a kid, that she was crazy just like her mother. So she always says that if I'm not good, she'll probably wind up there too. I'm glad she doesn't say that my father doesn't love anybody but himself at the same time though because that would really scare me, especially if she keeps having all these kids.

But I get confused about how much I can laugh and cry, so I figure if I were an actress, I'd have a director and then I wouldn't do things wrong all the time.

June 1st, 1955

Summer vacation is almost here. I usually can't wait until it comes, then midway through, I get bored. It's really hot in the city. We get a shower and get dressed up every night and go outside. I have to walk my brother and sister up and down and everybody says how cute we are. We all wear white shoes rimmed in black. I like to polish shoes. That's one of my jobs. I also have to dust, and sterilize Larry's bottles.

This year coming up, I'm going to start working in the store. My grandmother had a grocery store from when my father was born, and my parents took it over. That's why we moved here. My father says if I don't work, I can't eat. It doesn't seem that he works as much as he eats, but I'm not allowed to say that.

I'm not allowed to say much of anything these days. They say I have a big mouth and that I don't think before I speak. I'm working on that as well as my laughing and crying too much.

I'll probably get to stack the shelves, and maybe even cut lunchmeat. I wonder if I'll get paid. My father says a mother and father can raise four children, but four children cannot take care of one parent. He also says he should have raised pigs because, at least, he'd have pork. I just can't understand this. I do really well in school, I try to be obedient, I stay out of their way. I admit that sometimes I do get carried away and laugh or cry too hard, but still he thinks the pig is better.

June 21st, 1955

School's out. "No more homework. No more books. No more teacher's dirty looks." I like things that rhyme. I read it in school. I'm writing some poems myself. Everybody says they're pretty good too. I wonder if I don't become an actress if I can be a writer. That might be fun and also I could tell the truth and pretend I made it up, instead of the opposite which it seems I do now. Sometimes I can't tell the truth about what I'm feeling because if I do, I will be sent to my room or won't be allowed to go to dancing school. So I just smile and pretend I don't mind. Like when I get hollered at for no reason. The other day I was sitting reading a book minding my own business and my father barks, "Where's your brother?" No one told me I should be watching him, so I shrugged, I guess. And he slapped me right in the face and I peed myself, I was so shocked. There were lots of people in our house and I was really embarrassed. He sent me to my room and I cried because how are you going to stop doing things that are bad if you don't even know what they are? He does this a lot to me. He'll just yell for no reason. But you can never be mad at them, even if it's obvious they're 100% wrong. My mother always says, "Bee-bee-braciole," or she'll say, "Get mad, get glad."

My friend, Mary Lou, says that her father hollered at her for something she didn't do and then he apologized with tears in his eyes, and even took her out for ice cream. My mother and father never would have apologized, never. They don't ever feel bad if they are wrong and buy me ice cream. You know, I'm going to have to start watching how they treat the other three to figure out once and for all whether I am adopted.

September 1955

I started back to school. I'm in the fifth grade this year and I got a new school bag and it's real leather. I love the smell of it. I'm going to have Sister Xavier. I can't wait until I'm 10. I think September is the perfect month to have a birthday because everybody's in school. I feel sorry for the summer birthdays because sometimes the kids are away when you want to have your party. I think December (near Christmas) is a terrible birthday time too. September is a nice month. My brother's being christened Sunday. I'm really happy about that because I spent a lot of the summer over his crib ready to do an emergency baptism. And I'm going to have my birthday party on the same day and we'll have cake and soda and play games. I'll get gifts and everyone will sing happy birthday to me, and my mother and father will smile, and I'll feel like maybe they are happy I'm here. My mother says your life is over when you have kids. But sometimes I think I do make her laugh, and she does brag about how smart I am in school. And I think she likes that I have lots of friends. She always asks questions about them, whether they are Italian, where they live, what their parents do for a living. My father doesn't think any job is as good as having a business. "We're business people," he says. I have no idea what that means. He also says that I'm a Maroni like that's something special. My mother thinks I shouldn't help my friends with their homework and all, but I like to do it.

Sometimes it gets confusing because I don't know whether being a Maroni and the daughter of a business man means I'm special or whether I'm no better than a pig. I love going to the movies. I buy all kinds of candy and sit there and look at all those beautiful people. Sometimes they even have double features. Mostly we go every Sunday after dinner, which is at 12. And then sometimes we go for a hamburger. It is the most fun of all. I like to read too. I read books but really I'm into comic books right now, like Archie and Little Lotta. My friends and I trade them. My grandfather, my mother's father, bought me a whole stack last week.

Those comic books and Bazooka bubble gum are my idea of heaven. Once, when I was about 7, I went into my mother's apron and took some change, bought some gum, and lay on the bed and read and read and read. When she came back, she wasn't even mad, but she keeps on saying I'm not going to have a tooth in my mouth by the time I'm 20. That reminds me, when I was about 4 or 5 years old, I woke up and couldn't lift my head from the pillow and I screamed and screamed for my mother because I thought I was dying. What had happened was that I fell asleep with bubble gum in my mouth, which fell out during the night on the pillowcase, and the pillowcase stuck to my hair. My mother was really mad. She cut all my hair off and said that that should teach me. While I'm on hair, every time she cuts my bangs, they wind up one inch long because she keeps saying they're uneven and she has to make them even. After she's done, all you can see is miles of forehead. Even though I'm pretty mad and I really don't want to go to school looking like I've been scalped, I pretend it's okay. I fight back the tears and pretend because if I say the truth, I'll still have to go to school and she won't talk to me. It's just easier to pretend sometimes.

October 15th, 1955

Halloween is coming and it's my favorite holiday on the day. I like thinking about Christmas but when it comes, I'm all disappointed, especially when I get four stupid, unwrapped games. But Halloween is different. It's fun to think about, but even more fun when it comes. The only problem is my father thinks, because we're business people, I shouldn't go trick or treating. He says I don't need to beg. That's how you know when people are really old, when they think trick or treating is begging. I try to be obedient most of the time, but I have to go trick or treating. My mother says I can go to my cousin's and go with her, but under no circumstances am I to go down our own street. Doesn't she know that you get the best treats from the people who know you? Well, it's better than nothing, I guess. After it's over, I'm going to have to decide whether I actually committed the sin of disobedience since my father said no, but my mother said yes. I don't want to confess to something that's not a sin because that might be a sin of lying to a priest.

But first things first—my costume. I was a flower girl in my Uncle Carmen's wedding when I was 6, and I have this beautiful green gown which I wore for three Halloweens at my other school. I always went as a princess. I kept thinking I'd win a prize, but I never did. Andrea Cassali won every year. Her father's a doctor and she got to wear really neat costumes. She also has a colored maid. I told my mother they must be very rich and all to have a maid. My mother said that's because her mother died and I should feel sorry for her. I didn't though, because she won the Halloween contest every year for three years and she has a maid. Maybe we should feel sorry for me who has had to wear the same costume for three years in a row. My mother and I disagree on this. She says jealousy is not a pretty thing and that the worst thing in the world that I can be is jealous. And here, I thought the worst thing I could ever be is like my father. It's this kind of thinking which always gets me in trouble because sometimes I slip and say these things out loud, and then she says that I have a smart mouth and I'm to wait until my father comes home, and then he's going to fix my boots. I learned to keep quiet when she says this now because once, when I was trying to be funny because my cousin, Rosalie, was over, I said, "Good, my boots need fixing." She sent my cousin home immediately and sent me to my room. My poor cousin isn't here five minutes sometimes before she gets sent home. It's usually because *she* does something though.

Anyway, we're going to have a party in school in the afternoon, and then my cousin and I will go trick or treating until it gets dark. Not only is the day so much fun, but then you have all that candy to eat.

There's a lady on Walnut Street who gives out candy apples which she makes herself. They're not the caramel kind (although I love them too), but the red shiny kind. Sometimes she puts coconut on them. I don't like coconut, and I have thought about it and there is just no way I can be polite and tell her to leave the coconut off. It would be like looking a gift horse in the mouth, my mother says. Isn't that the most stupid thing you ever heard, like we ever even saw a horse, and if we did, be close enough to want to look in its mouth?

But I put my foot down this year and told my mother I must have a new costume. I told her if I wear that gown one more year, I will have to go as a ballet dancer instead of a princess since I've grown three inches. I'm still very skinny though, and might fit into it. She's okay with buying me an outfit. Now, the decision is, what do I want to be?

I do have a cowgirl outfit my Uncle Don bought me I could wear, she says. I think that horse remark got to her. Or, she says, I could go as a tap dancer and wear one of the outfits I wore in the show. She also says that maybe I could be a queen instead of a princess. Does she think I'm that dumb? She also suggests a hula dancer because I do have a skirt, but I'd have to cover up because it's cold in October in New Jersey.

Mary Lou is going to be a fireman. She has the hat and her treat bag is shaped like a hose. That sounds pretty good. Carla, my other friend, is going to be a ghost. Somehow I think there will be lots of ghosts. My father says I could go as a toothpick. He really thinks he's funny. He said I could be wrapped in brown paper; and as skinny as I am, it would be cheap. Then he says I could put something on my head and I'd be a match. Isn't that original, he says, you can be two things on the same day. Sometimes I really don't like my father.

I have a notebook now in which I put all my sins, and then if I commit them more than once, I add a line. This way, I don't have to spend one-half hour trying to remember what I did. It seems though that I commit the same sins over and over, like lying, and answering my mother. I never answer my father. Not liking your father is a serious sin though. Honor your father and mother. It's one of the Commandments. I get really confused about the Commandments though. I understand most of them, but the "covet" ones confuse me. My teacher says covet means to desire, but I can't understand why anyone would covet a neighbor's wife. I know you shouldn't steal or kill or want what everybody else has, and that you must not take God's name in vain, and you must always honor your parents and put God before everybody. Most of them are pretty easy to follow. I think the Pope added three more for Catholics. They are that we must go to church every Sunday, unless we're dead or dying; we must not eat meat on Friday; and we must never think bad thoughts. I guess we can't eat meat on Fridays because Jesus was a fisherman and He died on a Friday. Every time I wish somebody would disappear, I feel really guilty because I know that's wrong and I tell myself I'm not going to think that, and the more I try to put it out of my mind, the more it comes and the longer it stays. Sometimes I go to church when it's not Sunday and try to get rid of those thoughts. I tell God I'm not leaving until I do. Once, I went home after school and told my mother I was going to church. I was there for two hours trying to get rid of the horrible thought that I'd be better off without any sisters or brothers, and I fell asleep right there in the pew. When I woke up, it was dark outside; but as soon as I felt good about having gotten rid of that thought, I thought it again.

It isn't that I don't like them, I do. But they break everything I have, and when I need to ask my mother something, she tells me to leave her alone because my brother, who's retarded, is sick; or she's changing my little brother's diaper. She says she doesn't have time for my nonsense. Doesn't she know it isn't nonsense to me? And if I hear one more time, "you're the oldest, "you should understand," "know better," "do it," "not be so selfish," I think I'm going to scream. I wonder if it's a sin to scream or to want to. I don't really want them to disappear. I'm used to them now.

October 17th, 1955

I decided to be a pirate for Halloween because I'll get to wear an eye patch. I thought about it for a long time and decided I would have liked to be a pirate in real life because they get to go on ships and sail on the water and see all those far away places we learn about in geography. I have a problem with the stealing part, but I'm not going to steal. It is just pretending. And when those pirates died, I read, they were buried at sea. I think that's better than being buried in the ground.

Every Sunday afternoon before I had friends and started to go to the movies, our family used to go to the cemetery where my Aunt Boot would clean up all the weeds on some relatives' graves, while my cousin and I looked at all the pictures, ages, and birthdays on the tombstones. There was one nun buried there called Sister Clovis Young. I always wanted to remember that name because when I'm famous, that will be my name—Clovis Young. I think it's pretty exotic.

I think being buried at sea is best because everybody's equal there. In the cemetery, it's very obvious some people don't have anybody who loves them because there's all weeds and leaves on their graves. I don't want to be one of those people when I die who has a grave that makes people sad. And since most of my family will probably die before me and I'll never be able to depend on my brother, who's retarded, and my sister, who doesn't like me, I'm probably better off in the sea. The priest says cremation is wrong and we can't do it, so I'll probably wind up in one of those cemeteries. I wonder if it hurts when you die. I wonder if you're afraid and all. Sister Xavier says that Jesus meets you at the exact moment you die, but suppose 100 people die at the very same minute and He's busy? I can't imagine not being me or not being at all. Sometimes when I think about it, it almost scares me to death.

My mother says God lights a candle when we're born, and when that light goes out, we die. I wonder who picks out how long the candle is and whether it's fat or skinny? She also says we have a book with our names on it; and on one side, God puts all the good things we do, and on the other, all the bad things. Then when we die, He adds up each side and that decides whether we go to heaven or hell. I ask her if He knows whether the bad things are mortal sins or venial sins just by looking at them. I have determined my mother will answer only one question at a time. Every time I ask another question, she gets really huffy and says I have to stop asking so many stupid questions, but Sister Xavier says there *are* no stupid questions. It's no wonder I'm so confused all the time.

I could talk about death all the time if I thought about it, but I don't. But I did ask my mother whether she knows when she'll die. "When it's my time," she answered. "We'll all be big though?", I asked. She said, "Maybe." I wish she would have just said yes. I get really scared when she says maybe. What if we're all orphans and we have to go into an orphanage.

My Aunt Boot took my cousin, Rosalie, and me to an orphanage one time. It made me sad and scared. All those orphans were in a procession and were dressed in white. My friend, Angie, said that's because they go right from the orphanage into a convent and become nuns. I don't want to be a nun because they don't have any hair. Everyone knows they're bald and they have to wear those dark, long, hot outfits, even in the summer. Sometimes they're really mean too. I heard that one nun threw a boy in her class in the wastepaper basket because she said he was trash. He had to stand in that basket all day. The worst thing a nun has done to me, other than the slap when I was in the third grade, is hit me across the knuckles with a ruler because she says I don't write right. They think there's only one way to write. I start out like they say, but then my hand moves faster and faster so that I can keep up with my head, and it isn't right any more. I'll never win a prize for penmanship, that's for sure. But I do win spelling bees, and maybe I'll win the prize for best costume on Halloween.

Getting back to death though, sometimes I lie on my back and look up at the sky and wonder what heaven's like. It's probably bubble gum and comic books. I bet they hug you and kiss you a lot there, and that there is no oldest. I hope.

October 31st, 1955

I'm really, really excited today. We have classes in the morning and then we go home and put on our costumes. I ask my mother if I can wear rouge and she says no because pirates don't. Mary Lou says she's blotting her face with ashes so it will look like she just came back from a fire. I guess I could wet my face so that I would look like I just returned from the sea. My mother says that's not necessary and besides, it's cold outside. She says I better not get sick or she'll kill me. I have to think this through because I'm not quite ready to die. I've got a lot to figure out yet. The morning is never ending.

One of the boys, Joey Luongo, misbehaved and he has to stand in the corner, and Sister says none of us can leave until he apologizes for calling her a penguin. Everyone's restless but we're being punished too because we laughed. Nuns do look like penguins from far away, there is no denying that. How come they always tell us to tell the truth and then when we do, we get in trouble? We finally were allowed to go home. Joey apologized and then each of us had to stand and do the same. I wonder if it's a sin to apologize when you don't mean it? Probably. It might be lying.

We have 30 kids in our class and 15 are ghosts. Sometimes I scare myself with how much I know. There's one fireman, two brides, one princess, two cowboys, one clown, one pirate, two witches, one old lady, one fat lady, a baby, and the winner, someone dressed like a nun. Isn't that a surprise? Miss Goody-Two-Shoes, brown-noser, kiss-up, Frances Serano, wins the prize.

She's always telling Sister Xavier how she wants to be a nun. Her hand shoots up so fast to volunteer to clean the blackboard, one day it's going to come out of its socket, and I know things. And she also tells Sister Xavier everything everybody does when she leaves the room. Nobody likes her. I'm starting to think I'm never going to win a Halloween contest as long as I live.

Joey didn't come back in the afternoon. Apparently, Miss Goody-Two-Shoes, who lives next door to him, told his mother he spent the morning in the corner, and he wasn't allowed to come to the party or go trick or treating. Something has to be done with Goody, and soon.

After school, I went to my cousin's to go trick or treating. I didn't mention why though, because I don't want her to have anything to blackmail me with later. Sometimes if I don't do what she wants she says, "I'm going to tell your mother/father you did so and so," and then I have to do what she wants. She always wants to cook from her cookbook because my uncle said how special she is because she made him an egg when she was only 8. So whenever I tell her I win a prize at school, she brings up that egg. I try to tell her she has to do new things, but she doesn't listen. Her book is *The Humpty Dumpty Cookbook*, and when I go there, she always wants us to make dinner and surprise her mother. The pictures look really nice. There's one recipe we've been trying to make for a month. It's a Humpty Dumpty salad and it has a peach base and cottage cheese. But there's always one ingredient that she doesn't have, and it never looks quite like the book. One time, instead of cottage cheese, we used whipped cream and it looked really good. We even made a mouth with cherries, but by the time my aunt came home, the whipped cream began melting so we just ate it. Of course, that meant I wasn't hungry at dinner and got in all sorts of trouble. Another time we had the cottage cheese but no peach halves, so we used pears. But we found out that colors are important. It just looked like a blob of white. It didn't seem like my aunt was too impressed either.

Anyway, she doesn't have to know my father doesn't want me to go trick or treating or I'll have to spend the rest of my life cooking from the Humpty Dumpty book. The first place we go is to the candy apple lady before she runs out, who says she was sorry she didn't have any coconut to put on this year. I think this might be the right time to tell her I don't like coconut, but then I think again, because if I say it and for some reason she thinks it's cute, then she might tell my father and he'd know I'd disobeyed him. So I just smile and say that was fine. Everybody always tells me I have to think before I speak. Sometimes, though, it comes right out of my mouth as I'm thinking it. They're usually the nights I spend in my room.

And then we knock on all the houses on Walnut Street. Somebody gives us a bag of those candy corns, which I hate. There aren't too many candies I don't like, but they are awful. When we leave, my cousin's all happy because there are so many of them. People always surprise me. She doesn't like them either, so I can't figure out why she'd be so happy there were lots of them. After Walnut Street, we hit Chestnut. By this time, it's starting to get dark and we have a full bag of treats. Now I realize I have a big problem. How am I going to get the candy home without my father knowing I went trick or treating? So I have to tell my cousin about my father. She suggests I leave my bag at her house. Somehow I don't think this is such a good idea. I figure she'll probably eat most of it, and I won't know it until it's gone and won't be able to prove it. Or she'll put all the candy she doesn't like into my bag and keep the good stuff for herself. But I don't say anything because she usually hits me when she doesn't like what I say, which is often. So I lie and tell her my mother will expect me to share the candy with my sister and brother. She doesn't have any answer for this, and believe me, that's unusual. So we devise a plan where I'll go home first and then she'll come in with my bag and pretend it's hers. And then when my father's not looking, she'll sneak it into my bedroom. I tell her to come in about five minutes after I get home, I figure how much can she eat in five minutes? So that she won't swap candy, I tell her she should follow me right then and wait the five minutes across the street, where I can keep an eye on her. I don't *say* this last part though, but do tell her she has to leave her bag home. She likes this idea a lot because she's in the sixth grade and they're learning about spies. But now she's got something on me and I don't like that very much at all.

I go home. She waits one minute. I know because I was watching the clock. She says I'm lying, that it was five. She couldn't have eaten any of the candy, though, because she was pretending to be a spy and we both know a spy wouldn't stand on the corner in broad daylight drawing attention to herself going through and eating a bag of candy.

My father's sitting in the living room when she walks in, and she goes right up to him and says, "Uncle Larry, look at all the treats I got, and Missy didn't go trick or treating at all." She doesn't worry about committing a sin because her teacher told her that it's okay to lie to save somebody from being hurt. I thought she did pretty good, but for some reason, my father got suspicious. He told her to come over and sit on his lap. "You're my favorite niece, you know." She likes this. He only has one other niece and I never told her that he tells my other cousin, Mary Rose, the same thing, although I've been tempted to when she tells me that both my mother and father like her better than me. I sometimes think it's true because they're really nice to her. I think it's because she really likes to eat.

So my father says, "I know you're a good friend to Missy and all, but you'll tell the truth to your favorite uncle, won't you?" And she looks like a cat ready to purr. I know the spy is ready to spill her guts and I look around to see where I could run. And then my father looks at me, smiles, and says to her, "Why didn't Missy win the Halloween contest, do you think?" I'm breathing again, when the spy says, and I'm quoting her, "Probably because she couldn't wait to go trick or treating." I think she'd better read that spy book again. My father laughs, my mother laughs, and I laugh too. I don't know why they're laughing, but I'm laughing because I thought I didn't win the contest because I wasn't wet, and should have been as a pirate, and now there's all this pee running down my legs.

November 10th, 1955

It's Thanksgiving time again and I've decided that it's my least favorite holiday. I don't like turkey. All we do is eat. As far as I'm concerned, there's nothing in it for me.

December 7th, 1955

Today is Angela's birthday. All she's been talking about for months is this big party she's going to have and how we're all invited, Mary Lou, Carla, Carmela, Bernadette, Jeannie, and me. She's going to have cake and we have to bring presents. It seems she's always bragging about something, how her hair is naturally curly, how she doesn't need braces, and how good she is at ballet. She says her ballet teacher said she's a natural. She says she's going to be a ballet dancer when she's big and probably dance in New York. It might sound like I don't like her, but I do. It's just that I don't understand how she can get away with saying nice things about herself, when I can't because my mother says she doesn't like people who brag. Her list continues on forever about the people she doesn't like. She doesn't like jealous people, hogs (kids who take things from the table), kids who don't eat, anybody who's like my father, show-offs, and *scustimads*. That's an Italian word, she says, that means a scorch. I'm afraid to ask what a scorch is, because she only answers one question at a time. So I store it and decide to ask her tomorrow. The word *scorch* we learned in school means to burn something, but I figure that can't be what she means. So far, I don't eat, I'm like my father, and I'm not sure whether I'm a *scustimad* or not. So I either have two or three things on her list of things she doesn't like. Cassandra said her mother tells her that she loves everything about her and she wouldn't trade her for anybody else in the whole world. So I'm trying to eat a little more and trying not to be like my father by feeling sorry for people all the time. I'm also trying to help every one I know to show her that I care for others instead of just myself. I'll have to find out what exactly a scorch is to see if I am one. Then I can figure out how not to be one and she'll love me like Sandra's mother loves her. The way things are going, I think she might trade me in for my cousin any day.

Angela's party is set for 6 o'clock. It's a Wednesday, a school night, so it will be over by 7:30. Everybody eats dinner at 5 in this neighborhood, so I guess it will be okay. I bought Angie a keychain because she's always bragging about how she has a key to her house. I asked my father for a key to our house and he said I don't need one because somebody's always there. And then he says, and everybody laughs, that he'll give me a key when they move out. I should have known it was a joke because they were laughing, but sometimes I'm a little slow, so I asked if we were moving and he said they were, but they decided not to take me. He said he has fed me long enough. To hear my mother tell it, he hasn't worked a full day in his life and if it wasn't for her, we would all have starved to death for sure. My father thinks this is really funny. They all do. But I don't. I don't think it's funny a bit.

Anyway, I went to Angie's party and we were six girls. Each plate was filled with candy. We played Pin the Tail on the Donkey and Spin the Bottle, but we didn't kiss each other because there were only girls. I hope I never have to play this game with boys, for sure they'd expect us to kiss them. Yuck.

We play it so that when the bottle points at somebody, they leave until there's one left and that person wins a prize. It's like musical chairs without the chairs and music. We could have played musical chairs but there wasn't enough room in the kitchen, and Angie's mother doesn't want us making a mess in the parlor. I came in next to last and received no prize. I can't seem to win anything lately. Angie got a beautiful, and I do mean beautiful, red bike for her birthday. Just what I've wanted my whole life. Now I have to figure out how not to look funny when my mother asks me about the party or she might say I'm jealous, and jealousy is the worst thing anybody could ever be. And then I'll be three things on her list, maybe even four, if I'm a scorch. Then I thought up a plan to look sad and maybe she'd feel sorry and buy one for me. But it didn't work. She told me the problem with me is that I was never satisfied. Most of her sentences begin with the words, "The problem with you…" or sometimes, "You know what your problem is…" There seems to be an awful lot wrong with me. My mother and father keep saying good things about themselves. It makes me wonder how I could be their child with all my problems when they're so perfect. If you're adopted, I wonder if they could give you back.

December 25th, 1955

This Christmas there were no games left on the chair, but I got stupid things again. After five minutes, I turned around and looked under the tree for another present and there was none.

But my mother's really mad because my father bought her a Singer sewing machine. Somehow she feels insulted by this and she's been slamming things all day, and she let me know what my problems were at least six times, I counted. I wonder, though, if they're not her problems because they don't bother me at all.

February 1956

I'm going to have to make my Confirmation with a bunch of second graders. It's just too embarrassing. When I went to Sts. Peter and Paul's, the kids made Communion in second grade and Confirmation in fourth. But I left after third, so I am the only one in the fifth grade who's not a soldier of Christ. That's what Confirmation is. The bishop comes and slaps every kid in the face so he'll be able to take pain for Jesus. I'm really worried about the slap but my Aunt Lissa, who's going to be my godmother, says that it's only a love tap and it doesn't hurt. But the neat thing is that you get to pick a middle name. None of us have a middle name. My mother says she couldn't be bothered with that. I've always liked the name Anne, and Milissa Anne sounds really nice. But my mother says that, out of respect, I have to take my godmother's name. That's the way the Italian people do it. I tried to explain that Milissa Lissa is really stupid, but she won't budge. She says my aunt's real name is Elisa, so now I'll be known as Milissa Elisa Maroni. Why don't they just shoot me and get it over with? I go to my father and tell him that I'm not very happy at being called Milissa Elisa, but he gives me a speech about respect and agrees with my mother. Respect is really big in this family. We must, under all circumstances, respect our parents, our aunts and uncles, our grandparents, the priest, the nuns, and any one older than we are; and out of respect, I must take my godmother's name. Confirmation is in May.

May 5th, 1956

It's Confirmation day. In an hour, I will have a new name, be a soldier for Christ, and have seen the bishop. This, according to Sister Xavier, is a real honor. I'll also be walking down the aisle with 60 seven year olds and I'll get slapped. How's that for something to look forward to? My mother thinks it's hysterical. She says I'm going to look like a big galoot and nobody's coming either. Aunt Lissa gave me a beautiful Bulova watch as a gift, and we're going to have a party after. I hope my face isn't broken or anything. We've been practicing for a week. The only thing worse than a classroom full of seven year olds is two classrooms full of seven year olds. All we have to do is walk down the aisle with our godparents, hands folded, genuflect at the altar, and then we kneel before the bishop and he asks us whether we are willing to be soldiers for Christ. When we answer yes, then he wallops us. And that's it. We go down the aisle by height. Guess who's in the back? I guess this is good because by the time they all go up, maybe the bishop's arm will be tired and he'll be gentle.

Sister Cassia, who gave us the instructions, said that after we leave the altar, our faces should reflect that we are now soldiers for Christ, that we should look happy and tough (or strong). I don't remember exactly. One of the second graders peed right on the altar. Luckily, it was on the way up and not where you have to kneel. Finally it's my turn and the bishop asks whether I want to be confirmed and be a soldier for Christ. I say yes. He then blesses my head with some holy water and hits me hard, and I do mean hard. My head moved sideways and my Aunt Lissa starts laughing and then everybody starts laughing when he announces my new name is Milissa Elisa Maroni. The kids probably think the bishop made a mistake. I told my aunt that was hardly a love tap and she laughed. I was probably hit so hard because that kid peed. It seems I always get blamed for things that are not my fault.

At the party, they're all laughing at me saying they're surprised I didn't start to cry and they make the *cry* real long. I do have the reputation for being a cry baby. Every time my cousin hits, pinches or bites me, I cry and that's why she gets sent home. But my mother says it's about time I learn to fight back because she can't stand a cry baby. I forgot to add that to the list of things she doesn't like. My father is telling everybody a story about when I was seven and a little girl threatened to hit me. I didn't do anything to her at all. I didn't even know her, but she said she didn't like my looks or something. Well, one day when I was coming home from my cousin's, she made good on her threat and she pushed me down on my knees and started punching me all over. I started to scream for my father and he came running out and she ran away. But he said I was a disgrace screaming like a little baby in front of the whole neighborhood, that I was nothing but a cry baby. Now they all call me that. If the list of things wrong with me gets any longer, I'll have to quit school because I won't have any time to study with all the time I'll need trying to make myself okay. My father is now telling them that all he has to do is look at me like he's mad and I start crying. You know what's the worst part, he's right. But he forgets that I remember when he broke my mother's nose and used to hit her. Sometimes I'm afraid that if I get older, he'll start hitting me too because sometimes I do things wrong that nobody told me were. So it's sort of like not having a choice whether to be good or bad because I just don't know sometimes. I know it's wrong to answer anybody back and I shouldn't lie or steal or hit my sister or brothers. That's obvious stuff. But sometimes my brother's bottle will fall and my father will say I should have been watching him. Or my sister will do something and I'll get blamed for it. When she says she didn't do it, they believe her. One time last week my brother, Vince, who's retarded, walked into the kitchen where I was sitting doing my homework, opened a cabinet door and didn't close it. I kept on doing my homework, and when my mother came in and saw the cabinet door open, she blamed me. When I told her Vince did it, I saw him, she said that even if that were true, I should have closed it anyway. Things like that when I'm just minding my own business, yet managing to do things that are wrong. My father doesn't hit us, but I still don't trust him. My mother told me that once when we lived in the other house and they were fighting, my father threatened to throw my sister out the window if she didn't shut up. I'm glad she did.

My mother keeps saying that if a good, swift wind comes along, I'll be blown away because I'm so skinny. They're giving me an awfully lot of things to worry about at 10. My friends don't ever seem to worry about anything. They're happy all the time. I'm happy, but sometimes I'm sad too. I go to church when I'm sad and I pray to Jesus and tell Him I'm sorry I'm such a mess. I always feel better after, and I always eat a lot that night.

July 1st, 1956

I decided I want to learn to talk Italian, but my grandmother says I live in America, only she says "mediga", so I should speak English. I tried to tell her I already do speak English, but she won't teach me Italian anyway. So I'm tricking her. She speaks one-half English and one-half Italian, but never two times in a row. So when she slips and says something in Italian, I ask her what that means and she tells me. My Uncle Tony, my Aunt Boot's husband, taught me to count to 25 in Italian, and I can really rattle them off now. There are some words I learned like *stachazite* which means shut up. *Viniqua* means come here. *Co-mastad* means how are you? *Manja* means eat. *Cockyaone* means big mouth. When I told Mary Lou all the words I learned, she was impressed. There are two words I'm not sure are Italian. I don't want to ask my grandmother because she might find out what I'm doing and stop talking to me in Italian at all. Those words are *stupida* and *grandamom*. I'm not sure if these are the Italian words for stupid and grandma, because sometimes when my grandmother talks English fast, she puts a lot of "a's" in the words. Like for instance, she'll say *whereza your momma? Comea here. Sita downa* and *eata*. My father says he has a good Italian word for me, *stewnod*. He says that I give new meaning to that word. He's smiling too, so it must be something really good. He never compliments me so I'm really excited. When I ask him what it means, he says to look it up in the dictionary, and when I ask him how to spell it, he says I'll know because my picture will be next to it. I do go through the dictionary, not every page, but I can't find it. I really feel good about it, having a whole word he made up just for me. When my cousin Rosalie and I are making another horrible dinner from the Humpty Dumpty cookbook, I tell her what my father said, and she tells me never to tell anybody else what he said because *stewnod* means dopey. I thought she was just jealous and being mean because I had my own word and she didn't, so when she wasn't looking, I ate the banana we needed for our dinner, and she can't prove it either.

I think my grandmother's catching on, though, because she's speaking more English these days. My Aunt Lissa calls me *liegeasacod* which they say means a dried out fish. And now I have another nickname, *liege*. This family is really big on nicknames. They call my Uncle Joe "Porky Pig" because he's fat, but sometimes they just call him Porky. They don't call him this to his face though. They call my Uncle Jack, "Jack-Ass-Blues" because they say he's always complaining. Also they call him "Jonah" but nobody knows why. They call my father *Jabish* because he peed the bed. I finally found out why we call my aunt Bootie, because the family thought she looked like Betty Boop (she has big hips), but we kids couldn't say Boop, so she became Boot. Also they call her "Rosanelle."

Another Italian word I learned is *goomah*, which sometimes sounds like *camar*. That really means a godmother, like my Aunt Lissa, but it is also used for good friends or the family of your godmother. *Pizon* is a friend. *Amore* is love. I think this is a really pretty word.

I started to work in the store this summer. I pack the shelves, sweep the floor, and wash the front glass of the lunch-meat case. I want to cut lunchmeat for people, but my mother says she doesn't trust me. There's all these little bottles in the store and stuff like that, and I like to display them. I like little things. When I got the measles last year, I had to stay in bed and the Bond bread man brought me up a miniature loaf of bread. It looked exactly like the regular sized one. It made me feel good. I guess the Bond bread man likes me. Too bad he doesn't have beautiful dolls like the man who likes my cousin. When I had the measles, my mother said I had to stay in my room with the blinds closed or I could go blind. I guess she remembered that I'm very sensitive to going blind because one night when I was about six, we were going to see my grandmother and it was really cold. Because it was so cold, my eyes began to water and my eyelashes must have stuck together. All I know is that I couldn't see so I started to scream, "I'm blind. I'm blind," and my mother slapped me across the head which made my eyelashes part, and I could see again. I remember thinking at the time it was a miracle, you know, like when Jesus made the blind man see in that Bible story. Now I know better, I think.

My favorite Bible story we learned last year is the one about the loaves and the fishes. It seems that one night a whole gang had been following Jesus around all day and night and they got hungry. But the apostles told Jesus there wasn't enough food and Jesus said, "Oh, ye of little faith." Don't quote me on that. He might have said that in the story when he walked on the water. Anyway, there were some fishes and some bread, and Jesus said to the apostles, "Bring me those fishes and that bread," and they did. He blessed them and, presto, they had more than enough for everybody. In fact, they had some left over, I think. I like that story because my mother says that food is a little like love. So I think Jesus might have been trying to tell everybody that the more love you give away, the more you have. It's hard to tell though, because Jesus often spoke in parables. A parable, Sister Xavier says, is a story told so that the listeners can understand some important God stuff. She says they don't always mean what we think. But I think his followers understood. I hope so anyway.

My problem is I always have about a million questions, well, maybe not a million, but a lot. Like in the story about the loaves and fishes, I often wonder whether that bread was Italian. It looks like it from the pictures, but I don't understand how Italian bread could get to Jerusalem because they didn't have any airplanes or anything in those days. I'd like to know if Jesus ate last. My mother thinks that's important. She says it's good manners. But what I'm most interested in is why the apostles weren't more surprised. If I looked into a bag and there were three fishes and more fishes kept coming, I would probably just fall down and die because I would be so shocked. But those apostles acted like it was normal. And why didn't anybody say thank you? You always have to say thank you.

I don't ask any of these questions though because I'm afraid they're stupid. I don't care what Sister Xavier said, some questions are. Like one kid asked her when we were learning about

Jesus walking on the water, if Jesus could swim. As far as I'm concerned, this is stupid for two reasons. One reason is that Jesus is God and everybody knows God can do anything. And the second reason is what difference did it make since He was walking on top anyway.

We have Religion class every day. When Sister talks about Limbo, I raise my hand to ask if I can go to the bathroom because I'm still worried about those pagan babies we adopted.

I don't like when Jesus calls his mother "woman." That's really fresh. I did ask Sister Xavier if Mary got mad when he talked to her like that. She said he wasn't being disrespectful or anything, because that's the way they spoke in those days. But, besides that, it's obvious he doesn't want to change that water into wine. The way I look at it, there are lots of times that I don't want to do what my mother says but I do it without any lip. I could just picture saying to my mother when she wants me to walk my brother, "Woman, my time has not yet come." Trust me, my time would come in my room for a couple of weeks. And she'd probably not talk to me for a month.

She sent me to the store once and when the cashier gave me change, I put it in my pocket. When I gave her the bag without the change, she said, "I'll bet you lost the change, didn't you?" And I put my hand in my pocket, smiled, and said, "Oh, ye of little faith." My head still hurts from the slap she gave it. It isn't her fault, though, because I always do lose lots of things, like the watch my godmother gave me for Confirmation, I lost it already. Aunt Lissa says she's never buying me another thing as long as she lives, and I think she means it. Anyway, my mother says I'd lose my head if it wasn't attached to my shoulders.

My favorite subject in school last year was literature because I like to read. I hate geography except for our projects, like English, and can live without math. History's fun, depending on what we're learning. I love music class and I like doing book reports. After we handed in our last report, Sister Xavier said someone was guilty of plagiarism. I didn't know if it was me since I didn't know what it meant, so I looked it up in the dictionary. But I didn't steal. The way she looked at Joey, I knew it had to be him. Seems his brother is in the sixth grade and they both handed in the same book report. Joey really is not too bright. He didn't even copy his brother's report in his own handwriting. Some people do deserve what they get. Of course, Miss Goody-Two-Shoes is smiling and she probably can't wait to leave class and run home to tell Joey's mother. I would hate, and I do mean hate, living next door to her, and for that reason I feel bad for Joey. I got an "A" for originality and content in my report, but only a "B+" for handwriting. Goody got two "A's" because, as Sister Xavier always says, she has perfect penmanship. I told Goody a hundred times that penmanship doesn't matter much to me, because when I go to work, I'm going to have a secretary, and I'll never have to write. She says I am just jealous. I never have had a desire to hit anyone except Goody, and never more than when she says I'm jealous, because she's right. I am jealous because no matter how I try, no matter how slow I go, my penmanship is still not that good. I know there are probably more important things, but right now this writing thing is getting to me. According to my mother, my problem is I'm too sloppy and I do things too fast. She says it's only going to get worse as I get older too. I just mumble under my breath, "Woman, my time has not yet come," and leave the room.

August 12th, 1956

My mother has a picture of Jesus in her room which I really like because He has such a kind face, even if he might have given His mother some lip. His eyes are blue. I don't know anybody with blue eyes except my grandfather. Everybody I know has brown eyes, except for Mary Lou, who has hazel. My mother says my grandfather came from northern Italy, and all the people there have light skin and blue eyes, and that the people from southern Italy are dark. We must be in between because we have dark eyes but our skin is light. In fact, Mikey, a kid in my class, calls me "milk bottle," and then he laughs like a demon. Not that I ever saw a demon, but if I had, it would probably laugh like him. And I thought "macaroni" was bad. Now he said today that macaroni should eat some macaroni so she would have some color. I was really upset and I told my mother that all last year, Mikey followed me around the school yard yelling "milk bottle" and "milky way." My mother says I should tell him that I can get dark by getting a tan, but that he never can get light. The next time he did it, I used my mother's words exactly, and he looked surprised. So for today, he's left me alone. My mother is lighter than me, so I guess she has experience in this area. My father is darker and he has a mustache. Mikey asked if I know how you can tell if an Italian girl looks like her father. And when I asked how, he said, by her mustache, and started to laugh again. I think Mikey should get some help or something. He keeps on bothering me and I just try to ignore him all the time. My mother says he probably has a crush on me. She says a crush is when someone likes you like a girlfriend. Yuck. I wish Mikey and Goody would both move away and leave me alone. I don't hate them because Catholics don't hate people, but I don't like either of them a bit. Sister Xavier says we don't have to like everyone, but we should love everyone because we're Catholics.

September 6th, 1956

I found out today in Religion class that Catholicism is the only true religion, and any one who belongs to any other religion is not getting into Heaven, no matter what they do. I guess the Pope talks to God. I guess I'm lucky I'm a Catholic, but if I wasn't, I wouldn't know that Catholicism was the only true religion, so I guess I'd still be okay. I'm in the sixth grade now. We have Sister Mary Catherine. She seems nice, but from my experience, they all start out nice. Sister says we're going to have to do a report with pictures showing either ourselves or somebody we know receiving all of the sacraments. The sacraments are Baptism, Holy Communion, Confession, Confirmation, Marriage, Extreme Unction, and Holy Orders. I'm sure glad I made my Confirmation last year. We can use pictures of our parents' wedding for holy matrimony. I'm a little confused how to show Extreme Unction because that's the blessing you get right before you die, when the priest comes to bless you and forgive your sins. I guess I could ask my Aunt Bootie to take me to the cemetery and take a picture of one of the graves and say, this is the stop after Extreme Unction but before Heaven. I'm going to be 11 soon. My friend, Carlotta, was born in January 1945, so she's been 11 for a long time. She told me she got her period and she didn't know what to do, so she put Band-Aids on herself. When her mother saw all the bloody Band-Aids, she wanted to know what was going on. And then her mother told her about her period and all. Thank God for my cousin. I don't know where she gets her information from, but she's usually right.

My cousin's going to be 12 and she likes boys now. She drags me all over with her and makes me stand there when she talks to them. We went to Atlantic City for one week during the summer and she liked this guy, Greg, who ran the Tilt-a-Whirl. I went on the Tilt-a-Whirl 37 times, not all in one day. One day, I went on four times in a row and when I got off, I was really dizzy and I walked two steps and fell. She said I was immature and an embarrassment. I asked her what immature meant, and she said I was nothing but a baby, not a woman like her. When she was saying all this, I was still on the ground and her face looked like a monster's. It made me sick to my stomach and I threw up. She left me there and I had to find my way back. I was dizzy for a long time, so by the time I got back, she wasn't mad any more. She doesn't ever stay mad long. But, from what she's saying, it's probably because she now has a crush on the guy who runs the bumper cars, Lou. Her father would kill her if he knew she was talking to boys. I think when she's with me, he thinks there's no chance of that happening (or that's what she says anyway). I don't know whether that's a compliment or an insult, but I don't really care either. I think she's really silly about boys. When we went on the beach, we changed our names and told these boys big lies about how we were rich and all. I think they knew we were lying, though, because my cousin says I told them I was an only child 15 times during a 15 minute conversation. And, she says, people don't do that unless they're lying. She's starting to think she knows everything. She forgets that she told them that back home she smokes; and when they asked her what brand, she said Lucky Hits. Miss Know It All meant Lucky Strikes, and now she denies that she said it at all.

She keeps telling me she hopes I get boobs. I said, "What's it to you?" She says that I look like a child. I think she thinks I'm interfering with her love life, a love life which is only in her mind, I may add.

Anybody would get dizzy riding on the Tilt-a-Whirl four times, and she didn't have boobs when she was 10 either. That doesn't mean I'm a child. I think the fact that I am a child means I'm a child. I don't want boobs or boys, and I surely don't want any blood coming out of me. What I do want is an ice cream, and she won't get me one, even though I spent all my money on the Tilt-a-Whirl so she could talk to Greg. It seems to me that it wasn't too long ago that the most important man in her life was Humpty Dumpty.

September 18th, 1956

My birthday's over and I am officially 11. My father says I am built like my age, straight up and down. Anyway, we're going to hold an election in our class right on the real election day in November. Everybody's father is a Democrat but mine. He says Republicans are for the businessman. I don't tell anybody though because I don't want to be different, so I lie. I can't wait til both elections are over because every week I usually have to confess to about ten lies just for the elections. I lie about other things too, but 10 above my regulars doesn't sound too good. Last time I had to say 10 Hail Marys and 10 Our Fathers and do the Stations of the Cross. I was in church for an hour. By the time I got out I couldn't do what I normally do after confession, and that is stop at the bakery and buy six cream puffs, which I eat before I get home. We don't have dinner at 5 on Saturdays because the store's busy, so I can get away with it. Sunday's dinner is at 12, and even though cream puffs are my new most favorite things, if I'm full, I'm full. It seems so simple really. I try to explain it to my mother often, but she says I wouldn't be full so much if I stopped eating junk. They're calling me *lick-a-lick* these days. Out of the whole family, it seems I'm called the most names. In addition to the descriptive ones (we're learning about these in school this year), my grandmother calls me *granda-mom*, my father calls me *daddy*, and my mother calls me *mommy*. And they say I'm a *stewnod*.

Anyway, I'd like to be elected president, but when anybody mentions it, I pretend I'm not good enough. But honestly, I am. I don't even bother to confess this because Sister says humility is a good thing, and the way I look at it, I'm being humble just like Jesus.

Miss Goody-Two-Shoes has to learn to be humble. She told Sister she's going to hold a campaign like they do in real life. I don't know who she thinks is going to vote for her, nobody likes her. We love her though because we're Catholic. I notice since she said that, she's been smiling at everybody. She even brought in chocolate chip cookies. Sister says if we hold campaigns, we need slogans. I think hers should be, "Get the winter blues, vote for Goody-Two-Shoes," or maybe, "I will rat on no one during my term in office." That way, at least she could be sure to get Joey's vote. I also notice that when Sister asks for volunteers to clean the blackboard, not only didn't she put her hand up, like she usually does, she actually smiled at the rest of us who did. It's fun to clean the blackboard. The smell of chalk is great. Mary Lou gets picked. I think it's the first time in two years anyone had a chance because Goody's arm is usually in the air as soon as Sister says "Do I have..." Sister doesn't even get the word "volunteer" out. Most of us are daydreaming a lot of the time, so Goody's always picked. She says her campaign song is going to be "You Gotta Have Heart." She seems to have it all mapped out. Sister explains to us the importance of elections and how we should elect someone who's going to uphold everything we stand for. That person has to have leadership ability, be smart, fair, and willing to listen to everybody's gripes, and be able to fix them. She said our president should also act as a voice between his or her classmates and the nuns.

I'm perfect for the job, but I can't act as if I want it because then I wouldn't be humble. People might think "I think who I am." It is a difficult position I'm in. I don't even have to ask my mother because I already know what she'll say. She'll say that I should let other people think I'm right for the job, that she can't stand show-offs, and also she'll say she will not bake any cookies. So I guess I have to figure this out on my own. We have until October 1st to declare our candidacy, that gives me two weeks.

September 20th, 1956

Although I don't really want to ask my cousin about the election, I do because she does know things. Of course, being in the 7th grade and into boys (her words), this is silly to her. She says that I have to face facts, that I'm not a leader, just a crybaby. I remind her how brave I was doing all those dangerous physical things when I was 7 and 8, but she says I was just stupid, not brave. I then remind her how I went to the dentist myself to have a tooth removed, and she reminded me that when I left the dentist's office, I was so dizzy that I sat in front of the building and fell asleep, and she had to come get me. I remember that the dentist made me bite on this black thing that looked like licorice, but wasn't. The only thing worse than a know-it-all is a know-it-all with a good memory.

I remind her about all the times that I stayed alone on St. John Street when my mother was working. Her answer to this is not only did she do that, but cooked dinner too. Hah! That's a joke. Then I bring up the time we were in a Christmas pageant and we each had to say Merry Christmas in our forebears' native language, mine in Italian and hers in Polish, and how she forgot the words, and I said them for her. When I tell her this, she pushes me because I promised never to tell anybody. I try to explain that I never did and that telling her doesn't count because she was there and already knows. But she's mad and she leaves. And I don't know anything more than I did before our painful discussion.

September 21st, 1956

I finally know what I have to do. I have to get a campaign manager because if somebody else tells everyone what a great president I'd make and brags about my good qualities, I could still remain humble and win the election too. I know just the person, Mary Lou. Mary Lou is the nicest girl I know. She never judges anybody. Once in a while, though, Goody-Two-Shoes even gets to her.

I don't know how to ask her because I don't want anybody really to know how much I want to be president. I don't even know why winning the election is so important, but I know every time I get an A in school or do something special (which is rare), it makes my father really happy and I become his daughter. Every time I do something wrong (which is often), he tells my mother that she'd "better straighten her daughter out." Winning the election would surely please him. My mother has this new saying that I better straighten up and fly right. I know what it means. I just wonder where she hears these things. Now that I'm 11, instead of saying "Your problem is..." or "You know what the worst thing you could be is...", she says that the "best thing I could be is..." It's a slight change, but makes me feel as if I may be improving. Her ideas on how to be a "best thing" are awfully hard though. She says that what she admires in a person is somebody who never thinks of herself, but only thinks of other people. That's another reason why I don't want to tell her about the election. She also likes generous people, people who share. One day last week I had a bag of potato chips so I thought I'd try this sharing thing out. I was eating lunch with my friends, and by the time they all took some chips, there wasn't one left for me. My stomach growled all afternoon, and I couldn't concentrate on anything except those chips. So I went home thinking she'd be real pleased that I shared and reward me. But she said that I should "do good and forget, do bad and remember," and that it was too close to dinner for me to be eating chips. She also said that anyone who brags about doing good things is disgusting. I think this might be a game I can't win.

<u>September 22nd, 1956</u>

I can't wait too much longer to discuss this with Mary Lou because I have to declare my candidacy by October 1st, and that's only eight days away. I have to give her sufficient time to toot my horn so that when I declare, I can act as if I'm doing it just to please everybody. The Old Testament says that somebody else should toot your horn, not you. It doesn't say it exactly like that, but that's what it means. And my mother has this theory that if you're pretty and/or smart, people should see it and you shouldn't have to tell them. Or, she says, maybe you're not so pretty or so smart at all. Time is running out. Sister says when we're confused about how to do things, we should make a list first. So I did, and here it is.

<u>Presidency</u>
1. Swear Mary Lou to secrecy.
2. Tell her I'd like to be president.
3. Tell her it must seem like it's her idea.
4. Tell her she must remind everyone of my good marks.
5. Tell her she must say that I'm a leader.
6. Tell her she must advise that she already has ideas for a slogan. She has to say it just like that because if she says she wrote it, when I did, she will be lying. I don't want to be an occasion of sin for her.
7. I have to write the slogan.
8. She must (and this is important) poll the class to see if I can get a majority vote, because I'd rather know this before I declare my candidacy.
9. She must tell the kids that I never get in trouble, and also remind Angela, Carla, Theresa, and Rosie how many times I help them with their homework.
10. And then she is to report to me.

I think she can handle it. There are 29 kids in our class right now. Joey's mother has sent him to military school. I hope Goody is happy. So I have to get 15 votes. I wonder if I should vote for myself.

September 23rd, 1956

It's Saturday and I've spent all day trying to think up a slogan. Sister says a slogan should be short, to the point, but contain all the things we stand for. I think I stand for liberty, justice, and happiness, but none of these words rhyme with Milissa, Missy, or Maroni. Sister also says that people remember slogans better if they rhyme. I haven't told my parents about the election because if I don't win, my father will call me a loser. Sister says there are no losers, only people who don't try. But it's really easy to be a loser in my house, no matter how hard you try.

September 27th, 1956

Mary Lou is reporting back that, counting her vote, I can be sure of 13. She isn't sure about the boys. We're both sure about who Goody's voting for, though. I think probably, if none of the boys declares his candidacy, I may get most of the boys' votes because they don't like Goody any more than the girls do. But I wonder if that means, being Catholic, they love her more. We are going to have a secret ballot, just like the real election, so I've decided I'll vote for myself. And if anyone asks, I'll just say we have to honor the secret ballot system, and remind them that the Bible says your left hand should never know what your right hand is doing. So if the secrecy explanation doesn't work, I can always use the Bible to get out of answering.

The Bible also says if your left eye commits sin, it's better if you tear it out of your head than sin with it. I hope voting for yourself is not a sin. I can't afford to lose my right hand, my writing is bad enough as it is. I think a guaranteed 14 votes is a good start, so I decide to take a chance. After all, I only need one more vote, and if my mother's right and Mikey does have a crush on me and votes for me, that will do it.

September 29th, 1956

I've come up with some possible slogans:
Don't be a sissy, vote for Missy.
If Missy can't do it, it can't be done.
Vote Maroni and have some fun.
Milissa stands tall for fairness and fun.
Vote Maroni and it will get done.

I think they're good, but I think Sister might comment about the fun part because she keeps saying that holding office is a holy challenge and that one must give a lot of thought for whom we vote. That "for whom" really gets to me. I mean, we learned to use whom when it is an object of a preposition, but nobody I know says "for whom." My mother says there's a good book entitled _For Whom the Bell Tolls_. Isn't that a great title? I wish I knew Hemingway. I'd ask him to write a slogan for me.

Anyway, I think I have to rethink this slogan business and maybe give up on the rhyme. Although I know the kids like rhymes. I've started to write poems this year for fun, and all my friends always want to read them. They say "I loooove this," just like that, stretching the word "love." I like to write poems. Usually after you do something that's fun, when you're done, it's over. But when I write a poem, I always have something to keep, and I'm going to keep them forever. The way I look at it is you can write the truth about your innermost feelings and if people ask you if it is about you, you just can say no. They can't prove it because no one really knows what your feelings are. I know it might sound like I'm a big liar, but I'm not really, at least I won't be after these elections are over. Sometimes I tell a lie, but not about anything important. Well, not important to me anyway. Like, for example, once my cousin asked me if I liked the new white lipstick she was wearing and I said I did. She really looked like a stupid ghost, but I said that because she might have pinched my arm. She's into pinching arms these days, a form of discipline previously used by both our mothers in public places. My mother always used to say then she pinched me, "If you cry, I'll kill you." I think it must be a sin to pinch your kids and threaten their lives. But who can I possibly ask?

Today my mother wanted to know if I had a snack at Mary's after school and I said "No," because I am not allowed junk food in the afternoons. I lied because I didn't want to be sent to my room, but I forgot to wipe the red from the red taffy I had off my mouth. That's why I'm thinking up slogans now because I'm in my room. No TV after dinner, even if I eat my dinner. The punishment is for lying. Lying to your mother, apparently, is the new worst thing I could ever do. Someday, if my mother is ever in a good mood, I might ask her if we could sit down and she could tell me, so I could write down, all the things she thinks are the worst things I could do in order of importance. I think it would be easier for me to figure things out if I had a list, because now, it seems, every time I do something, it immediately becomes the worst. It's really hard to keep track, and there must be some order to things. But, maybe not. Miss Know-It-All says there's no rhyme or reason to anything. Things just happen. I think she's becoming philosophical these days because one of the boys she had a crush on during the summer is going steady with someone else. She says it's not easy being jilted. She never even talked to him. And she says *I'm* dramatic. Once I was really excited about something and I was saying it, apparently dramatically, and she stood up and clapped. She said I deserved an Academy Award.

There's two things I wish would happen. One—I hope to get bigger than her; and two—I wish I could get a two-speed bicycle. Then who knows what might happen.

Anyway, when she clapped, I got mad and called her a Miss Know-It-All, and she said if she's Miss Know-It-All, then I must be Miss-Doesn't-Know-Nothing-at-All. All I will say is that it is obvious why I was so impressed by Sister saying "for whom."

October 1st, 1956

I have declared my candidacy today. It was no big deal, Sister just asked who would like to run for president and I raised my hand, as did Goody and Thomas Renna. Thomas is the smartest boy in our class; but because of that, most of the boys don't like him much. And he's not real cute or anything, so the girls don't like him much either. I may have a chance. Sister says that we must conduct this election as Catholics, which means that we cannot lie to get votes, or bribe anybody, or promise anything we cannot deliver. Sometimes I think there are three parts to me: my mind, which I'm always aware of; my soul, which I worry about a lot; and my heart, which holds my feelings about the other two. I try to make my mind stop thinking about what I'm feeling, because sometimes it's sad. But my mind's not sad. It makes me say things that everybody laughs at, but my mother, who says I'm not funny a little bit, and my cousin, who says I'm not funny, just silly, and that I get on her nerves because I laugh too much. I found out what a scorch is. It is a pain in the neck, somebody who gets on your nerves.

When my heart is sad, I go to church and I tell God what's bothering me because my mother says my problem is I don't know what real problems are, and that I should have had her life, then I'd know. Sometimes I sit on my grandmother's lap when I'm sad, but I only cry when I'm alone. It's not the same kind of crying like when I'm scared. It's a different kind. I really can't explain it. I try to remember what I'm thinking about when I cry so I'll know why, but I can never remember thinking anything, I just feel really sad.

Sometimes when I see old people alone, I cry too. I think it must be terrible to be old and nobody wants to be with you, and nobody loves you. One time I started to cry in a restaurant when I saw some old people all alone, and my mother told me to stop because if they could go to restaurants, there was nothing to cry about. I try to tell her that their faces look sad, but she says I'm imagining it. Maybe everybody's sad sometimes. My mother used to be sad a lot, and she'd cry and cry when we lived in the other house. Sometimes she'd say she wanted to die because my father was no good, she had to work all the time, and we never had any money. I think she was so sad because she didn't have any mother. I tried to be really good after she cried because I felt so sorry for her. And even though I was scared when she sent me to pay the rent by myself, or when I was all alone in the house, I tried to act as if I wasn't. I also tried to be really good in school because I thought maybe if she was proud of me, she wouldn't think her life was a waste and that she should never have gotten married or had kids. But she's so much better since we took over the store and moved to this house. She isn't so sad any more, so why am I? I write lots of poems when I'm sad, but I don't show them to anybody. I only show them the funny ones.

My friends who are only children say they are lonely and they are sad sometimes. But I'm not an only child, and there's always lots of people around, so loneliness can't be my problem.

I hope I'm not sick like my mother's mother, who was in love with a young man who got killed in the war. She was forced to marry my grandfather who she didn't love and who didn't treat her very nicely, and she had seven children and no money.

So one day, she sat on the floor with my mother and the other kids and put the gas on. That's when she had to go away to the hospital. My mother goes to see her sometimes and she's awfully unhappy when she comes home, even now, and I never know what to do. She scares me after she goes to see her mother. She said that soon she's going to bring her mother to visit on a Sunday from the hospital. That scares me a little too. I never met anyone who is not in her right mind. We are never allowed to use the word "crazy." Sometimes the kids in school use it and it makes me feel funny just to hear it. Somehow I feel I'm doing something wrong by not saying anything to them.

Sometimes my mother says she should just kill herself because we don't appreciate her. I really love my mother, I always try to make her happy, but she's never happy for very long. She says I must never do anything that's wrong because people will talk about her being a bad mother and say she shouldn't have had kids so young. I don't know why this bothers her so much, but she says it all the time. She's always making sure we're clean, we're never allowed to get dirty or bring any dirt in the house. She always says, "What will they think?" I asked her one day who "they" were, but she says I was trying to be smart. I wasn't though. She and my Aunt Bootie always talk about "they," and I just wanted to know who "they" were, that's all.

One time she even said she'd be better off where her mother was. That really scared me a lot. I remember in the other house, when I was about 7, she and my father were fighting and she told him that if it wasn't for me, she would never have married him. It took me a long time to try and figure out how I had anything to do with it, so I had to give up thinking about it because I probably was small and don't remember. My father said he wouldn't have married her either. So sometimes I think I'm sad because I caused both of them to be unhappy. It's my fault she has to work so hard and that my father used to hit her, because if she hadn't married him, her life would be different.

I really try to make her proud. I want her to think that I was worth her marrying my father. Sometimes I do make her happy too, like when I was small and she used to dress me up and tell me to sit on the step because probably somebody from Hollywood would see me and want me to be a movie star. I heard her tell somebody once that I was her ace in the hole. I didn't know what that meant, but it seemed to be good by the way they smiled at me. She likes when I get good marks and when I get along with everybody. She doesn't say it, but I know she does by her eyes. Sometimes she makes me feel like the most important person in the world, but sometimes I feel she doesn't even see me. It's okay really. I'm happy a lot, and when I get sad, I get happy again fast.

I always try not to get mad because if I get mad, I might say things I don't mean and wind up hurting people. I don't like to look at people's faces when they're hurt. Besides, I'm not allowed to ever get mad. It confuses me how I am expected to defend myself if I'm not allowed to get mad.

October 4th, 1956

My slogan is either going to be "If you like M&Ms, you'll like <u>Mi</u>ssy <u>Ma</u>roni." Or "Go with Maroni or you'll <u>miss</u> your chance to pick a winner." Or "Be sure of this, with Maroni you can't <u>miss</u>." I'm going to discuss these slogans with Mary Lou because she's my campaign manager. I like them all, but the third one rhymes.

Sister says we have to give a speech before the election and tell the class what our platform is. Apparently, a platform is what you believe in and want to accomplish during your term. I figured I'd better ask around to see what the kids think is important, and then figure out if I can deliver. But, so far, all they'll tell me is that they want longer lunches, longer recess periods, less homework, and fewer tests. But there's no way I can get those things. I don't even have to ask, I know. They think we should have movies shown every week, instead of once a month. That has possibilities.

I told my parents about the election, and my father said anything I need to know I should ask him. He always says this about school work too. But every time I ask him, he says to look it up in the dictionary or encyclopedia, so now I just go directly to the books.

I decided to ask him about the way I should give my speech so that I don't promise anything I can't deliver, but let the kids know I will try. He says that people in politics do this all the time. I had to remind him we're Catholic. He says my speech should show that I'm aware of the desires of my classmates and I will do everything in my power to bring those desires to the attention of the appropriate people. I'm writing it down as he says it because I want to make sure I won't be lying. But it is perfect. He is really smart. I will mention the longer lunches and recesses and also fewer tests and less homework to the nuns so I will be fulfilling my promises. That is the only thing I can do. Our speeches are on the Friday before Election Tuesday. This way, Sister says, everybody can have all weekend to think about their choice, as it is very important. Although I think most of the kids already know who they're voting for, Friday's better for me, then I won't have the whole weekend to write and rewrite my speech. I get like that sometimes. My mother says I have a one track mind and she is right. Sister said that when we give our speech, we have to address her first, then the class. I haven't written it yet, just the opening, in case I forget what she said. Sister Auxilia says we should begin with something like, "My worthy opponents and ladies and gentlemen." I'm not sure whether opponents should go after ladies and gentlemen, so I'll have to check with my father. I found out he's pretty good about these things. He says it always helps to put in a joke because people like you when you make them laugh, like I didn't know that. But, he said, most of the speech has to be serious and strong. He also says to stand up straight because I have a tendency to slouch. He didn't say he was proud of me, but I knew he was because I've been "his" daughter since he found out. He told Danny, his friend, that I get my brains from him. And he told me that I can be anything I want, and that marriage is not always the answer. Every once in a while he asks me what I want to be when I grow up, usually after I get my report card. He never says that my report card is good, just to get the B's up and to practice my writing. But he does smile when he hands it back and that's good. My mother said she can't figure out how she got such a smart kid because she wasn't any good in school. I think maybe she should ask my father because he seems to know, and I'm not about to tell her.

October 13th, 1956

Mary Lou is 11 today. I'm older by 27 days. She had a real neat party at her house and we did our new tap steps for everybody. We practiced it before so we would do the moves at the exact time. "Synchronize, synchronize," Mrs. Bowman says all the time, so I looked it up in the dictionary and that's what it means. We had lots of practicing to do. It's just about how long you hold the beat. Mary Lou is a really good dancer, I am too but I don't tell anybody I think so. But they tell me all the time. Mary Lou and I love to dance. I think I probably love it better than anything, even candy, and that's saying something. I'm not certain if dancing beats bubble gum though. I think they're tied. Now I have to stop telling Mary Lou that I'm older than she so she has to respect me because I was 11 and she was only 10 for three weeks. I just did it to be funny because she's always so nice to me. She never laughs at me. She laughs at all my jokes though and tells me how smart I am. I think we'll probably be best friends forever. I hope so.

November 2nd, 1956

I gave my speech today. I didn't slouch and tried to speak in a forceful voice. My father says women have screechy voices and I should speak slowly and loud. Once in a while, I get worried because if I don't win, I think my father's going to say I'm nothing but a loser and I take after my mother's family. I really like it when I make him proud and he says, "My daughter is just like me." Even though my mother says that's the worst thing I could be, I like to be like him, in some things anyway, not the bad parts though. Sister says we all have strong points and weak points and we shouldn't judge other people. Jesus says it too. He says, "Judge not lest you be judged." Sister Mary Catherine says that everybody is the "best" at something, even if it is being the best at not being the best at anything. I don't judge people too much except for Goody, and I'm trying to figure out what each person I know is best at. It's pretty easy too. My cousin is best at knowing mature things. My mother is best at working. And my Aunt Boot is best at cooking. My grandmother is best at hugging. My father is best at talking. Mary Lou is best at being a best friend. Goody is best at ratting everyone out. I have to admit, though, she's been nicer since she's running for president. I think I'm best at making people laugh and also writing poems. This is easy to be best at though, because nobody else does it. I showed my father one of my poems and he didn't believe I wrote it, but I did.

I was relieved when the speech was over. Thomas Renna

spoke first but he was too serious and he tried to use all these big words, which I think went over everybody's head. I think it's a good thing to be smart, but not a good thing to act smart. Then I give my speech. Mary Lou was smiling at me all the time and that made it easier. We also had some secret gestures. I told her if I started to slouch, she was supposed to let me know by sitting up straight in her chair. I don't know if I didn't slouch or she forgot, but she never did make the gesture. If I started to talk too fast, she was supposed to clear her throat. She did this two times and I did slow down, but she told me later she was really clearing her throat, so now I'm worried I might have talked too slowly.

Then Miss Goody-Two-Shoes got up. She gave a pretty good speech, I'll give her that. Even though she's a pain and all, I wish she gets more than her own vote because that would be awful. I did go with the third slogan because it rhymed, and I thought all the kids would like it. The election is on Tuesday, November 6th, 1956. Unlike the real election, where the president will be sworn in in January, the winner of our election will be sworn in on the same day. I think it's because America already has a president between November and January and our class doesn't.

I talked about lunch, recess, homework and tests just like my father said to, and I told the class I stood for safety in the halls and school yard, less tests, more movies, less homework, and longer recesses and lunch. I think the thing they liked the most is when I said if they have any problems, I would take them to the proper source and try to have them resolved. My father says you always have to use weasel words in politics because weasel words allow you to weasel out later. Sister says the new president will get to choose her vice president, secretary, and treasurer, and she'll even be allowed to choose the person who will clean the blackboard. Well, that should eliminate Miss Goody if either she or I win. She wouldn't dare pick herself, or would she? That's the problem with Goody, you just never know.

November 6th, 1956

I won. I received 18 votes. Sister didn't tell the class who received the other votes, which was probably better for Goody. Sister says there are no losers, but Goody looks like she's ready to cry. I can understand that because I'd probably look the same way. I don't know what she's thinking, but I know what I'd be thinking. How am I going to tell my father? Because if I lost by one vote, it wouldn't matter. Only winning matters to him.

Since he says all the time he only married my mother because of me, if he thinks I'm a loser, I'm afraid he'll leave. Once when I was small, about six, he sat me on his lap and told me he was leaving. I started to cry and when my mother came home, I was still crying. She said he wasn't going anywhere and that I should stop being such a baby because she already had a baby. And that she didn't understand what the big deal was anyway because he was no father. I wanted to tell her that he was "my" father, but I didn't because then she'd get mad at me or cry, and I hated it when she did either.

My father got a real big smile on his face when I told him I won. He rubbed his hands together, which he does when he's happy. Sometimes I'm really happy to be me. My mother was pleased too. Maybe if I just keep winning things, I'll make them happy I was born and then they'll be happy they married each other and had kids.

Sister says important positions carry important responsibilities, and she hopes that I will remember that. How can I ever forget that, being the oldest child?

Sister swore me into office and said I was to pick the vice

president, treasurer, and secretary by Friday, November 9th. I already know who my vice president is going to be—Mary Lou. But Sister says that the treasurer should be somebody who is good at math, and the secretary should have good penmanship because she'll have to take the minutes down at our meetings. I'm not sure what those meetings will be like, but I think they're probably like giving a book report except there's no book and no opinions. I want to show Sister that I take my responsibilities seriously so I nod my head. I found out that nodding your head without smiling makes people think you understand or are agreeing with them. Everyone seems to like it when you do this. At first, I didn't understand but when I was explaining to Mary Lou my plans to be president, she did it and then I understood. So I decided to use this gesture often during my term. That'll be easy. What I think might be hard is having no expression on my face. I'm always getting in trouble for making faces I don't even know I'm making. The other day my mother said something and I apparently rolled my eyes. TV was really going to be good that night. So I have to be careful about this.

I watch all the people in my family and they make faces at each other all the time. I guess it's okay for adults to do, but not for kids.

November 11th, 1956

My mother's trying to teach me how to knit and it's not pretty. I can't seem to do one line without dropping a stitch. Once you do that, you have to fix it immediately so I have to keep bothering her and she doesn't have much patience. She tells everybody that knitting makes her relax. Well, it makes me nervous, especially when I have to tell her that I dropped a stitch again. She's making a large blanket of different colored squares which she'll sew together. She thought with my help that she would get it done sooner, but I think, after a week, we both know better. She told me today that I'm slowing her down and maybe she'll teach me another time since she really wants to get this blanket done. I think these are probably weasel words because she stresses the word *maybe*.

My mother knits, sews and bakes, and I can't do any of those things. She doesn't even try to teach me to sew or bake, but that's all right. I don't have any interest anyway. Everyone says I'll never be like my mother. What I don't understand is how I'm expected to be like both my father and my mother when they're nothing like each other. My father says what he's forgotten I'll never learn, and I ask him what good learning is if you forget it. He sees no humor in this remark. Maybe he's "forgotten" how funny I can be. I like to make him laugh. I can too, sometimes. I know he laughs at me a lot, mostly because I'm skinny, slow, and a "stewnod." I think both my parents should talk to Sister so she can tell them about not judging people. It must be another one of the things he forgot.

I really don't like to be laughed at, but there isn't much I can do about it but pretend I'm laughing. The way I figure it is you can either cry or laugh, and from where I sit, laughing is better. And besides, they stop faster if you laugh. If they know it's bothering you, they seem to do it even longer.

December 4th, 1956

We had our first class meeting today and it was stupid, if you ask me. I have to name my cabinet. I chose Thomas to be treasurer because he's the smartest boy and I figure he must be good in math because Sister always says boys are better at math. I picked Cathy as secretary because her handwriting is excellent and also because I like her, because almost everyone has good handwriting in this class, except me. I can't figure it out. How can I be so smart in everything else and not be able to figure out how to write the way they want. My father always says success comes from figuring out what people want and giving it to them. I think he's right about this. He just bought a new hi-fi with a PA system and plays Mario Lanza records all day. He says it brings all the Italians into the store. It seems to me the same people are coming in, but when my mother told him this, he said she was not a business woman, that's for sure. She said he was right, she was a slave. My father then said, "Work is made for fools and mules." I don't think he should have said it during this conversation with my mother though. She's been in her room for two days.

My question is, if family is the most important thing, why doesn't he apply his success rules to it and try to give us what we want? But he doesn't.

December 12th, 1956

I don't care if I burn in hell for eternity or if the sky opens and I'm struck by lightning. I hate, hate my sister. We have a project to hand in tomorrow on China. In addition to a written report, we have to submit visuals showing all the important things for which China is known. We could draw it or cut out pictures. We are to be graded both for content and originality. I bought a large sheet of construction paper and, after reading about China and writing my report, I thought I would paste pictures on the construction paper of things which reflect China's culture. I got some rice, some real rice, a tea bag, and beans. I couldn't find soybeans so I substituted coffee beans instead. I also got some chopsticks and a large picture of Asia on which I colored in China only. I had it all ready to be glued and my intention was to do it after dinner when my little brother was asleep because he makes too much noise and I needed to concentrate. I was also afraid he might upset it before I got it finished. I put everything in place right after school, and after dinner I went upstairs to the bedroom I share with my sister and found that she had absolutely destroyed my whole project. It had taken me weeks to gather everything and she just took the glue and glued everything all over the paper. I started screaming and my mother came running upstairs. I was angry and I didn't care that I was angry. Sister says that sometimes there is righteous anger, like when Jesus got angry in the temple. I wanted to hit my sister but I didn't. Hitting people is usually not the first thing I do or, in fact, ever do. My mother asked her why she had done it and she played all innocent, but she knew what she was doing. My mother told me to stop carrying on. I was yelling, "It has to be in tomorrow. I'm going to fail. It took so long. I hate her." My mother reminded me that she was only 5 and that she was my sister, like that makes everything all right.

Luckily, there's a PTA meeting tonight. My mother said she'd tell Sister and she was certain Sister would give me an extension. She did tell my sister that was a bad thing to do and she should go to bed. I'd like to see what would have happened to me if I had done something like that. Why am I always supposed to know what's right and wrong and the rest of them get away with murder? Then, after my mother went to PTA, I started to cry. I knew the rice, tea bag, and beans were easy enough to replace, but it was going to take a lot of time to find another picture of Asia, and forget those chopsticks. We never go to restaurants because my mother says we have the best of food at home, and I had never eaten Chinese food because she thinks I won't like it. So it was a problem getting those chopsticks. I told my mother that Chinese people in the restaurant on Broadway always smiled at me and called me "Miss," and they seemed so nice so maybe I could just go in and ask them for some. She said that would make me a "cavone." A "cavone" is an Italian word for someone who has a hard face and no manners. I said I could ask to buy them, but she wouldn't hear of it. Just when I had given up on including them in the project, although I did think they were absolutely necessary, our neighbor, Ro-Ro, said she was going to the Chinese restaurant for dinner. Now I knew if I asked her to get me some chopsticks that would make me a "cavone," so I started talking to her about how I was doing this project for school on China and what an interesting culture I found it. Then I asked her if their food is good, and she said she loved it. I told her that I was doing a written and visual report and that I was including rice and tea, blah, blah, blah. I asked her how they cooked their rice and if it was eaten with a spoon. Her face lit up when she told me how the Chinese always used chopsticks. I asked her whether they were hard to use and she said she'd bring me some home and show me.

Now, for the record, I never asked for those chopsticks and I was polite, and when my mother asked me how I got them, I knew I wouldn't get in trouble. I think I did a good thing because Ro-Ro seemed happy to help. My father always says it's a good thing to get people to do things for you, but what's even better than that is convincing them they've enjoyed it. I don't like myself when I'm not honest. I would rather have just asked right out. I think she would have been just as happy to help, but I think I would have been happier. And now that my horrible sister has ruined it, I think God is punishing me for my dishonesty. But frankly, as bad as felt after I tricked Ro-Ro, I wish I could do it again. Those chopsticks really did make the project special.

I'm sitting here waiting for my mother, hoping that Sister at least gives me a week. My mother comes home about 8:30 p.m. beaming and she said Sister understood and gave me two weeks' extension. Apparently Sister told her I'm very smart and a pleasure to have in her class. She also said I'm nice and the kids really like me and that I'm college material. I know my mother can't wait to tell my father and the rest of the world. I do like it when I make my mother happy. It makes me feel all warm and tingly inside. I wish she could be happy like this all the time.

Sometimes I look in my mother's eyes and they're shining with love. They used to shine when I was little and she'd sing "Baby Face" to me or "You Ought To Be In Pictures," or "Daddy's Little Girl." I used to feel so beautiful and special and that being Missy Maroni was a good thing to be and that she was happy I was born. She never hugged or kissed me, but in those moments I knew. Once I asked her why she never hugged and kissed and she said that she was too busy working so I could eat and she didn't go in for all that mushy stuff anyway. She said that kisses didn't iron my dresses. I used to think sometimes that I would rather have had wrinkled dresses and a kiss.

December 16th, 1956

I've totally ignored my sister since she destroyed my project. I won't be like the rest of them, always screaming at each other. Sometimes I think that's why they think I'm "stewnod" because I try not to pay any attention to them. It's intentional.

My mother is always hollering at my father because she said he's nothing but a lazy bum and she's nothing but a slave. My grandmother is always fighting with my Aunt Boot who usually starts it. My aunt is the worst of them all. She actually screams, stomps her feet and bites her fingers all at the same time. She slams doors, calls people terrible names, and throws things. I'm a little afraid of her. My father basically yells and screams at everybody, me, in particular. I'm not sure why he's always so mad. Like yesterday, he started screaming because he couldn't find his comb. I ran upstairs and gave him a comb, but he started yelling even louder because he said he wanted his "blue" comb. I admit that I don't always know what's important, but somehow the color of the comb doesn't seem important to me at all.

Sometimes people talk to each other in normal voices, usually when company is over or somebody's in the store. I hate all the noise, so I go to my room and read, or I go to a movie, or I daydream. The worst part of it all is that I can't find any way I'm like these people.

Sometimes at night, when my mother starts yelling at my father after my aunt and grandmother go home, I wish she'd stop because when he yells back, there's a certain tone of voice he gets that makes me afraid. So I lay on my back and say over and over in my head, "Stop, stop, stop." It works, too, so far he hasn't hit her. But it's awful when they have these kinds of fights because they're both in bad moods for days. He hollers if I walk across the room, and she doesn't have time for me and doesn't want to talk about anything. They just give each other these dirty looks and a cold shoulder. I know the Church doesn't believe in divorce, but sometimes I think we'd all be better off if they did.

My sister is angry often too. Instead of apologizing to me for what she did to my project, she said she was glad she did it. I can't figure out why they're all so angry. The only one I can talk to is my cousin because I'm not allowed to tell anyone what happens in this house. Not that I would. I'd be too embarrassed. But sometimes I talk to Rosalie. I know I tease her and all, but she understands. I think we're going to be the best of friends as soon as I become a woman and stop acting like a crybaby.

When I go to my friends' houses, it seems like everybody talks really nice to everybody else, but my mother says I don't know what goes on behind closed doors. I don't but I don't think their families carry on like mine does.

The other night my Aunt Lissa and my Uncle John were

over. Everybody was sitting around the table having coffee and cake, when my aunt and uncle started arguing. My uncle got mad, took my aunt's mink coat off the chair and threw it on the floor. When he did this, I think he may have pushed her shoulder, but I can't be sure because it happened so fast. The next thing I knew, my father jumped up from the other side of the table and threatened my uncle. My uncle got up and they started arguing about how my father should stay out of his business and my father punched him right in the face. My uncle staggered backwards until he was stopped by the pickle barrel in our store, which he wound up sitting in. It was funny so I left the room to laugh. My uncle wasn't hurt or anything.

My father says nobody's going to hit his sister. Two months ago, he beat up my Uncle Jack, his own brother, for hitting my Aunt Estelle. Since he stopped hitting my mother, it seems he has a lot of righteous anger. Sister says that converts to Catholicism are much more serious about it than those born into it. Maybe it's the same thing with my father and hitting women. My mother's tough too. She said once this girl was spreading lies about her so she rang her doorbell and when the girl answered, she punched her right in the face. You can see they're really proud when they're telling these stories. I don't like hitting people; in fact, I never even think about doing it except that once with my sister and once or twice with Goody. That's why I don't fight back or anything. They think I'm a wimp and laugh about it all the time.

January 15th, 1957

My mother's furious. When I got weighed in school I was four pounds below normal weight. You would think I killed somebody. She thinks it's a disgrace, especially when they have all that food. I've been getting these horrible sore throats all year. The doctor says I should have my tonsils out, but it hasn't been scheduled or anything. My glands get all swollen and I can't swallow, let alone eat. I get these high fevers too. My mother says I've always been sickly and that when I was small all she had to do was take me out in the cold and I got sick. She blames my sore throats on my skinniness, but I think maybe I'm skinny because of my sore throats. Also, I'm anemic and I have to get B12 and liver and iron shots every week. When I went for a blood test, the woman said I needed to eat oranges. My mother became extremely angry and she told the woman that we have a store filled with oranges and maybe *she* should come over and see if she could get me to eat them because she, my mother, couldn't.

I think she's really embarrassed by me and can't understand why I don't like to eat. She said I look like a scarecrow and if I stand sideways, no one would be able to see me. You know, for someone who is so concerned with my thinking before I speak so I won't hurt anybody's feelings, she sure hurts mine left and right. My parents are good at doing one thing and telling me to do another. Although I must go to Mass every Sunday, they never go. This worries me too because Sister says anybody who doesn't go to Mass on Sunday is committing a mortal sin and if you die with a mortal sin on your soul, you go to hell. I'm trying really hard to get to heaven but I don't want to be there without my mother.

They also tell me I'm not allowed to get angry, but they do all the time, and I'm not permitted to say curse words, but they do all the time, especially my father. He says "Jesus Christ" every time he gets mad and that's every day about 12 times. But the best one is when they tell me I shouldn't judge people. They call me skinny, *liege*, speedy, *stewnod*, petsey (because I look like my father), and *dradrool*, which is an Italian word meaning cucumber, but it also means dopey. Don't they know that these words are all words of judgment?

February 2nd, 1957

My friends and I have discovered the Mickey Mouse Club, which comes on TV every day after school. That's all we talk about. Our favorite Mousketeer is Annette Funicello. We all want to look like her, especially me. She has this beautiful black curly hair, so I had my mother give me a permanent. She did and it smelled awful and it looked like somebody fried my hair. My mother is no hairdresser. Even she knows it because she said next time, she'd send me to one. Annette is close to our age, and I think sometimes we all pretend we are her. She's Italian but that's only part of it. She's pretty, talented, and sings nice too. We go to Tina's house almost every day, stand in a line like they do on the Mickey Mouse Club, and say their names just like they do on the show. We try to do the dances and sing the songs, especially "M-I-C K-E-Y M-O-U-S-E, M-I-C K-E-Y M-O-U-S-E."

I'm always buying movie star magazines, especially those which have stories about Annette. I found out she has two brothers, like me, but no sisters, lucky her. Her father is a car mechanic and her mother doesn't work. Somehow I think that behind her closed doors is nothing like behind mine. Pretending I'm like her is lots of fun. I always, well almost, always pretend I'm someone else. That's why I like reading books and going to the movies because they provide me with new people I can pretend to be.

When I was about 7, my two cousins and I went to see *Three Coins in the Fountain* and pretended to act out the parts when we got home. My two cousins, Rosalie and Mary Rose, are alike and they both wanted to be the same character. I didn't care who I was. But they started to fight. My cousin Rosalie is one year older than me and my cousin Mary Rose is four years older. They're both pretty sturdy, but Mary Rose is also very tall. So when they decided I had to pick sides, I sided with Mary Rose because she could probably beat both Rosalie and me up with one hand tied behind her back. So I thought if I picked her, my cousin Rosalie would give up. My thought processes were pretty good, but not good enough. Although they didn't fight, after Mary Rose left, Rosalie beat me up good and called me a traitor. She said I was a Benedict Arnold and that she was never, ever going to allow me to play with any of her toys. I worried a little bit about this because she has thousands of toys, but not too much, because she forgets she was ever mad really fast.

Pretending is the best thing I do. That's why I think I'd make a really good actress.

When I really hate it around my house, I sit and stare into space. If I stare long enough, my mind turns off and when my mother yells for me, it is almost like I've been asleep. It's really fun to do and sometimes when my parents are especially mean, I pretend that I'm going to be someone really famous and that they'll be sorry that they didn't treat me better. I don't think it's right that they're only nice to me when I do something special, like win a prize, because you can't win a prize every day. I thought about it a long time and it just can't be done. My friends don't win any prizes and their parents are nice to them. They even hug and kiss them.

We are now starting to learn new vocabulary words and I love it. I like learning new words. Sister says if you use a new word in a sentence three times, it's yours forever. I love words. So I decided to read the dictionary. I didn't tell anybody 'cause I thought it might sound really stupid, so I started with A. My plan was to learn a word beginning with each of the letters and then start back with A. The first word I picked was "abate" because it's someone's last name in my class. It means to lessen, but it's tricky because you can't say, "Sister, please abate our homework." I know because I tried and Sister said it was nice I learned a new word, but I also needed to learn how to use it properly, so she gave me some examples. "Her tears abated." "The humidity was abated by the thunderstorm." I knew I was missing something so I decided it would be easier just to pick another word. I like the word "arrogant," which is an adjective that means full of pride. I think I'd better start with adjectives because they're easier to use. Anyway, my cousin can be arrogant so I know I'll get to use the word three times without a problem, maybe even in one day. I have to wait though until she tells me what a baby I am or how she is a woman and I'm not. My time will come, I'm sure of it. So between school, my presidency, the Mickey Mouse Club, and reading the dictionary, I have a lot to do. Even so, Mary Lou, Carla and I decided to make up a dance to "Thumbalina" and try out for the school's talent show which will be in May. Mary Lou and I have learned enough tap at this point to do this. Carla never took any tap lessons but we'll teach her the steps. She picks up pretty fast. Tryouts are in April so we have plenty of time. I like being on stage. Everybody looks at you and smiles, even my parents.

March 1957

We meet three times a week at Carla's house to make up our dance routine. We chose "Thumbalina" because we like the song. It's happy and it's a perfect tap dancing number. Luckily, Carla was able to get a pair of tap shoes from somebody because you absolutely must have them. Part of the fun of tap dancing is the noise the shoes make. We also have to synchronize, not only our tap moves, but our hand gestures and voices. It's not easy, but it sure is fun.

The words in Thumbalina are "Thumbalina, Thumbalina, tiny little thing," so I suggested we put our hands down toward the floor to emphasize the word "tiny." The next line is "Thumbalina dance, Thumbalina sing." Mary Lou says we should extend our right hand and then our left hand to show Thumbalina does two things. I think it was a really good idea. The next line is "Thumbalina, what's the difference if you're very small." I suggested shrugging our shoulders at this line. And the last line is "When your heart is full of love, you're nine feet tall." Carla said to act out this line, we should extend our hands way above our heads. This is really a lot of fun because nobody's fighting like my cousins and nobody is bossy. We are all contributing.

March 30th, 1957

Now that we know the words and hand gestures, we are concentrating on the dance steps. The hard part is doing everything in synchronization. We also have to be careful that the tap steps allow us to make the hand gestures comfortably. I stressed that because we don't want to do anything jumpy when our hands are extended above our heads or it will look stupid. We could even lose our balance.

April 14th, 1957

We're finished our song and dance and we're good. Tryouts are next week. We intend to practice every day because everything has to be letter perfect for us to get in.

April 24th, 1957

We're in the show. Now we have to get matching outfits. So we go up to Broadway and pick out an orange jumper which is very, very flared, and a white blouse. We have to wear lots of crinolines under the jumper so it will look like a dance outfit. I made Mary Lou twirl when she was wearing it, and it twirled exactly right. All you can see is skirt and slip. Because if you could see anything else, for instance, panties, we'd be excommunicated from the Church.

Now that we decided what our outfits are going to be, we have to go home and convince our parents we're going to wear them again. This won't be a problem for me because my parents like to spend money and it probably won't be a problem for Mary Lou because she's an only child, but Carla thinks it might be a problem for her. She says the reason she couldn't take tap lessons is because her mother wouldn't give her the money. I never knew that and I never knew she really wanted to take them. Mary Lou and I told her that if her mother said, "no" to buying the outfit, we could all save up our allowances until May. I already had $3.00, Mary Lou had $4.00, and Carla had $3.00, so we were halfway there. Carla was really happy when we told her this. I guess that's why my mother always tells me that I should be generous. I got a really warm feeling when I saw how happy Carla was.

April 25th, 1957

Carla's mother said she'd give her the money on Friday and we'll go to the store on Saturday and buy the outfits. I'm happy Carla's mother is giving her the money, not only because I get to keep my allowance, but Carla's mother agreed because she thought our routine was really good. They give prizes out at the talent show. We might win, but probably not because there's this fifth grader, Phyllis, who is the best tap dancer I've ever seen. She has won the talent contest every year. She takes private lessons and all. I hate to admit it, but she's a better dancer than me. But we still have a chance because we're not only dancing, but singing too, and it's an original dance. My mother says as long as there's life, there's hope, so who knows?

Easter Sunday, 1957

I've always loved Easter because it is the holiday for candy and because every year I get a whole new outfit from head to foot. I get new shoes, a coat, a dress, a hat, and a handbag. My shoes and bag match. Almost everybody gets a whole new outfit. It's even fun going to Mass because everybody looks at what everybody else is wearing. This is the first year I'm allowed to get black patent leather shoes. My mother's in love with white shoes because she says they look so clean, so it took a lot of convincing to be allowed to buy black ones, believe me. But I am 11, and white shoes are so babyish. My mother insisted I get this straw hat that has a hole at the top. It's in style, so she says. I think it's stupid looking, but I don't make any fuss or I'll be wearing white shoes for sure.

Mary Lou and her parents go to Atlantic City on Easter Sunday. They have a parade on the boardwalk. She says it's fantastic and she learns about the newest fashions this way. Once I go to church and invade my Easter basket, the rest of the day is like any of the other "big dinner" holidays. I shine the least at these.

About a month before Easter, we get these Easter egg cards from school. The card has all these neat names on it like Eric and Ellen. My mother calls them *medigan* names. Anyway, it's a contest. You pay a dime, pick a name, and after all the names are chosen, you punch in the winning name which is on a different part of the card. The prize is a big Easter egg made of dark chocolate, cream, and coconut. Now I don't like dark chocolate or coconut, but I do like to win. I don't this year. I have never won any year.

I used to get upset, but I don't any more because, as my mother pointed out, I won't even eat that egg. She doesn't understand the point about winning, feeling lucky, and how winning makes you happy like you're God's favorite. I remind her that she gets really happy when she wins at Bingo and she says that's different and tells me to drop it and I do.

About six weeks before Easter, Lent begins on Ash Wednesday. We have to go to church to get ashes which are to remind us that from dirt we come and to dirt we shall return. It's really quite dramatic. Then, as Catholics, we're supposed to give up something we like for the whole six weeks because, Sister says, it's a small price to pay since Jesus gave up his life on the cross for us. I decide to give up ice cream, but my mother says this is cheating because I don't really like ice cream that much. She said I should give up bubble gum, potato chips, or candy. The Catholic part of me knows she's right, but the other part doesn't want to do it. I ask her what she's giving up and then she gets mad and says I should worry about myself, not her. Then I think I could live without chocolate candy for six weeks, but not JuJu beads, taffies, or Dots, which my mother calls junk candy. I know I could never live without bubble gum or potato chips, so I compromise. I decide to give up chocolate candy, ice cream, and potato chips, but I'm allowed to eat chips two days a week. By this time, my mother has lost all interest in this conversation because I apparently insulted her. So I promise Jesus that I'll have no chocolate candy or ice cream for the duration, and I'll try my best with potato chips. I feel good about my decision because it will be a sacrifice, just not an overwhelming one.

The week before Easter is real important to Catholics. I love Palm Sunday but I hate having to braid those palms because I'm not very good at it, and Sister is constantly unraveling my mess and telling me to redo it. It's very embarrassing.

On Good Friday, I sit in church from 12 p.m. to 3 p.m., which are the hours Jesus spent on the cross, and I think really hard about how He must have felt, how scared He must have been, how those thorns must have hurt His head, and how those nails must have felt going in His hands and feet. I know I couldn't have done it. Every year I'm saddened by the fact that everybody loved him so much on Palm Sunday, and only five days later they crucified Him. I'm sad because that's the way things are around my house. My mother says, "You can do 100 things right and people love you, but as soon as you do something wrong, or don't do what they want, they hate you." I think it might be impossible to do everything right all the time, but I don't want people to hate me either.

Sister says that Easter is the most important holy day to Catholics because it's when Jesus rose from the dead. But that doesn't make much sense to me because I think Christmas is. After all, if Jesus hadn't been born, He couldn't have died and been resurrected.

April 28th, 1957

Our project on the sacraments is due in two weeks so I ask my mother if we have any pictures from my baptism. She says we don't and I ask why because all my friends have pictures and she tells me, once again, for the zillionth time that I am lucky that I have food to eat. I'd like to remind her that I really never liked food, but figured that would lead me down a path I dare not go, my non-eating being such a sore subject and all. So I'll just use my baby brother's pictures. Since all babies look alike and since he's wearing a long gown, I probably could get away with telling everybody it's me in the pictures. And, although Sister says lies are usually venial sins, lying to a nun is probably a mortal one and I don't think I want to suffer eternal damnation over a christening picture. So my plan is not to be specific. This way I won't be lying, but if everyone thinks it's me, I can't help that. I have pictures of my Holy Communion and Confirmation so they're easy. I need my parents' wedding pictures which I've never seen, and I need to figure out what to do about Penance, Extreme Unction, and Holy Orders. But I don't want to ask my mother about her wedding pictures today because she's been talking under her breath about all she does and it's never enough, ungrateful kids, and once I even heard the word "pigs."

April 30th, 1957

I love the Blessed Mother. When I was little, my mother bought me a statue of her with a big wooden rosary attached. I pray to her all the time now. I used to pray just to God, but sometimes I get on my knees and look in her face and pray to her and I think she understands. Other than my encyclopedias and Bible, this statue is the only thing I have left from the other house. We didn't have much money when we lived on St. John Street and my mother had to pay for these things every week and she didn't make much money or anything. She says these are the things that shows she loves me and I agree.

Once when I was in the second grade, I remember coming home for lunch and my mother told me we didn't have any food. As if that weren't bad enough , she also said that she had to take all the money out of my piggy bank which I had been saving for as long as I could remember. I didn't like putting that money in my piggy bank either, but she made me. I would rather have used it for comic books and bubble gum. But I had to do it, so I did. And now it would all be gone. She said she'd give it back though.

I thought it was really scary not having any food, so every day after that in the second and third grades, I would wonder if there would be any food. I don't have to worry about that now because we have a store full of food. The day we had no food I went to church and I prayed to Jesus, God, and the Blessed Mother. I asked them to leave $100 under my pillow so I could give it to my mother and we wouldn't starve to death, like my mother always says we would if she didn't work. My father doesn't work and he's usually in bed when I come home for lunch while my mother's at work. Other than that one time, we always had food, even if it was only tomato soup. My mother worked for Campbell Soup and someone gave her a whole case of tomato soup and we ate it every day. I didn't like tomato soup before we had to eat that whole case, and I hate it now.

Whenever I don't finish my meal, my mother says that before I throw it in the garbage, I must kiss it up to God and apologize for wasting good food. She says there are kids without anything to eat, and that if I did this, God would forgive my waste.

Even though it never happened again, I worried about starving until we moved here. Although we were poor, except for that time Sister called me in front of the class and said my uniform was too short, I never felt poor. I don't know why I didn't, but I didn't. Sometimes my mother put cardboard in my shoes because I had holes in them, but no one knew it but us. The cardboard worked fine except when it rained, then my socks would get wet and I hated that.

My mother says I'm too particular about everything. She says I *skeeve* things I shouldn't. I don't like my vegetables to touch each other or things all mixed together. I like things to look pretty because only then do they taste good to me. One time I asked her what we were having for dinner during the tomato soup marathon and she said meat. I remember feeling really, really happy, but we had stew that night. The meat was mixed with potatoes, carrots and peas. I hate things mixed. But it sure did beat tomato soup. So I picked out each piece of meat, ate it, then the potatoes, and then the peas. I didn't eat the carrots because I don't like them. That's another thing I do. Even if everything is separate, I always eat one thing at a time and always my favorites first. That way if I get full in the middle of the meal, which usually happens, I would have eaten what I liked. I thought it was pretty smart of me. My mother thought otherwise. I loved two things she used to make—cheese steaks and pizza. She used poppyseed rolls for the cheesesteaks, added lettuce and tomato. Everyone said her pizza was out of this world. My cousin Rosalie always wanted to come home with me when my mother was making either of these things, and usually did. She really liked me a lot, it seemed, on those days and then she used to butter my mother up by going on and on about how delicious they were, so my mother always made me ask her, whether we were fighting or not, and whether I wanted to or not. My mother says it's a pleasure watching my cousin eat because she really enjoys food and when she says this, she looks at me. She doesn't say anything but I know what she means and I think my cousin has caught on too.

I was really disappointed when there wasn't any money under my pillow because I could not have prayed any harder than I did. I couldn't understand why God or Jesus or the Blessed Mother didn't answer my prayer. I didn't think they would want kids starving to death. I tried to find out if maybe they left it under my mother's pillow, but I didn't ask her because I didn't want her to know they didn't answer my prayer because then she might have thought that I wasn't very good. She always said that God answers the prayers of good children. I couldn't ask my teacher either because she would have thought the same thing and she would have known how poor we were. Nobody was supposed to ever know that.

Even though we were so poor, my mother would never let me wear anyone else's clothes. I had a friend, Bonnie Bern, whose parents owned the grocery store where we shopped. Her mother really liked me. Bonnie was a year older so she was bigger than me, and her mother sent all these beautiful dresses for me to wear. My mother said her kids didn't wear second-hand clothes. I really wanted those clothes too. My mother said I could just have one. Sometimes it is really hard to understand adults.

Bonnie's mother fed her sour cream every day when I was there and she never asked if I wanted any. It looked good so I told my mother and she said I wouldn't like it. Bonnie had a ton of toys. One thing she had was a ventriloquest dummy of Howdy Doody. Unlike my cousin, she always let me play with her toys, even the dummy. I was pretty good at it too. I could talk without moving my lips. Bonnie told me if I wanted, I could take it home and practice. When I asked my mother she said, "No way," because I might break it and she couldn't afford to buy another one. Bonnie had this big closet full of games like Tiddley Winks, Monopoly and Checkers. She even let me choose what we would play. I wanted to introduce her to my cousin so my cousin would learn how to share, but Rosalie said I was making it up. She said nobody did that. But Bonnie did do it. Her parents even took me out with them. They said I was very mannerly and that Bonnie really liked me. My mother let me go too.

One day in the summer, when I was 7, Bonnie and I decided to open up a lemonade stand. I figured if God didn't leave that $100 under my pillow, maybe it's because he wanted me to earn it. So Bonnie's mother, Mrs. Bern, made a whole pitcher of lemonade. We put the lemonade and paper cups on an egg crate and charged five cents a glass. The only people who bought it were Mr. and Mrs. Bern and it was really hot, so we drank the rest. Although my mother always said I didn't understand the value of money, I knew enough to know that five cents was not going to buy any food for us, so I bought some bubble gum instead.

It was fun though, and I did have that gum after. Bonnie and I thought that maybe we could sell old things that we had around the house. I didn't want to tell her I didn't have anything old, because then she might think we were poor. My mother broke most of our toys. She hated it when my brother, Vince, who's retarded, and I would fight, so she'd break them right in front of us in the yard. So most of my old things were gone because my brother was and is very selfish. This didn't seem to matter to my mother though. She used to tell me he didn't understand, but I think he understood all right. The one thing that belonged to me my mother didn't break was my Betsy Wetsy doll, but my sister took care of that. She took Betsy's head off and then said, "See." Of course, she was a baby and according to my mother, she didn't understand either. It seems nobody's expected to understand anything but me. My mother threw Betsy away because we couldn't put her head back on. It's true I was bored with Betsy, but it was the only doll I had. My mother said I shouldn't give my sister crayons any more because she took a bite out of an orange one and they're full of poison. But to tell the truth, when she pulled the head of my Betsy Wetsy doll, I was tempted. When I got home, I told my mother about our sale and she gave me a few stupid things. So I told Bonnie that everything we had was new and I didn't have anything to sell. She understood too. She said we could still hold the sale and whatever money we made we would split it. This was really a shock to me after my cousin.

I always have to beg my cousin for everything. As soon as I get mad and tell her I don't want to play with something she says, "I was going to make you play with it, but since you're so smart and really don't want to play with it, you can't now." So

I've learned to beg a really long time, but no matter how long I beg, she'll always say I might have been able to play with it, after I stop begging. My mother says I should have had pride. I didn't know what pride was, but I would have rather had toys and Bonnie's dresses than pride any day.

I think if I had a lot of toys I would have been like Bonnie, not like my cousin. Maybe, maybe not. But I think so.

My cousin has some neat things too. She had a toy type-writer which I loved. I wanted to be a secretary until I told my father and he said I'd never make any money doing that. She never allowed me to play with that typewriter and I really loved it. We did enjoy coloring and puzzles, and we used to have con-tests. In one contest my aunt would pick the one who colored the best or the fastest, and in another contest she'd pick the one who could put the puzzle together the fastest. My cousin always won all the contests. At the time, I thought it was because they were her puzzles and coloring books and she practiced, and besides, she was older. But now that I'm 11, I think maybe it was because my aunt was the judge. I don't blame my aunt though. I saw what happened when I had to pick sides between her and Mary Rose. When I picked Mary Rose, it wasn't pretty. And my aunt still had to live with her after I left.

May 1st, 1957

May is the Blessed Mother's month. On the first Sunday of every May, we have a procession in her honor made up of all the children who made their First Communion in their white dresses. One girl is usually chosen from the higher grades to crown the Blessed Mother, and this has never been me. I pray to Mary and Jesus every day, and I always light candles to her for specific requests and thanks. You have to pay a quarter for a small candle and one dollar for the larger one, and the difference is that the one dollar candle lasts longer and I think you're more likely to have your prayer answered if you donate the one dollar instead of a quarter. My mother gives me money to put in the basket at church every week too. Priests constantly talk about donations, but it seems to me that Jesus didn't like money too much so I get confused about this all the time. The only time Jesus got angry was over money. He thought people were being disrespectful in God's house, the temple, by trading and selling. Jesus was born a Jew and He came to earth so everyone would follow Catholicism. Sister tells us that Peter was the first pope and that Jewish people don't believe in Jesus as Savior. She also says that if you don't accept Jesus as your Savior, you're doomed. I think about this sometimes because if the Jewish people knew Jesus, I can't understand why they didn't all follow Him and become Christians. Maybe it's because sometimes when you pray, it doesn't seem like He pays you any mind. But Sister says Jesus always answers prayers, He just says no sometimes. This makes sense to me because my parents say no to me a lot and they always say it's for my own good.

I wonder if Jesus has righteous anger against those who knew him and died without becoming Catholic. I think it must be sort of insulting to Him. I know that sometimes when I tell the truth and nobody believes me, I get insulted. Sister says that Jesus was both human and divine so maybe the human part gets mad and the divine part doesn't and He forgives them. When Jesus was on the cross, He asked God to forgive all the people because they didn't know what they were doing.

I hope I don't get excommunicated or anything, but I can't understand if Jesus is so forgiving and all, how only Catholics are going to get to heaven. And I also don't understand if He already died for our sins why we have to go to confession and do penance. And besides, Bonnie Bern is Jewish and she is the last person I know who should go to hell.

But when I pray to Jesus or Mary, I think I understand. It's like you have a mother and father who love you no matter what you do and who give you a million chances if you're trying to be good. I think the difference between regular parents and them is that they really know what's inside you. Sister says you can't fool God. My parents always think I'm not trying hard enough, but I'm always trying hard. I try really hard every day, and Jesus and Mary know it, I think.

May 10th, 1957

I'm almost finished the project on the sacraments when I ask my mother for pictures of her wedding. She tells me she doesn't have any, but she doesn't say it like she usually does, which is that she was too busy worrying about food and had no time for silly things like pictures. She then says she has something to tell me, and goes on to explain that she was only 17 when she got pregnant with me and that my father and her were not married, and that they went to Elkton, Maryland to get married because she was under age. She said I was born in September and they got married in March. She looks really embarrassed while she's telling me this, and I'm feeling very sorry for her. For some reason, it's not a big surprise. I feel like I might have known, but I don't remember anyone ever telling me. I tell my mother that it's okay. She says she wasn't a bad girl or anything. She really didn't know what she was doing. She also says that I have to be very careful that it never happens to me because it was hard having kids so young. I tell my mother that I understand because I don't know what else to say. It doesn't seem too big a deal to me, except after about 10 minutes, I realize I have no wedding pictures for my project. I don't want to bring up the subject again because my mother's been very quiet since our talk, so I call my cousin. I explain the situation to her and she understands and says that she'll get me pictures of her parents' marriage. Sometimes she can be so nice, it makes me want to cry.

May 15th, 1957

I overheard my mother telling Marge, one of our customers who doesn't have too much money, that God will provide. She says that a few years ago when we lived on St. John Street, she didn't have any money at all and there was absolutely no food in the house except one slice of cheese. I remember that day too. And then she said the very next day her brother, Junior, came over for no reason and handed her $50. I literally jumped in the air when she said this because I knew that Jesus had said "yes" to my prayer. I remember I asked for $100, but that doesn't matter. I tell my mother I have to go to church and light a candle and ask her for a dollar because Jesus deserves a big candle for this. Now that I'm 11, it makes perfect sense to me. Then I was only a kid. Of course, Jesus wouldn't come down and leave the money under my pillow. I probably had him confused with the Tooth Fairy who left money every time I lost a tooth. But my mother did get the money, and so my prayer was answered. I wonder if she ever put the money back in my piggy bank.

I thought about Jesus when I lit the candle. Even when I thought He said no, I still loved Him. Sister says God works in mysterious ways. She's got that right.

June 3rd, 1957

My mother told me that there was no TV until after I was born. She said people used to listen to the radio instead. When we lived in the other house, we had a really small TV with a bubble on the front. I used to watch Howdy Doody and really liked Buffalo Bob Smith and Princess WinterFallSummerSpring. There weren't too many shows in the beginning; but one day after school, when no one was home, I watched a show that made me very scared. I remember that it was about kids being kidnapped. When I told my cousin about it, she asked why I didn't turn the TV off. What scares me now is that I never thought to turn it off and should have.

I also used to watch a show called *The Honeymooners*. It was really funny. My Aunt Lissa says Ralph and Alice are just like my parents. They look like them, but I think she says it because they were always fighting and Ralph always made a fist and told Alice one day he was going to send her to the moon. The only thing different is that Ralph didn't hit Alice like my father hit my mother, and Ralph worked, he was a bus driver.

The first time I saw *I Love Lucy*, I laughed until tears ran down my face. We used to go to my grandfather's to watch it every week. I was really surprised the first time I realized it was going to come on again. I used to like when Uncle Miltie dressed like a woman at the end of his show, but *I Love Lucy* was always my favorite.

Now that I'm 11, there are lots of shows on. My favorite is The Mickey Mouse Club. We're allowed to watch TV after dinner every night until bed time. I like *Father Knows Best*. The father, Jim Anderson, calls his daughters "Princess" and "Kitten." I wish my father would call me nice names like that and be nice to me like Jim is to his kids. And he knows everything too. By the end of every show, he solves everybody's problems and then they're happy again and nice to each other. I wish my family was happy like them. It's true they laugh a lot, but they can't be happy being so angry all the time. When I ask my mother why our family can't be like the Andersons, she says because that show is make-believe and has nothing to do with real life. Maybe that's true, but somebody had to think up the show and how could he think it up every week if some people weren't like that. What I like best is nobody yells. I think you learn better when people don't yell, at least, I think I would. Sometimes when my father yells, my mind freezes and I can't remember anything he said because I begin to think that maybe at 11, I'm old enough to be beaten.

There have been lots of good movies out too. When I was younger, my Aunt Bootie took me to see *White Christmas* and it was so beautiful. This wasn't the first time I had been to the movies though, because my Uncle Junior had taken me to see *Cinderella* when I was 5 or 6. And even though I used to see lots of movies when I lived in the other house, for some reason, I only remember these two. My mother and father never go to the movies.

I remember once when I was about 7, my mother told my father she was taking me to the movies. He was going to babysit. But after we left, she told me we weren't going. She was taking me to my grandfather's house. I was disappointed but I didn't say it because I would have been in trouble. I did go to my grandfather's and played with my Aunt Lucy. My mother went somewhere else and then picked me up later. On the walk home, she told me what the movie was about in case my father asked. I didn't like having to lie to my father, but I had to.

My cousin says once her mother was hiding down the cellar from her father and her father made her swear on a Bible that her mother wasn't home. She did too. She said she would have done anything for her mother. I was real impressed. She became a hero to me, but only until she became arrogant (one time) again.

But I figured it was okay to lie if your mother wanted you to. The priest said we should do everything our mother tells us because our mothers would never steer us wrong. My father only asked if I liked the movie, and I said yes and went upstairs. At the time, I remember thinking how my guardian angel was watching over me, since I didn't even have to lie, because I had nothing against that movie.

Guardian angels are with us from the day we're born and protect us all the time. Whenever I did something and thought I could get hurt, I would always ask my guardian angel to help me or protect me. I think it was awfully nice of Jesus to pick a guardian angel for each and every kid that's born. It must have taken a lot of time. I always feel better knowing that I have an angel.

After that night, every time my mother said we were going to the movies, I could never be happy about it because I was never sure. Sometimes we did though.

June 6th, 1957

For our class trip, we went to the Philadelphia Zoo. Everyone was all excited but me. I've been to the zoo before and it smells really bad. I "skeeve" everything that looks or smells bad, and I can't help it. My mother acts like I can, but I truly can't. It makes me want to throw up. Once my cousin was making sounds like she was going to throw up. Her sounds made me throw up and she didn't. I hate when my mother had to change my brother's diapers or when people don't wash. Even stains on clothes make me sick. My mother says she doesn't know what I'm going to do when I have my own kids. I probably won't have any kids for this reason alone.

Anyway, all everybody talked about was going to the zoo, and I dreaded it. I thought maybe I could wear a mask, but my cousin said that would be extremely childish and then she said, "Get over it." Don't they know if I could, I would? I don't like being this way. One day I went home for lunch and my grandmother had fried cheese. I walked in and it smelled so bad I walked right out. I had no lunch that day.

The nuns are taking us to the zoo and several mothers are going to chaperone, not mine though. On the morning of our trip, I ask my mother for a paper bag in case I have to throw up. She says I'm a disgrace and she doesn't know where I came from. I wanted to say I often wonder that too, but didn't.

We get to the zoo and the boys go crazy at the monkey cages. They think it's funny to imitate the monkeys. Quite frankly, I don't see much difference from the way they usually act, but I smile anyway because it's polite. I have no idea what I'll be when I grow up, but I'll guarantee that I'll be polite. My parents will see to that.

Sometimes when the smell gets too much, I move to the sidelines with the mothers. They don't seem to mind and no one seems to notice I'm close to throwing up.

I often wondered when I saw cows just lying in the grass if they weren't bored with doing nothing all day long. And now seeing these animals so close, I wonder if they think and feel useless because they're bored. I wonder if they ever wish they lived someplace else and if they can smell what I smell. I can't wait to get home and for me, that's something.

There are certain smells I love, like my mother's perfume, not the kind I bought her, the kind she buys herself, Youth Dew by Estee Lauder. I used to love smelling my baby brother when he was all clean and powdered, and I love smelling my clothes when I first put them on. They smell like starch and soap. I just hate foul smells.

I don't want to be *skeevy*. Most things that bother me don't seem to bother anybody else, but most things that bother other people don't seem to bother me. That should count for something. Sometimes it's hard being different. My cousin always says she's my grandmother's favorite. I don't care about that because I think my grandmother can love lots of people. My cousin always wants to be everybody's favorite, but I don't. All my friends worry they're not going to have time to finish their homework, but that doesn't worry me either.

Finally our class trip is over and I didn't throw up once. I did pray to Jesus and asked Him to help me not to. I told Him if I didn't, I'd be nice to my sister for a week. We all get on the bus, including the monkeys, still believing they had been so amusing.

June 15th, 1957

Tonight is the annual talent show. Carla, Mary Lou and I had a dress rehearsal yesterday to make sure our jumpers twirled just right. This is really, really important.

We were really excited today, a little nervous too, but we know that song and dance backwards and forwards. My mother's coming tonight, but not my father. He only comes when I do something alone.

I can hardly eat dinner, but fortunately no one thinks it's unusual. What I don't need is a lot of screaming before the show. The program says we're second to last, Phyllis is last, and I'm certain she'll win.

We were good, I could feel it. Everybody was happy and smiling. "Thumbalina" is a happy tune. When we were introduced, Sister told the audience that we choreographed the dance ourselves. I thought the audience was impressed because I heard a couple of gasps, but my mother told me afterwards somebody dropped a soda on two people's laps. We lost. My mother told me it's okay to lose sometimes as long as you do your best. And we were very good, she said. She didn't seem disappointed or anything. I was disappointed though. Phyllis is a great dancer, that's for sure.

When we were walking home, my mother said that there will be times in my life when I'm disappointed and that's part of life. Everybody gets disappointed and that I have to learn to be a good sport about it. I asked her if she ever was disappointed and she said, "Every day." That makes me sad, but I can't ask her why because her answer might be too sad and I'm feeling sad enough.

My father was pretty good about it too. I don't think he thinks dancing is too important, not like school and manners. Since he was being nice, I asked him if he ever lost and was disappointed and he said, no, he never loses.

June 21st, 1957

School is over. In September I'll be going into the seventh grade. My baby brother is 2 now and he is really cute. Every night we both get dressed and I have to walk him around the neighborhood. The other night this Chihuahua was barking at him and I grabbed him because I thought the dog was going to bite him, but he bit the dog instead. Laura, the dog's owner, had to take the dog to get a tetanus shot, but my brother didn't get one. He is really an embarrassment. Somehow he learned the "F" word, and when we walk down the street he says it to all the old ladies, and there's nothing that I can do about it. The more I tell him to stop, the louder he gets.

I tell my mother when we get home, but she says he's just a baby. It doesn't feel that way when you're the one standing next to him. She does tell him he shouldn't bite dogs though.

I try everything I know to get out of walking him, but I can't. It's one of my jobs, I'm told. I also have to polish his shoes. And now, my father's been making red wine, he calls it "Dago

Red," down the basement. And every night I have to take a jug downstairs and fill it up. It's always during my shows and I hate everything about it. The cellar is damp and I absolutely hate the smell of the wine. I especially hate it when it gets to the bottom of the barrel because then it takes a really long time to fill up.

July 4th, 1957

My mother and father went down Atlantic City for a couple of days and my Aunt Boot watched us. When they came home, my mother's face was all swollen. She said she got too much sunburn. It's probably true, but my stomach was real nervous because I thought maybe my father hit her again. I know I shouldn't think about those things because that happened a long time ago, but I can't help it. I'm always so afraid he's going to start again and that he might even kill her someday. He says he's going to, sometimes he says he'll cut her up and put her in the freezer. He seems to be kidding, but I'm never quite sure.

My sister has friends now, which is good, because she's more pleasant. She has this one boyfriend and they get married every week in the back yard. My mother says she pulls him by the nose. She calls him a *mamuch* because he's skinny like me. A *mamuch* is a puppet.

Our yard has this cement aisle between flower beds on both sides, so it is perfect for weddings. My father's new hobby is growing roses. He mixes colors and they're really beautiful. He even has black roses.

I would like to put a shrine to the Blessed Mother in the yard because I'd have lots of flowers to honor her, but my mother says someone will knock over my statue and then what? One thing is for certain. Whenever she ends a sentence in "then what," I never have an answer. I wish sometimes I could see ahead to the future because if I'm not sure, and answer her and I'm wrong, I'll hear, "I told you so," about a million times.

My cousin says, "I told you so" all the time and I hate it. She doesn't realize the only reason she knows is because she's lived longer than me. She thinks she's smarter. She's not though. She's just arrogant (two times). I called her arrogant (three times) the other day, and even though I don't think she knew exactly what it meant, she did get the idea because she punched me really hard. Well, I used it three times so arrogance is mine.

August 16th, 1957

Since I mastered the "A's," I go back to the dictionary and start reading the "B's." I like the word "balderdash," which means nonsense, but if I used it, everyone will think I'm arrogant or stupid. I picked the word "barren," which means boring and dull and empty. I should have no problem using this word. This triggers my thinking on why everybody else can be boring, dull and empty, fresh and dumb, and I'm supposed to understand, but nobody lets me be anything. I'm always hearing, "He's sick" (Vince), "She's a child" (Cathy), "He didn't mean it" (Larry), "She's not as smart as you", "That's who she is and you have to accept it, she doesn't know any better." Why am I supposed to know better all the time? Every time I say, "I didn't know," my mother or father will say that I should have known. There seems to be two sets of rules, one for me and one for everybody else. I ask my mother about it and she tells me that's because I'm the oldest, and people expect more of me. But she never has a good answer when people older than me don't do the right thing. She says she is tired of hearing me ask why people do the things they do. She says they just do. My question is, why can't they think that way about me? Why am I expected to do everything perfectly and never make a mistake? I'm human just like everybody else.

My cousin and I were playing with this girl who lives down the street from her, and my cousin got mad and pulled her hair out. I only stood there, yet I got punished and my cousin didn't. My cousin is older than me so you would think she would have known better. I didn't pull the girl's hair out and I'm still unsure what they expected me to do. Sometimes I feel that I'm being tested every minute of every day. I feel that they want me to be perfect. Don't they know, like Sister says, that nobody is perfect but God?

I remember when I was 7, my cousin and her family went to the Shore for a week. I wanted to go and I missed her so I started to cry. My mother told me to get out of her sight. I didn't understand why I never got to go to the Shore and why I wasn't allowed to even be disappointed. It seems my feelings are always wrong. Everybody else can yell and scream, but I'm never allowed to be angry. Everybody else cries and everybody hugs them, but I'm not allowed to cry, and if I do, no one ever hugs me. I just sit all by myself. If I laugh too loud or too much, I get in trouble too. I don't know how you can stop your feelings because I've tried and I can't.

Wasn't my father expected to stop his feelings before he hit my mother? He doesn't hit *us* when he's mad, so he can. When my mother cries, I want her to stop, but she doesn't. Sometimes she used to cry all day when I was younger, and no matter what I did or said, she didn't stop. She used to say she'd be better off dead. Sometimes I wanted to hug her, but I was afraid to. I don't know why I was afraid, but I was. I don't know how to hug anybody but my grandmother. She likes it, that's why.

When I make a mistake, my grandmother hugs me and says it's all right. She tells me she loves me too and calls me *facha belle* which means "pretty face" in Italian. At least she doesn't pinch my cheek real hard like some people do. It really hurts and I have to smile because my mother says they do it because they like me. I wish they wouldn't like me so much.

Other than Mary Lou and my cousin, my grandmother is my best friend. She's the only older person who doesn't expect me to be perfect all the time. If my father hollers at me because he's in a bad mood, she hollers at him in Italian. I don't know what she says to him, but he stops. Sometimes she hollers at my mother in Italian too about me, and my mother stops too. That's probably why she doesn't want me to learn Italian, because then I'll know what she's saying to them.

Some days, I think she's the only person in the world who loves me. My mother says nobody could love me like her because she carried me in her body and all. Maybe my mother and father do love me, but most of the time I don't feel it.

Sometimes when I'm at my friends' houses, their parents just hug them for no reason at all except that they love them. I want to cry then because I think there must be something really wrong with me if my parents don't hug me. I know my friends like me and all, but that's probably because they don't know me as well as my parents. That's why I try not to get too close to anybody because I'm afraid they'll find out what my parents already know. My grandmother is pretty close to me though, and she loves me. But she goes home at night so I figure that's when I'm not lovable, at night.

My father says I'm not allowed to get B's in school or ever make a mistake, and I told him my cousin gets B's and she's older. He says what my cousin does is the business of her parents, but as long as I'm living in his house, under his roof, I'll follow his rules. Sometimes it's hard to get all A's and it's either impossible never to make a mistake or I'm not as smart as they think. My father tells other people I have brains I haven't even used yet.

I wish I knew how to use them so I could figure out how to get all A's and never make a mistake.

Every one says seventh grade is really hard too.

September 3rd, 1957

Today was the first day of school. We don't have to wear our uniforms the first day and it's fun. Our uniforms are brown jumpers with tan cotton blouses. You could have nylon blouses, but my mother won't let me because she likes to use starch. She thinks everything looks better starched. Last year, she used so much starch in my blouses that I had a permanent red ring around my neck. After that, she used a little less, but that ring stayed around a while. My father said that she starched his pajamas when he went into the hospital and he was uncomfortable all day in his bed. It felt good that he agreed with me because this doesn't happen very often. It's nice to wear our uniforms. It makes it easier to get ready in the mornings because you never have to waste any time on what you're going to wear, but sometimes it does get boring.

My mother says uniforms are good because it makes all the children equal and the kids whose parents can't afford to buy them a lot of clothes don't feel bad. This is what I mean though. She always allows everybody else to have feelings and even feels sorry for them, but never me. If I were one of the poor kids and felt bad, I know she would tell me that I was lucky to have food to eat. I guess that's why you get smarter as you get older, because people do and say the same things over and over, and there comes a time when you just know things.

I'm really into music now that I'm almost 12. There's a new kind of music out called rock and roll and we all love it. Not my parents though. They say it's just a lot of noise and they also say that I don't know what good music is. I do know what good music is though. I like all the old songs plus Italian music and some opera, but you can dance to rock and roll and I'm just learning to do the jitterbug. It's really fun and two girls can do it with no problem. Mary Lou and I are learning together and I lead. I'm also teaching my cousin, Rosalie, so I have to lead her too. I hope this does not become a problem when I dance with boys.

My mother asks why it is I have a lot of energy and move fast when I'm dancing, but move like a snail whenever she asks me to do anything. I have learned that this is one of those questions you just don't answer.

Elvis Presley is really getting popular and he can really move. He's handsome too. My favorite record used to be "All Shook Up" until my Aunt Boot said it was a dirty and disgusting song. Now every time I listen to it, I wonder if I'm committing a sin. I wonder if they danced in the time of Christ. I never read it in the Bible, but there was that wedding and I think that people have always danced at weddings.

October 1957

I was watching _The $64,000 Question_ on television and one of the questions was to spell "antidisestablishmentarianism." I think it's the longest word in the dictionary. For some reason after the show, I knew how to spell it. My father was extremely impressed and every time someone came to our house, he made me spell it for them. I can only spell it if I don't think about it and I have to say it really fast. Of course, I didn't tell anyone because that would be showing off. Somehow, though, Sister John found out and made me stand in front of the class and spell it. The kids' eyes got really big. They couldn't believe there was such a long word. I'm not sure how I did it, but I'm sure glad I did because I've been my father's daughter for weeks now.

Sometimes when I study and there's a list of things I have to memorize, I try to make the first letter of each word make up a separate word. That way if I forget one of the things on the list, I'll know the first letter, which helps me to remember what I forgot. And sometimes during a test, I can see where an answer is on the page. My father says I have a photographic memory. It may be true. It's like I take a picture of it when I'm studying but I don't even know I'm doing it. I remember things for a long time too. My friends say I never forget anything with a smile, and my parents say the same thing, but they're usually not smiling.

I am also a very good reader. When I first learned to read, my teacher always said I was very good. So one day when my father was watching TV, I started to read out loud because I wanted him to know how good I was. He just said, "Can't you read that book to yourself, I'm watching TV here." So I've been reading to myself ever since.

One thing about me is that you only have to tell me once. I've heard my aunt scolding my cousin and saying, "How many times do I have to tell you?" Nobody ever can say that to me. Once they tell me, I don't do it any more. I guess that's one problem I don't have, but according to my mother, I have plenty of others.

My teacher in the seventh grade is Sister John Boniface. All she does is talk about how wonderful her other children were and how they never did, said, or thought the horrible things we do. It gets sickening sometimes. I know she's telling the truth though because nuns never lie. I wonder what nuns have to confess when they go to confession. They don't lie, steal, cheat, curse, disobey their parents, or take God's name in vain. They do get angry and hit some kids though. I wonder if that's a sin or considered righteous anger. The kids usually have it coming, but not always. Sister John is particularly upset by my handwriting. She walks up and down the aisles and usually smacks my knuckles with the ruler, sends me to the front of the class, and makes me write on the blackboard so she can correct it in front of everybody. The more she does this, it seems the worse I write because I get nervous. In my opinion, her anger over my handwriting is not righteous because I try my best and I really can't help it. I hope she confesses what she does to me.

My father says I'll probably be a doctor because I don't write well, but his humor fades fast when I come home with a B in penmanship on my report card. I heard that people can hire tutors to help kids if they're having problems in any subject, so I ask my mother if I could get a tutor to help me with my handwriting. She says that it's unnecessary, that all I have to do is take my time and not be so sloppy. Sister John makes me so nervous about my handwriting that today I spilled some ink on my desk. We use fountain pens. I'm not sure how I did it, but the more I tried to clean it up, the worse it got. I'm going to have to try to hide it until the end of the year because destroying school property is one of the worst things a Catholic can do. If Sister John finds out, she'll embarrass me in front of the whole class, and only God knows what else she'll do. I may even get expelled.

Whenever I go to church now, the first thing I pray to Jesus about is that ink spot. I would like it to disappear, but every day I look and it is still there, and I can't tell anyone, not even Mary Lou. And the very worst thing is that spilling the ink was probably just a venial sin, but every day I don't tell Sister John about it, that sin is probably growing into a mortal one. It's probably like lying, and lying to a nun has got to be a mortal sin. We're learning about sins of omission this year in Religion class. A sin of omission is when you're supposed to do something and don't. Sister says sometimes sins of omission are worse than sins of commission.

The reason I won't tell Mary Lou is that she might have to tell or she might be committing a sin of omission too. The way I look at it is if she tells, I'm in trouble with Sister, the principal, the priest and my parents. But if she doesn't tell, not only will I be committing a sin, but I will be leading her to commit a sin and I'll be in trouble with God. Besides, I like her too much to do that. But I do worry I'll be found out. Every morning when I get up and every night when I go to sleep, I pray that Jesus will remove that ink spot. It's hard for me to understand why He won't because it wouldn't be hurting anybody. So far, it's been a week and Sister hasn't noticed it.

November 3rd, 1957

It's been a month since I spilled that ink, and I have to tell somebody. So I swear my cousin to secrecy and tell her that even if she has to swear on a bible, she can't tell. She says the best thing to do is face the music. I thought about it, but can't do it. I have even thought that it would be better because I do worry about it all the time, well, not all the time, but a lot of the time. My cousin says I'm a worrywart. I hate when she says this because it makes me feel weak. Strong people probably don't worry about anything because they're never afraid. I know I'm weak, but I don't want other people to know it.

I'm afraid often. I'm afraid every day when I go home that I will be in trouble because I never know until I do something that it's wrong. It seems like every day I commit some new offense. I'm also afraid that my mother will be in one of her moods. Last week, I won a spelling bee and ran home because this usually makes my parents happy. My mother was in the store cutting meat and I was so excited that I told her. She said I had no right to be so happy because my brother, Vince, was sick and the problem with me was that I only cared about myself. I was surprised because I didn't know he was sick. That's what I mean, I never knew I couldn't be happy if he was sick. I thought it was always good to be happy, but I guess I was wrong. I also worry that my mother will go the hospital like her mother or that my father will start hitting her again. One thing I don't have to worry about now is that we will have nothing to eat. We have so much food in the store that we couldn't possibly starve to death for years.

Sometimes I worry when I get a B in a test because I'm not allowed to get B's. But I don't worry too long because there will be other tests, so I just study harder.

It might seem like I worry all the time, but I don't. I don't worry when I'm having fun with my friends, or when I'm reading, or when I'm at the movies, or when I'm watching TV. I don't even worry during class once I cover that ink spot because I'm usually trying to concentrate real hard on what Sister is saying.

And when I laugh real hard, I don't worry then either. But I do think I might worry while I'm sleeping because sometimes I have nightmares and wake up in the middle of the night. But I just lay there and then I fall asleep again.

None of my friends know I'm a worrywart because I always try to make them laugh and I never tell them what I worry about. I don't think they have anything to worry about, and I don't want them to think I'm different. But I am different, I think.

December 4th, 1957

Mary Lou and I really dance well together now, and that's good because Carla is having a birthday party and is inviting the cute boys. I don't think the boys know how to dance, so Mary Lou and I will probably dance together. Carla wants to play some games. I hope we don't play spin the bottle, because the last thing I want to do is kiss Mikey, and with my luck, I'll probably get him. There is a boy in our class, Tommy, that both Mary Lou and I like. He's not only cute, but real nice; but he talks to Mary Lou more than me so I think he likes her better. She says that's not true, but she's so nice she'd say that whether it was true or not. Carla is having six girls and four boys to her party, and everyone's really excited. She has a finished basement, not like ours with that smelly Dago red. I ask my mother whether I could get a new outfit and she says yes. She's going to take me to Lit Brothers to pick something out. My mother loves Lit Brothers. She says they sell quality. I think, though, that she likes their chocolate best because sometimes that's all she buys. I like chocolate, but not as much as other candy. She says I don't know what's good. This doesn't make any sense to me because what's good for one person is not always good for another. She tells me that all the time. I don't understand why it doesn't apply to candy.

Well, my cousin was little help about that ink stain, but she won't tell anybody and now when I get real worried about it, at least I can talk to her. She'll probably call me a worrywart and a coward, but it's worth it to be able to talk to her about it, especially since I am a worrywart and a coward.

December 16th, 1957

I have tonsillitis again. I seem to be getting it more often and each time, it is worse. This time, I have to bow my head until my chin touches my chest to even swallow. Dr. Glass is pretty mad when I go to see him. He said these tonsils must be removed. I think he scared my mother because he said that this one was so bad that the whites of my eyes had turned yellow from infection, and if I didn't have them out immediately, I could die. As soon as we got home, she told everybody that the doctor was going to send me to a surgeon. I have to go to Children's Hospital in Philadelphia. I'm not too thrilled about having surgery, but it looks like I don't have much choice. Dr. Glass says I have to get over this bout first, which he thinks will take about 10 days. I'm scheduled for surgery after New Year's. No one seems worried that I'm going to miss so much time from school. Sister says that my friends can bring me the assignments so I don't fall behind. I'm scared because I don't know how I'm going to feel after, but I don't think my throat can hurt any more than it does now.

January 6th, 1958

I had my tonsils out today. Yesterday when I came to the hospital, there was a girl here with big bandages on her nose. I knew she had had her tonsils out so it made me really scared. The doctor said the bandages were because he removed her adenoids and she bled. I made him promise that he would not remove my adenoids, but I found out, he did. Luckily, I didn't bleed so I didn't have any bandages. My only memory is that when they brought me up to my room and shifted me from one bed to another, the back of my gown opened and I think a bunch of kids saw my rear end. But, there isn't anything I can do about that. I wish I could pretend it didn't happen, but it did.

I am in a room with a younger girl who is very sick. I've been here for two days and no one has been up to see her. She's the oldest of five children and she says her mother can't come because she's got all those little kids at home. It makes me really sad. My mother and father come to see me, and I whisper to my mother that she should talk to Sally, the little girl, and she does too. Sometimes my parents are the best parents in the world. The next day, my mother even brought Sally some comic books and fruit. Sally was really happy. I think my mother feels sorry for her too because she's so sick and so alone. The third day I'm here, her father comes up and that makes Sally extremely happy.

I try to talk to her a lot so she won't be lonely. I can't stand it when people are lonely. It makes me want to cry. I can't cry here though because she might think I feel sorry for her. No one wants people to feel sorry for them.

My parents come to take me home, and when we were in the car I started to cry. My mother asked me what was wrong and I told her I felt really sad leaving Sally because she was so alone. My mother said we would go back and visit her, but I don't think that will happen. My mother might want to, but she'll get busy or my father won't drive us.

My throat really hurts. I'm allowed to drink grape juice and eat vanilla ice cream. Everyone tells you how lucky you are when you have your tonsils out because you can eat all this ice cream. They don't tell you it tastes horrible. Vanilla was always my favorite, but I don't think I'm ever going to be able to eat it again after this.

During the day, I get to stay in my parents' bedroom. They gave me a bell to ring when I want something, but I have to write down what I want because I'm not supposed to talk. I don't want to anyway. It really hurts.

After I'm home a few days, my friends bring me my school work. Sometimes Mary Lou stays and we watch The Mickey Mouse Club together. We don't like it as much as we did because there's a new show called *American Bandstand* and we're starting to watch that.

My Aunt Estelle always makes a big fuss, in a nice way, because I can do my homework and watch TV at the same time. She says she can't understand how I can do both. Nobody stops me either because my grades are good. I like lying in bed reading, watching TV, and having people wait on me. I feel like I'm rich. Every day my throat hurts less and I think the entire family is going to be real happy when it's completely healed because a lot of the time I lie here and think of all the food I want to eat. I think not to enjoy food is the worst thing you could ever do in this family. Now they call me another name, *mooshod*. Most of my nicknames mean the same thing basically, that I'm skinny and slow. I think that if I ever start really liking to eat and gain some weight, my family's vocabularies would be cut in half. My mother has been really nice to me, so after a few days, when I was able to talk, I told her that I had been a little bit upset that none of my friends suggested I run for office this year, and I couldn't understand why because I tried my best in the sixth grade. I thought I had done a good job. This really made her mad because sometimes she says my friends take advantage of me when they call me about homework. But I don't think they do. She said, "Remember, too good is no good." And if I wanted to be a fool and let people walk all over me, then she didn't want me running crying to her. "You're too easy." "People take advantage of you and you're too stupid to know it." She said she was surprised at Mary Lou, but I told her that Mary Lou was the only one who said I should run. I think that made her feel a little better. Tommy won the election. I didn't even run because only Mary Lou mentioned it. I think I'm just too sensitive sometimes because my feelings get hurt quickly. I don't think everybody means to hurt me, but sometimes they do anyway. You would think I'd be used to it with all the insulting nicknames I have and how I'm always in trouble for doing things wrong and because I have "all these problems," but I don't think I'll ever get used to it. That's another reason I think I'm weak. My feelings get hurt and I cry about it. Nothing seems to bother my cousin. They tease her too, but it doesn't make her feel bad. Sometimes she even gets mad. I think my feelings, when I'm mad and sad, are the same. Either way, I cry. They say I have thin skin. It's true, I do.

My cousin says I have to get tougher and I shouldn't let people see how much they hurt me. She says I have to get some thick skin. I'd like to but I don't know how. She says I show everything I'm feeling on my face and that's not good. I know she's right, but I don't know how to do what she says. I think we're becoming best friends as we are both maturing. I can tell her things I can't tell anyone else, and although she does know I'm a crybaby, thin-skinned, and a coward, I think she likes me anyway. Nobody else really knows these things about me because I only laugh in front of everybody else, even my mother and father sometimes.

January 16th, 1958

I'm back to school and everyone said they missed me, and I missed them too. I did all the assignments and I'm not worried about my grades. One good thing about my tonsillectomy is that it made me forget about that ink spot until yesterday when I was thinking about coming back to school. I can see Jesus has not removed it, but somehow He has worked a miracle because Sister John hasn't noticed it yet. Everybody says I look real good, like I haven't even been sick. Even though I liked being in bed watching TV and reading all day, nothing really takes the place of friends, especially not vanilla ice cream.

February 1958

I've gained four pounds since my operation and everybody is happy. They're all saying my cheeks are rosy and for the first time I look healthy. Dr. Glass says I'll never get those terrible sore throats again and that makes *me* extremely happy. The first thing I ate after my surgery was ravioli. My Aunt Bootie made them especially for me. Everybody was smiling while I was eating them, because they said it was the first time it looked like I was enjoying myself while eating. I just hope that they don't think that surgery was some miracle and I'll just start loving food. I just think after a week of soup and juice and ice cream, those ravioli tasted mighty good. I still have to eat food that's a little mushy, although I'm dying for potato chips. My mother says they're too crispy and it will hurt if I eat them. Maybe I'll charge admission when I eat my first bag because it's been a long time and I'm going to be extremely happy.

Even my sister was nice to me when I was sick. She used to come up all the time when I rang the bell. I'd write a note and sometimes, if it wasn't liquids, she'd bring it back up. I think my sister has a very kind heart and she didn't like me being sick. Even though most of the time, when I'm not sick, she doesn't pay much attention to me.

All I can say is I'm glad it's over. I wasn't ready to die.

February 27th, 1958

Not being class president bothers me. I wish it didn't, but it does. I feel like I must have done something wrong. I'm afraid to ask anyone because, although a part of me wants to know, a part of me doesn't. It's so hard to figure some things out. I don't think my mother's right about my friends, though. They do like me. When I walk into a room, they always smile and they call me all the time. I just hope they never find out the secret only my parents know. I don't think they have, not yet anyway. Maybe I'll ask Mary Lou. She'll be nice about it, I'm sure of that.

Sometimes my friends miss a class or have trouble understanding something in math and they call me. My mother thinks they're using me, I think it's a compliment. My father always says a mark of true intelligence is not knowing everything, but knowing where to look for the answers, and I do think my friends are intelligent, so the fact that they ask *me* makes me feel that they know I'll give them the right answer.

My parents really confuse me on this issue. Every time somebody in the family is mean, they tell me he's my brother, or she's my sister or my aunt and that I have to forget it, but yet, any time they even think one of my friends is doing something, they go on and on about how stupid I am, that if I get hurt enough, I'll learn.

When I was 6, my brother, Vince, bit me on the chest and it hurt, but I was told not to make such a fuss because he didn't know what he was doing. Why don't they know that no matter who does it, a bite hurts? My Uncle Joe is married to my Aunt Carrie, who sometimes isn't very nice to me, but I'm never allowed to answer her back. And whenever I mention it to my mother, she tells me to shut up about it because she's my aunt, she's older, and I have to have respect.

I think that no matter who does it, if it is hurtful, it hurts. I don't think that they know that they're hurting me when they holler for no reason or when they laugh at me for being skinny or *stewnod*, or maybe they think they're allowed, or maybe they just don't care.

But I do have good friends who never hurt my feelings. But just in case they might, I laugh at myself first, so if they laugh, they'll be laughing with me. Sometimes I lie too. I'll say a test was hard when it wasn't, or that I'm worried about a grade when I'm not. I confess that sin, but I would hate it if my friends were mean to me because there wouldn't be anyone to run to for cover.

It gets really confusing because my mother is always so happy when Sister tells her how well I get along with everybody and how popular I am, or when my friends' parents tell her how much their kid likes me and how nice I am. That doesn't just happen. It happens because I'm nice to them and that includes helping them with their homework if they need it or lending them money or making them laugh. I can't act in two different ways anyway. I can't be one person with the family and a different one with my friends. So I'll either have to toughen up with everybody or continue to be nice to everybody. And being nice is easier for me. And besides, my mother is always telling me how she can't stand phonies. When she says this, I think she is talking about me, although she doesn't say it, because sometimes I'm really mad about what goes on in this house and I pretend it doesn't bother me. I wonder if that makes me a phony. My friends never get me mad so I'm honest with them except when I tell them I'm worried about tests and grades. But I don't want them to think I'm bragging or feel bad about themselves because I felt a test was easy. I don't like to hurt people's feelings. When I see their sad faces, it makes me sad. Jesus said that the Golden Rule is "Do unto others as you would have them do unto you." It seems clear enough and it's really easy to follow. All you have to do is not do to anybody else what has hurt you; and if you're not sure, just ask yourself if what you are going to do or say is kind. People have hurt my feelings a lot because I'm so sensitive, so I mostly don't even have to think about it, I just seem to know.

March 9th, 1958

My little brother, Larry, is three years old now. He's a little bad, but he gets away with it because he's the baby and he's a boy. They always call him the baby. I wonder if I was ever called the baby. Maybe I was before Vince was born. I don't remember it though because I was only two when he was born. I remember one time when I was about three, I had this terrible nightmare that he died and I couldn't go back to sleep. I was afraid to go near his crib the next morning because I didn't know if it was a dream or real. My mother says the doctor says he won't live to be 18. That makes me sad, real sad.

I'm starting to understand now that I'm 12, and he's 10, what being retarded really means. He doesn't go to school. He went to a special school for a little while, but my mother took him out because she said she didn't want anybody making fun of him. Sometimes people do, too. I remember once when we lived on St. John Street, some kid was laughing at him and my cousin and I beat him up. Nobody will ever make fun of him or do anything bad to him as long as I'm his sister. One day while I was thinking that he had no friends and didn't go out and didn't play with other kids, I felt really sorry for him. I try to play with him, but he doesn't do, or isn't allowed to do, so many things. He's not allowed to run because of his heart. He can't understand enough to play any games except for Fish, War, and checkers. He's really good at checkers, though. I taught him and now he can beat me. He doesn't seem to know he's different. When I told my mother how sad it made me, she told me that he was happy in his own world and that made me feel 100% better because it seemed to be true. She said that people were different, and that I shouldn't think that everyone was like me or like to do the same things I did.

I'm trying to teach him to dance now, and he's pretty good at slow dancing, but my mother says he can't fast dance because of his heart. I'm not supposed to make him mad either because he should never get upset. Sometimes I wonder if he understands enough to get upset when everybody's screaming and hollering at everyone else. I hope not.

Sometimes he does get me mad because he won't share any-thing. If he gets a new toy, no one can touch it. And if I do, he thinks it's his and I'm not allowed to fight with him about it because I'd be in big trouble then. He's cute too. His head is a little bigger than his body, but he doesn't look different to me. I don't think he's going to die when he's 18 because every-body takes really good care of him, and I think God knows my mother couldn't take it. All He has to do is listen to her, she says it all the time.

My mother says when he was little, she had to stay upstairs with him for a year. I remember that too. Every night she dressed me up and I went downstairs with my grandmother and aunt, and I stayed downstairs all the time. She thought he was going to die then, but he didn't. Maybe the doctors are wrong about his dying at 18 too. I pray for him all the time. I tell God if He wanted to take one of us, it would be easier if it were me because my mother would probably die too if it were my brother, and I wouldn't want to live if that happened anyway. So He'll prob-ably do that, and that will be fine. Sometimes I think they'd miss me, but sometimes I think they won't.

My mother says God made me so smart so that I can take care of my brother after she dies. I will too. I just hope I'm grown up if that happens because I sometimes feel that I can't even do what they expect now. I'm supposed to understand all these grown up things and I don't. I think that might be the se-cret that they know, that I'm just a baby and a coward and weak, because a lot of the times, I feel that I can't stand it. Sometimes I feel that I can never do anything right and I just want to run away.

I remember when I was about seven and my mother would go to the grocery store and it was night time and dark. She'd tell my brother and me to sit in front of the TV until she got back, she wouldn't be very long. I remember how scared I was and how it seemed so long before she returned, and how I would think that if we just sat real still and didn't move, everything would be okay. Then when my brother would start to move, it would make me even more scared. If we sat real still, I thought that nobody would come in and kill us, and that there would be no fire, and that my mother would come home.

My sister was sleeping upstairs, and I remember thinking that if something bad happened, I didn't know what to do and how I should probably know because my mother wouldn't have left us if she thought I didn't. She'd always bring home some cream soda when she went to the store, so I would try to think about that. I was in the house alone every day after school and I wasn't afraid then because it was light outside, and I figured if something happened, I would run out the door or jump out the window. But it was different when she went to the store at night because then there were three of us in the house and I didn't know what to do to save my brother and sister. When I couldn't think about that cream soda, I would pray to Jesus to keep us safe because no matter how much I wanted to be an only child, I didn't want anything to happen to my sister and brother, and I especially didn't want to be blamed for it.

One time I remember coming home from school and my sister was in her playpen. An old lady down the street used to watch her sometimes, but she didn't speak any English so I didn't like it when she was in our house. This particular day I walked in, closed the door, and the whole wall fell down. Luckily, the wall didn't reach into my sister's playpen and hurt her, but she started to cry really loud. I kept telling her it was okay, but she wouldn't stop, probably because she sensed that I thought it really wasn't okay. I thought my father would kill me for ruining the house. It wouldn't matter that I didn't mean to do it, that all I did was close the door, he would just see the damage and get really mad. Finally my sister stopped crying, and I remember getting down on my knees and praying to Jesus to make it all okay. I don't remember what happened after that, so I probably didn't get punished, but as hard as I try to remember, I can't remember where that old lady was that day or what happened with my father.

April 13th, 1958

I have reached the conclusion that there are some things that cannot be understood. Sister says the Trinity is a mystery of faith that we'll never fully understand, but that we have to accept it. The Trinity consists of God, Jesus, and the Holy Spirit, who are both separate beings and one being at the same time.

I think I do understand the Trinity because I feel that there are three parts to me: my body, my mind, and my soul, and I also think they're separate and one at the same time. I know that this can't be right though because it's not so hard, and certainly not impossible, as Sister says, to understand. So even though I think I understand, I probably really don't. It's probably the same thing around my house. When I think I understand something, I probably don't. Like how screaming and yelling makes you feel better. It makes me feel sick, but it must make others feel better because everybody does it around here all the time. I don't understand why my mother tells me all the time how much she hates my father, yet sometimes they kiss and have sex. I thought if you didn't like somebody (Catholics are not allowed to hate), you don't even want to be near them, the way I stay clear of Goody and Mikey. If you know somebody's going to hurt you, why would you put yourself near them at all? And I thought that if my brother was happy in his own world, that that was a good thing, and I could be happy in mine. But sometimes when

I'm happy in mine or have a problem in mine, my mother will say I should be ashamed of myself for being happy or having a problem, that I should look at my brother and his problems. I feel sometimes she wants me to feel lucky for not being mentally and physically disabled. But then if I do feel lucky, she says that I should be ashamed of myself because I get to do everything and get attention and my brother doesn't.

When I ask my cousin about these mysteries, she says that not everything is black and white, that sometimes things are gray. I guess that means something can be good and bad at the same time, just like the Trinity can be one and separate.

Maybe when I'm older, I'll understand the color gray. But, to me, something is either good or bad, happy or unhappy, lucky or unlucky.

May 31st, 1958

I am a woman now. It is Memorial Day and I got my period. I told my mother and she gave me some Kotex with a belt. I swore her to secrecy and told her not to tell my father. I'm not sure why, it's just embarrassing. The first thing I want to do is tell my cousin, Rosalie, but I don't want to call her from my house because my father might overhear. So I walk up to the drugstore and call her from a pay phone. When she picks up the phone, I tell her right away that I'm a woman, and she says she doesn't know what I'm talking about. I had to remind her that she told me I'd be a woman when I got my period and she said she didn't remember saying that. I think her problem, being a know-it-all, is that she says so much, she can't remember most of it.

Since my phone call woke her up, she's not being too nice, and tells me that it will take a lot more than my period to make me a woman, like boobs and knowing you should not call people at nine o'clock in the morning. I try to tell her I do have boobs, and my mother said she is going to buy me a training bra. And she said they looked like fried eggs and that my mother shouldn't waste her money.

So when I get home, I ask my mother if my breasts will grow now (only my cousin calls them boobs), and my mother says they will. I ask her whether they will get as big as my cousin's, and she says not if I take after her. I hope I don't because hers are no bigger than tangerines. My Aunt Boot and grandmother have big breasts so maybe I'll get lucky and take after them.

My stomach feels funny all day and my mother gives me two aspirins. I hope I don't feel like this every month, especially because I started crying for no reason this afternoon. That's one thing I don't need in my life—to cry more.

My mother says when you get your period, you can have children, and I ask her what you have to do to have children, not because I want them, but because I don't. As far as I'm concerned, we have enough children in this house. I told my mother that my cousin told me that a man puts his thing down there and then you get pregnant. She says that was true and that I mustn't ever make a man do that to me until I get married. I think my mother told my father though because about a week later, he sat me down at the kitchen table and said, "If you ever get pregnant, don't come home. But if you don't come home, I'll find you wherever you are and then I'll kill you, the baby, your boyfriend, and your mother." Having said that, he left the table. Now there are many things I don't understand, I admit it, but what my mother would have to do with it is really beyond me. But his message was crystal clear—don't get pregnant or he'll slaughter everybody.

My mother told me later that he had just heard that his friend's daughter was pregnant and unmarried, and he didn't want it to happen to me. I just wonder why my father's explanations of anything always involve violence, and why he always says that he'll disown me. I didn't know parents owned their children. I thought only slaves were owned. But I could be wrong. I'm wrong a lot.

June 15th, 1958

For some miraculous reason, Sister John never saw that ink stain on my desk. I was so happy that I made a mistake and told my mother and she said, "She had to see it when you weren't in class and covering it with a book." I hadn't thought of that, but now I feel guilty about all the bad things I thought about Sister John and how mean she could be, because my mother was right, she had to see it and chose not to embarrass me in front of the class or punish me or throw me out. I think it would have been better, like my cousin told me, to face up to it when it happened because it sure made many of my days a gray color. I don't know why I didn't, but I didn't.

Everyone says when you do something wrong, it's better to admit it and face the music, but the music gets awfully loud and ugly around my house whenever I do. My mother says she can tell if I'm lying by my face. This face is going to get me killed. I just know it.

July 6th, 1958

School's out. Since we had that little talk, my mother's been really nice to me, except that she still says I'm just like my father because I get really interested in things, and then as soon as I get everything I need to do it, I lose interest. She says I'll never get anywhere in life if I'm like this.

What happened is that I decided to take up painting. I made her buy me an easel, paints, brushes, and a smock, then painted for one hour and didn't want to do it any more. I point out to her that it was only this time, but she points out to me that I often lost interest in the games she bought after playing with them only one time. I guess she's talking about that stupid presidents' game again. Then she reminds me about the time when I was about seven and I begged her to allow me to scrub the kitchen floor. She says she got tired of hearing me and let me do it, and then she says, "Do you remember what happened?" I didn't have to think about it too long because she jumped in right away and said, "You ruined your slippers, soaked your pajamas, flooded the kitchen, and almost ruined the linoleum." She might be right after all, I do get bored easily. I always think I won't, but I do.

In my defense though, after I started to paint, I wasn't very good so I stopped. Those games were really *boring*. And the reason I wanted to scrub that floor was because my mother made it look like fun, but when I started to do it, I found out it wasn't any fun at all.

Sometimes I watch my mother's face when she does things, like iron, knit, bake and clean. There is such a look of concentration and enjoyment that everything she does looks like fun. I wonder if I ever have that look on my face. I bet I do when I'm reading or dancing. Maybe we just like different things. I don't like the same things my father does either. Now he's into aquariums. He buys all these expensive fish and seems happy for a minute and then doesn't look at them again. I wish when I grow up I'm like my mother and get enjoyment over and over from everyday things. I don't want to be like my father because he's always looking for outside things to make him happy, and then he's only happy for a minute until he's looking for something else. He seems to have lost interest in the PA system and the roses. I'm glad my grandmother is taking care of them. They're much too beautiful to let die.

July 10th, 1958

My grandmother is going down to Atlantic City for the rest of the summer. She'll stay in a hotel with a restaurant, and we'll be allowed to visit. Everybody says my grandmother deserves it because she worked hard her whole life. She was widowed when she was a young woman and she had six kids, one a baby. So she used to make whiskey and sell it, and then she opened the grocery store, which has always been open seven days a week. She was real good to her kids too. She bought them all a house when they got married. Everyone loves my grandmother. People tell me that during the Depression when no one had anything to eat, she would give them food for their kids and they would pay her when they could. They tell me my grandmother is a saint, but they don't have to tell me that because I already know it. She's always real happy to see everybody. When they stop in and we're eating dinner, she'll tell them to sit down and eat. If they do, she won't eat until she knows there is enough. What is most amazing to me is that she never lets anybody know she's doing this. She'll tell them she's already eaten or she's not hungry. I'd like to be like my grandmother when I'm an adult. I think it's a good thing to be like her, because she's always so happy and everybody loves her.

She really loves us kids too. She says her favorite is the one who needs her the most. I think that could be me because I'm so skinny and such a crybaby; but, although I would like to be her favorite, it doesn't really matter to me because she loves in such a wonderful way that it fills you up, whether you're her favorite or not.

Everybody says my father is her favorite child. My mother loves her like she was her own mother, and she loves my mother too. My mother says when I was a baby, she listened to everything my grandmother told her to do. For instance, she used to put diapers with pee in them on my face because my grandmother told her that would give me a good complexion. I sometimes question whether it was my grandmother who told my mother to throw my bottle on the ground in front of me when I was two and say, "No more." I hope not. That wasn't very nice. But my mother says when she had my brother, I had to get off the bottle and be potty trained, so I guess drastic measures were needed. My cousin was potty trained at nine months. I think that is unbelievable because my little brother couldn't do anything at all at nine months. And he's three years old now and still has accidents. But it's okay because he's the baby and he's a boy.

Whenever I ask my grandmother to tell me about when she was a young girl in Italy, she says that is the past. My mother says my grandmother doesn't like to talk about the past because it's too painful. I wish my mother would learn this from her because she is *always* talking about the past. I don't think anyone had a harder life than my mother did. That's what she tells me all the time. She says compared to her, I'm being raised like a queen.

I hope that when I get big, I don't talk about the past all the time and feel sorry for myself. I hope I'm just like my grandmother, except not fat.

July 23rd, 1958

I really miss my grandmother. Somehow with her gone, I feel a little unsafe. I think I may have convinced myself that she protects my mother and me against my father. It seems when she starts hollering at him in Italian, he stops whatever he's doing to us. One time she was so mad at him that she jumped up from her chair, grabbed a broom, and ran towards him as if she were going to hit him. He started to laugh and then we all laughed.

I think sometimes she should have hit him more when he was a kid because he's really miserable and unfair. My mother says that's because he doesn't want to work at all. It seems to me, he doesn't work much now. The other day I was up in my room and he called me downstairs to change the channel on the TV he was watching three feet away. Now that is really lazy. My mother, on the other hand, works all the time. She never sits still. She cuts meat, packs shelves, runs the register, cleans the store, and then at night she'll scrub the floor or bake or sew. It's been decided that I will soon start running the register now that I'm almost 13. My father says I'm not allowed to make any mistakes, and he taught me how to count out change, which is pretty easy. If someone gives you a five dollar bill and they spend $2.40, you count up, you don't subtract. You take a dime and say, *two fifty* and then two quarters and say, *three dollars*, and then two one dollar bills and say, *and two dollars makes five dollars*. He says it's easier that way, and I think he's right. My mother taught me how to pack the bags. Soap doesn't go in the meat bag, cans on the bottom but not too many in one bag or it will be too heavy. Sometimes you have to double the bag too. I sort of like it.

When people shop in the store, they always talk to me and ask me about school. It makes me feel important. I'm running the register a little now and when school starts in September, I'll run it after school and on weekends. They're not going to pay me because they said I get everything I want. I do too. There aren't many things I want that I don't have. My parents are very generous. My Aunt Boot says they spend money like drunken sailors on leave. My mother says if everyone were like my Aunt Boot, who doesn't buy anything, the world would stop because no one would be able to earn a living. I will have to do my homework in the store and I can't really get out of that because I always did it watching TV anyway. I am unable to say now that I can't do two things at once and have to concentrate when I'm doing my homework. One thing, though, I will be allowed to watch *American Bandstand*, which is a dance show in Philadelphia. It's been on the air a couple of years, but my friends and I just discovered it. We watch it and we know all the new songs, dances, and regulars. The regulars are high school students who go on *Bandstand* every day, and we talk about their clothes and who danced with whom. I like Justine Correlli and Bob Clayton, and Arlene Smith and Kenny Rossi. I'd like to go on *Bandstand* some time, and I think Mary Lou and I will do it. We're planning it out. My mother says that rock and roll is just noise, that when she was a girl, they had beautiful songs and good music. But I like rock and roll. Unlike my parents, I think it's going to last.

August 12th, 1958

My Aunt Bootie and Uncle Tony, Vince and I went to Atlantic City to see my grandmother and she looked beautiful. She was all tan and happy. She has two lady friends who stay at the same hotel and they knew each other before. She seems to be having a good time and I'm feeling a little guilty for wishing she would come home and protect everybody.

The hotel has this really great restaurant where I can get a combination dish of ravioli and gnocchi, which are my two favorite foods. I think to be able to get them together in one meal is really neat. My mother says I use the word "neat" too much, but all the kids say it and it just describes so much of what I want to say. And Sister says not to use three words when one will do. My grandmother seems pleased to see us, and introduces us to all her friends like she is really proud. She tells her lady friends how smart I am in school and when they say I'm *bella* (pretty), my grandmother says I will be when I gain some weight. I did gain some weight after my tonsillectomy, but apparently not enough. Everybody says my color is better though, and I have never gotten a sore throat since. We never did go back to see Sally in the hospital. I knew we wouldn't. I think of her sometimes and hope that her parents get some time to visit her, because it's not so great lying in a hospital bed all day. The days are very long and can be very lonely if no one visits you.

September 16th, 1958

I'm finally a teenager and it's really neat having so much in common with my friends. Until I had my friends and we started watching The Mickey Mouse Club, I never thought I was like anyone else. Now, especially with *Bandstand*, I feel just like everyone else and I like feeling this way. We have Sister Regis as our eighth grade teacher and she's really pretty and nice. I think she and Sister Veronica, my teacher in the first grade, are the prettiest nuns I have ever seen. Some people say that women become nuns because they're unattractive and can't get a man, but I never thought so because I see many unattractive women who did get men around my neighborhood. I just think the nuns are married to Jesus and want to help people. My mother keeps saying I'm going to be a nun, and my father gets really mad. Her reason is that my face is so innocent and, maybe, although she never says it, she thinks I'm nice. I hope it's not because she thinks I'm ugly.

Sister Regis is treating me like I'm really smart, and because she thinks so, I work harder to please her. It's better to work harder to please somebody who already thinks you're okay, than to work harder to convince somebody you are, like I'm constantly doing with my father. I think because I don't get nervous doing it, it's almost fun. This way seems to work better for me all around.

October 1958

Sister Regis has decided we're going to have a debate and the subject is going to be *Bandstand*. I guess she hears us talking about it all the time. She also decides that Carla and I, who love it the most, are going to have to argue against it. Personally, I don't have any arguments against it so I'll have to think long and hard about this. When I told my mother how unfair I thought it was that I had to argue against *Bandstand* since Sister Regis knew how much I loved it, she said that's because Sister probably thinks that I'm smart enough to come up with arguments against it, and that's probably true. I'd really shine if I could follow my heart and argue for it. After all, if you're going to be in a real debate, you would get to argue what you really believed. This is a really hard assignment. I want to get a good grade, for sure, but I don't want any of the kids to believe I'm really "against *Bandstand*." That would make me really weird and I don't want to be weird. I felt weird my whole life until now, and being part of things is so much better.

My mother says I am now in puberty, which has something to do with my body changing. I hope my breasts are listening because they're not changing at all. I can see that some of my friends' breasts are getting bigger, they even need bras. I'm still wearing undershirts with no change in sight. I think big breasts make you womanly and I still look like a child. But I do have lots of hair on my legs and under my arms now, and my mother says that's another side of puberty. We're negotiating on when I'll be allowed to shave.

I pray every day to Jesus that I'll be pretty. I know it's probably wrong to pray for this, but I think it's really important to everybody, including me. My parents always seem to be apologizing for the way I look. "She's going through the awkward stage." "She has to fill out." I think that if I don't fill out or get through this awkward stage, it's going to be impossible for them to continue to love me. Both my parents are nice looking people, as they keep telling me, so I don't want to be a disappointment to them.

Sister says we shouldn't care about how we look because that's vanity, and vanity is a sin. In fact, it's one of the Seven Deadly Sins. I think that means it's a really big one. But I think if I am pretty later, I'll never be vain about it, just grateful. It would be awful if two good looking parents have an ugly child. My mother says that happens.

Sometimes I pretend I'm beautiful, but I'm not and I know it. I think Jesus is going to answer me though because He knows that if I turn out to be ugly, I'm going to have big problems around here. This family likes beautiful people, that's for sure.

October 2nd, 1958

Two things have happened. I'm allowed to shave my legs. My first attempt was very bloody and I had to put pieces of toilet paper up and down on the cuts, which were all over. Luckily, I shaved at night or I wouldn't have been able to go to school. The other thing is that I got a pair of white bucks like Pat Boone. They're really neat, but I had to promise my mother I'd polish them every day. I like polishing shoes, so that's not a problem. She's probably happy because I'm wearing white again. Pat Boone has a real clean image, even my Aunt Boot likes him. He's married and has four daughters, but I like him anyway.

Movie star magazines are now my favorite things to read. Comic books are definitely out. I like Debbie Reynolds and Eddie Fisher, and my cousin likes Janet Leigh and Tony Curtis, and we have arguments all the time about who is the prettiest and most handsome. It's not like I don't like Janet Leigh and Tony

Curtis, because I do. It's just that I like Debbie Reynolds better. One of the first movies I ever saw was *Singing in the Rain*. I think she's a good singer and dancer, as well as an actress, and I think Janet Leigh only acts. As far as I'm concerned, Debbie Reynolds has a perfect face. All her features are the same size, and to me, that's what beauty is.

I have really big eyes, which are too big for my face, and I absolutely hate my nose. It's not that it's big, because it's not. It's just different and not perfect like Debbie's.

Photoplay Magazine is my favorite. It has stories and pictures of all of my favorite stars. That's how I know all about Pat Boone. Elvis is always in them too. I do think he's handsome and he can really move his body, but I still like Pat Boone better. Elvis is making movies too. I saw *Love Me Tender* and it was wonderful. He was on the Ed Sullivan Show and they only photographed him from the waist up because the critics are saying his movements are obscene. I don't exactly know what obscene means, but I think he can really move well, and obscene sounds like something really bad.

Mary Lou and I are planning how to convince our parents to allow us to go on *Bandstand*. We would have to take a bus to Philadelphia. It doesn't really matter right at the moment though because we're only 13 and you have to be 14 to get in. I'd love to see Dick Clark and the regulars. We are wondering if anyone will ask us to dance. We both doubt it because most of the kids who go on *Bandstand* are older and we're not even wearing bras yet, but Mary Lou will be wearing one soon, I can tell.

I wish my breasts would grow as fast as the hair on my legs. It's a pain to have to shave them so often. Of course, my mother is constantly reminding me that she told me that once I started, I wouldn't be able to stop and I wouldn't like it.

One day I was going in to take a bath and my father told me to wait. He went into the store, got a roll of toilet paper, and handed it to me saying, "You'll probably need this, there's only a half roll left in the bathroom." He just thinks he's so funny. Everybody laughing at him doesn't help either.

Also, I'm using deodorant and perfume. I feel just like a grown-up. In addition to the hair on my legs, I've developed some hair on the top of my lip which, my mother says, you can't shave. I'm very self conscious about it, especially in front of Mikey, who still tells that lame joke about Italian girls and mustaches. My mother suggests we bleach it, so she tries the bleach on my arm first to make sure that I'm not allergic, and I'm not. The bleach makes the hair lighter, but it's still there. My mother says I look like a different person. Maybe she won't keep saying I'm going to be a nun now.

I'm gaining some weight this year and even bought a straight wool skirt which makes me look like I have a shape. I feel really neat when I wear it. We used to wear really full skirts and loads of crinolines under them. The more crinolines you wore, the better you looked. But we're getting away from that a little. We still wear them, but we wear other stuff too.

I used to wear several crinoline slips and my mother didn't mind because she said that when I wore them, people couldn't tell how skinny I really was. But one of my slips was usually hanging, and this seemed to upset everybody. They then gave me a new nickname, *scumbaree*, which means sloppy. I'm always having to pull up my dress so I can pull up my slip, not in front of anybody, of course. Another thing that's big in fashion these days are sweaters with separate collars. Some of the collars are even beaded. I'm so glad I was born now, because when I look at old pictures, the fashions seem to be very boring. I have a picture of my mother holding me when I was a baby and she is wearing a suit that has shoulders like a football player. Why anyone would think that looked good escapes me.

My Aunt Lissa, my mother tells me, always wore black. My mother said she'd have a dozen black dresses in her closet and then go out and buy another black one. I can't figure out why somebody would wear just one color all the time. It seems boring to me. My mother says it's because black is slimming and sexy.

My favorite color is blue. Everyone says I look good in white and red, but I like blue anyway. I wonder if you can like one color to wear and another to look at? I like blue because everything that is really beautiful is blue—the sky, the ocean. Blue eyes are the prettiest too. I think what makes me like it so much is that it has so many different shades, more than any other color, and it can change shades in a minute. I mean black is always black, and yellow is always yellow. But sometimes the sky can be a pale shade of blue, and then in an instant, the color is more vibrant, the same with the ocean, the same with blue eyes. I don't like things that are always the same. My mother says I get bored too easily. My father can't say anything because he's worse than me and he's got to know it.

My favorite day is one in which I get to do many different things. But if I have to do the same thing all day long, I really can't stand it. I like working in the store, but it gets boring sometimes too. In between customers, I read books so that breaks up the monotony. Also, I do my homework. For some reason when I have to memorize things for a test or presentation, I walk up and down the aisles in the store. My father thinks it's really funny, but I learn better that way.

The other day in school, Sister was talking about comic relief, and when it's used or needed in literature. Sometimes I think I'm the comic relief in my family. So many things I do seem to make them laugh and I'm not really trying to do that. I guess that's the purpose. They never laugh at my sister because she gets really mad, and they never laugh at Vince because he's sick. They laugh at Larry once in a while, but for the most part, he's not very funny. Everything about me seems to make them laugh. If I don't think about it too much, I like it. But when I start to think about it, it makes me feel bad.

November 10th, 1958

My sister is 7 now and we don't get along too well. It's because we share the same room. I think there should be a law against sisters sharing the same room because it is unnatural. I'm not the neatest person in the world, but when it gets too messy, it does get on my nerves and I straighten it up. But it never seems to get on her nerves, never. Also, sharing the room bothers me because I don't have any privacy. Sometimes my friends come up to my room and my sister gets really mad when I tell her to leave. She gets mad all the time. She's pretty though.

One day last week, Angela was over and we were talking and I heard a thud in the closet. When I went to check it out, there was my sister sitting there. I asked her what she was doing and she said, "I'm looking for something." Now I know everybody thinks I'm *stewnod* or dopey, but this dopey I'm not. I told her to leave and I told my mother about it. My mother told her not to do it any more. She said, "It's my room too." Sometimes I think she's trying to get me in trouble, but then at other times, I just think she's nosy. She's real quiet because I think she listens to everything that's going on and thinks a lot. I don't remember what Angela and I were talking about, but I didn't hear anything about it from my sister, so I guess it wasn't anything bad. Sometimes I think she wants to get something on me so she can blackmail me, but I don't think she's a rat at heart. I hope I'm not wrong. She always gets into my things too. No matter how many times I tell her not to touch anything, she does anyway. When she touches things, she often destroys them and she never cleans up her mess, and I always get blamed for them because I'm older.

I wish I had my own room. I wish I had some privacy. The only privacy I have is in the bathroom, and only when I lock the door. But I feel really awful thinking like this because I just finished reading *The Diary of Anne Frank*. Talk about no privacy. I think this is one of the best books I've ever read. Maybe it's because we're the same age and I never read a book written by someone my age. But she seems so smart and charming. The whole Holocaust makes me very sad. It's hard to believe something like that happened and nobody did anything. She didn't even have to die if she didn't get sick. She could have made it because they didn't gas her or anything. Sometimes I think about Anne Frank and how she must have felt with all those people in those little rooms, and it makes me grateful that I'm Catholic and living in America.

Sister says the Holocaust was an atrocity against mankind and that Hitler was the devil on earth. She looks so sad when she talks about it, especially because she probably thinks that only Catholics go to heaven. I don't believe that. Since what I think is not hurting anybody, I don't think it's wrong. I just think that it doesn't matter what religion you are. As long as you believe in God and live a good life, I think you can get into heaven. The only reason I believe this is that there is a colored family, Mr. and Mrs. Butler, who live across the street from us. They are the nicest people you'd ever want to meet and I can't believe that they won't go to heaven, even if they are Baptists. And also because of Bonnie, my Jewish friend. I can't picture anyone that nice and that generous going to hell. We are never allowed in any other church but a Catholic one. I think if we go into a Baptist church, we might get struck by lightning. I'm not sure, but that's what I think. I don't talk about this to anyone because they might report me. I might get excommunicated, which means you can't receive Holy Communion or go to Confession. I've been praying to Jesus and the Blessed Mother to let me know if I'm right, because if I'm wrong, I'm going to try and convert Mr. and Mrs. Butler. They're much too nice to go to hell or limbo or wherever non-Catholics are supposed to go. I don't know how you go about converting people, but just in case, I'm always on my best behavior around them. Sister says actions speak louder than words, and we have to live our lives so as to set a good example for other people. So until I figure this out, I'll continue to be my most polite and kind. Not that I'm not polite and kind to other people, I am. I just try harder in front of the Butlers.

When we do extra work in school, we get extra credit. I wonder if God gives you extra credit for changing Baptists into Catholics. Probably. I'll bet it counts a lot in getting you out of purgatory, which is probably where I'm going anyway. But in the event you go straight up to heaven, it probably will get you a seat closer to God. But then I think, suppose the priests and sisters are wrong and Catholicism is not the true religion, and Protestant is, then what?

November 15th, 1958

We are learning about two new sins in Religion class—masturbation and impure thoughts. Since I don't know what they are, I don't know whether the Pope has just decided they are sins or they are old sins they're just teaching us about. I know they're not in the Ten Commandments or one of the Seven Deadly Sins. Sister is saying if we engage in masturbation, it is a very grievous sin and could result in blindness. It makes me think back to that night the miracle cured my blindness, and I start thinking whether I could have masturbated that day and that's why I went blind. Impure thoughts are thoughts which are not pure and have something to do with sex, I think.

I look around the class and everyone is listening intently to Sister. I can't tell by their faces whether they have any idea what she is talking about though. When you go to Catholic school, you learn to perfect a look on your face that says you're both listening and understanding. You learn it or you perish. I don't think any of my friends know because I've had to teach them everything so far about sex which I learned from my cousin. I remember last year when I told Mary Lou and Carla that "hoor" was spelled "whore," I knew they wouldn't believe me so I carried my pocket dictionary to school and showed them. I'm really careful how I tell them things because I don't want them thinking I'm a Miss Know It All. There's only one Miss Know It All, and she knows who she is.

The first thing that comes to my mind is whether you can commit sins of impure thoughts if you don't know they're impure. I have a zillion thoughts every day and I don't have time to decide which one of them is impure because then I'd have two zillion thoughts every day, and that's a little too much, even for me.

No one mentions anything at lunch or after school, so I decide that I can either ask my cousin or my mother, and then I decide that maybe I should ask each of them only one question. My mother was alone in the store making sausage and I ask her what masturbation is, and she says that means when you play with yourself. I thought I probably heard her wrong because she always told me to go play by myself when I was a kid. But she didn't say *by*, she said *with*. Now I learned a long time ago, if you ask my mother more than one question at the same time, she gets irritated and I get hollered at. So I say, "Oh," and go to my trusty dictionary. It says to masturbate is to manipulate the genitals for sexual gratification. I can't even figure out how you can do that, so I'm relieved I haven't committed that sin and won't go blind. But it does make me wonder, and then I wonder if that's what Sister means by impure thoughts. Sometimes I think about kissing boys, and sometimes my hand accidentally touches my breast and it tingles. And I have even wondered what boys look like naked. The only boy I have ever seen naked is my baby brother, and he's not much.

December 17th, 1958

I ask my cousin how you know when a thought is impure. She says any thoughts having to do with sex are impure. I forgot what she had told me about sex, so I ask, "Like what?" which was a mistake. She then went on and on about how she can't be wasting her time talking to babies about things they don't understand. But at the end she said, "If you have an impure thought, you'll know." Well, that made me feel a little better. It's impossible to confess sins if you don't know they're sins. And then I said, really just to be smart, "By the way, do you masturbate?" and she did something she hasn't done in a long time, punch me. There is only one reason I don't think I'm adopted, because if I were, she would tell me.

December 21st, 1958

I have my period today and my rear end hit up against a big cardboard box, causing my sanitary pad to move a little, and it tingles. I'm just wondering if this is only an impure thought or whether I have masturbated. So I go back to the dictionary and decide I didn't manipulate anything, so I'll only have to confess that I had an impure thought because when it happened, I remember thinking I wouldn't mind if it happened again.

These impure thoughts are driving me crazy. The more I try not to have them, the more I do. Last time I went to Confession, I told the priest I had one thousand impure thoughts every day. And he shouted real hard, "You what?" He then said that it was impossible to have that many each day because even if I had 60 one minute thoughts each hour and I was up 14 hours, that that would only be about 840. And he knows that, with school and everything else, I must be thinking of other things. I guess he's right, but I think it's better to be forgiven for more than you actually do than to confess to less and have those others remain blots on your soul. And we are taught that if we are not sure of the amount of times we did something, we should approximate to the best of our ability. It really does seem like a thousand some days.

December 25th, 1958

I received the best gift for Christmas this year, a hi-fi. I'm so into music, and now I not only can buy 45 rpms, but 33-1/3 albums. They even bought me Pat Boone and Elvis Presley albums. I want to buy a bunch of albums of singers, as well as Broadway musicals which I love because the songs tell a story. I think that life should have music, that when people are happy they should burst into song and dance, and that when they're sad, they should sing sad songs or sad music should be playing in the background. Whatever's going on in my life, music always makes me feel better.

As far back as I can remember, we always had music in our house. My brother, Vince, my penance is over now about being ashamed, used to love the song "Good Night Irene" and I used to love "How Much Is That Doggy In The Window?"

My mother used to have this small 45 rpm record player and we would listen to the same songs over and over again. Whenever I hear one of those songs, it always reminds me of the time I heard it before. And if that was a sad time, it makes me cry. I think I might be too sensitive, but I don't know what to do about that. I think it might be like trying to change brown eyes into green. You just can't do it. When I was little, I thought anything could happen. I thought I could fly, and I thought Jesus could put money under my pillow. I still do in a way, but I figure, although God can work miracles, He probably doesn't waste them on silly things. But miracles do happen. Both my mother and Sister agree on this.

When I was about 8, a friend dared me to jump off the library steps, which were quite high. I never liked being dared, so I did it; but before I did it, I prayed to God and my guardian angel to let me be able to do it without getting hurt. I remember doing that many times when I was small. And I don't ever remember getting hurt.

The only time I remember bleeding was when a neighbor boy pushed me down on a piece of glass and I ran home because I had a big hole in my knee and lots of blood was coming out. My mother hates whenever any one of us gets hurt. She asked me what I had done to make that boy do that, but I hadn't done anything. I was too much of a coward ever to make someone bigger than me mad. She was really angry when she was cleaning up my leg, and she kept asking me, "Don't I have enough problems without having to deal with you getting hurt?" She acted like I did it on purpose. I still have a scar on my knee too.

I have since learned that my mother is not very good during emergencies. The other day my little brother hit his head getting into my father's car and it looked like he was bleeding from the eye. My father and Frannie, a friend, took him to the hospital while my mother just ran up and down the stairs screaming, "His eye is out." When they came home, my brother still had his eye. He just had a cut on his eyelid.

I heard them talking about the time I was an infant and my father wanted to take me to Hammonton to visit relatives because I was all dressed up. My mother didn't want him to and they started fighting and I had a convulsion. It was my Aunt Lissa who ran with me into the street, hailed a car, and got me to the hospital. She basically saved my life.

Whenever there is an emergency, my mother either freezes or starts screaming. I'm glad my grandmother and Aunt Bootie are here all the time because sometimes I think if it was left to my mother, we'd all die.

I'm not good in emergencies either because I get really afraid. I hope it's because I'm only 13 and not because I take after my mother. But I don't worry too much about it because my mother and Sister Regis both say that when we're born, a guardian angel is assigned to us and keeps us safe, and that we only die when it's our time. That's probably why none of us has died yet.

Sometimes I talk to my guardian angel. I explain to her that I'm about to do something that I've never done and ask her to watch over me. Even if we're just playing baseball, before I get up to bat, I pray that she'll guide me to hit that ball. And I usually do too.

When I was little, I always left room on one side of me so my angel could sit, but since I'm older, I know that is silly. Guardian angels don't have to sit or stand beside you, they can fly about you if there's no room. I used to think when I was small that there was absolutely nothing I couldn't do, and that some day I was going to do something really important. Sometimes I still feel that way, but sometimes I don't because there are certain things I have learned I can't do. I can't lift heavy things, I can't fly, and I can't write in cursive too well. But I don't think those things are all that important. I'd like to do something special with my life. I hope it has something to do with music. I write poems because they sound like music to me, the way they have a beat (only it's called meter in poetry). When I write them, I feel their rhythm like my body feels the beat and rhythm when I'm dancing. It's the same thing. I don't know exactly what it is, but whatever it is, I'm sure glad I have it. Even when I'm trying to be funny, there's a certain beat and rhythm to that too. So I guess I only have one talent that can be applied to many things. I think some day I'll figure exactly what that talent is, but for now, I just hear it, feel it, and do it. I'm starting to write more and more. Sometimes I'm not sure what I'm writing about but after I write, I feel better.

My life is really very good now. I'm popular. My grades are good, and Sister Regis really likes me. I've gained weight and I haven't had a sore throat since last year. And just when I thought it couldn't get any better, someone told my grandmother that Sister Regis said that I'm so smart, I may win a scholarship to Camden Catholic High School, that is, if I get in. You have to take a test and it is a really hard school to get into because everybody wants to go there.

Everybody seems really happy I might win a scholarship. I have to keep reminding them that there are other kids as smart as me who write better and I might not get it because I might get a lower grade in penmanship than those other kids. They don't want to hear any of this. In their minds, I've already won it. Sometimes I wonder what will happen if I don't. I wish whoever told my grandmother about the scholarship hadn't. Well, at least worrying about winning that scholarship will cut down on my impure thoughts.

January 1959

We had our debate on *Bandstand*. I came up with the argument that to spend too much time in front of the TV could affect our grades and that there were more important things in life than dancing and music. I didn't believe it, but I had to argue something. Carla said that *Bandstand* is bad because you could fall while you're dancing. The class thought that was really funny because Carla is always complaining that her mother is always worried she'll get hurt, and doesn't allow her to do things because of that. And, besides, everyone knows that you can't fall while you're dancing, Carla especially, because she is a really good, safe dancer.

Sister says the debate is a tie. That makes everybody happy, especially me, because one of my competitors for the scholarship argued in favor of *Bandstand*, and everybody knows that's easier to do. I like debates, being on stage, and giving speeches. Some would say I'm a show-off and like being the center of attention, in fact, some in my own family do say it. Maybe they're right, but I think it's just that I'm pretty good at these things and everybody likes to do things they're good at, even my mother with her sewing and baking. The Bible says that before you find fault with others, you should see whatever is in your own eyes, something about smite and smoting. What it means is that before you criticize others for something, you should see if you have the same problem and clear that up first. It makes sense to me. My mother feels so good when people tell her she bakes the best cookies in the world or she knits the best blankets. And she does it more often. Why is it any different when I give a speech or dance on stage? It's the same thing, I think. But what do I know, I'm only 13.

February 1959

I'm really studying hard to win that scholarship for two reasons. One is I like to win, and the other is my family already thinks I have. My father has decided to buy this beautiful building on 4th Street which would give us a bigger store. I'm sorry it won't give us a bigger house, but he's taking what used to be the most beautiful house in the neighborhood and making it mostly into a store. It has four bedrooms. I'm still going to have to share a room with my sister though, but it is a bigger room. The downstairs will only have a kitchen and living room and no dining room, like we have now. It has no yard which makes me sad because of those beautiful roses. It doesn't matter what I think though. My parents usually do exactly what they want anyway. We just go along with the program. I'm trying to look on the bright side. It will be closer to school. Our bedroom will be bigger, and it has a real big closet. My father says it will be better for my grandmother because he's going to build a commode between the house and the shed so she doesn't have to go up and down the stairs to go to the bathroom. It seems to me he always uses this argument. I remember when I was about 7 we were walking down Spruce Street around Easter and he told me he only had enough money to either buy me an Easter basket or to buy my grandmother a flower. I knew what the answer had to be and felt bad because I sure wanted that Easter basket. He bought both though. I guess he was testing me to see if I was unselfish and I passed. I always feel guilty though because I sure wanted that Easter basket no matter what I said. Now it seems I'm not allowed to feel badly about the move because, after all, my grandmother is getting old and how could I live with myself if she had a heart attack going up and down those steps? And she's more important than any house. Sometimes she's more important to me than any person. So I tell him I think it's a good idea, even though I don't want to leave the only home I have ever had where I have felt safe.

February 13th, 1959

I realize that I have an ongoing problem of trying to figure out when, or if, I'm ever allowed to feel proud of myself. My mother says I shouldn't brag in front of Vince because it makes him feel bad, and I shouldn't brag to my friends because they'll think I'm a show-off and not like me. From experience I know I can't tell my cousin anything because she starts singing the hymn, "How Great Thou Art." So I'm starting to put down everything I do to the point that I think I have convinced myself I'm nothing special. When I feel like I'm nothing, I don't like it much. My mother says to be ordinary is fine, but yet when I'm only ordinary in things, they pay me no mind. It's only when I win a prize or get all As that they pay attention to me. I think everyone needs to feel special, but I'm afraid to feel that way. My father confuses me too. Sometimes he'll say if I just make a little mistake, "You're not as smart as you think you are." Part of me feels that you should feel good about who you are and what you do, but every time I do, somebody hurts me or puts me down.

It isn't that I think I'm better than anybody else, because I don't, but there are certain things I can do better, just like there are certain things they can do better. And when they tell me things that they do better or have more of, I think nothing of it. I don't even think it's bragging. Mary Lou told me when she was down the shore last summer, a man approached her about being a model. I thought that was really neat, and I also thought that she was pretty enough to be one. Sandy always has lots of money in her purse, and I think that's a good thing. When I told my mother though, she said it was probably the same money all the time. My cousin has more common sense than I do, and I think that's great because I can ask her about things I don't get. I think that everyone has certain gifts and talents, and those gifts and talents are fact. My question is why I'm not allowed to feel good about mine? I'm so afraid that if I keep denying them, I'll forget I have them and I'll never feel special. I think everyone should feel special, even me.

March 3rd, 1959

My father did buy that property and we'll be moving in September. I'm sad about that but I'm doing my best to accept it. In our house now, off of my parents' bedroom, is a balcony. It's so romantic to me, like Romeo and Juliet. You can even sit out there. I do too, especially when I want to escape the noise. I wonder if I'll have a place to escape to in the new house? Most of my friends live closer to the new house though, and there really are no kids on Cherry Street, where we live now, who are my age. On 4th Street, my friend Terry will live right next door to me, and Jenny lives next door to her. It will be fine, I hope.

My father's really doing it because he says we will have more business because we can carry more food. In fact, his newest project has been to send out flyers. To tell the truth, it is extremely embarrassing. One of his flyers says, "You've had the rest, now try the best." There is no way I am ever going to be comfortable with this new interest of his. All I can do is pray to God that he loses interest even faster than usual. He's also talking about buying a truck for deliveries since he thinks his flyers will bring in business from the outskirts of town. And the truck is going to have our name painted real big and say Maroni's Food Market, You've Tried the Rest, Now Try the Best. For Free Delivery, Call, and then have our phone number. Just the thought of it makes me want to throw up. I wonder why nobody ever tells him he's a show-off and needs to be the center of attention. I wish somebody would, and fast.

<u>March 14th, 1959</u>

Most of my class has taken the test for Camden Catholic High School, and we are waiting for the results. I really hope I get in. I hope all my friends do too. If I don't get in, it's going to be extremely unpleasant around this house because that surely will mean no scholarship. I haven't told any of my friends about the scholarship, not because I think they would think I was bragging, but because I may not win it. And that would be just too embarrassing for words. I think my mother told Mary Lou's mother though. We don't talk about it, but I think she knows I'm in the running. It doesn't bother her at all.

The test was on Saturday and when I came home, my Aunt Boot made me a sausage sandwich. It tasted great, but I know that I will, in the future, always associate sausage with failure or success based on the outcome of that test.

Everything always reminds me of something else, like perfumes and songs, foods and scents. Each brings back a memory so vivid that I feel like I'm experiencing it again. I guess everybody does this, but I've never discussed it with anybody else because maybe they don't and it may be really weird. Cream soda always reminds me of when we were left alone while my mother went to the store. No one can understand why such a *lick-a-lick* like me refuses to drink cream soda. I won't eat tomato soup either because of all the times we ate it at the other house. And I can't stand to hear the song, "Your Cheatin' Heart" because my mother used to play it all the time and cry. And every time my Aunt Boot makes breakfast sausages, I think of the time when I was sick in bed and no one was home, and my mother bought me this book about a little girl who had a yellow slicker and ate sausages. I kept reading that book over and over and I started to get hungrier and hungrier, but my mother was at work and I didn't know if I should eat. This was the only time I wished I knew how to cook eggs like my cousin. I have asked my mother to teach me to cook, but she says I'll never be able to do it and brings up the scrubbing of the floor-ruining of the slippers story again. My question is, how does she know I can't do things until I've tried?

I think when my mother was a girl and her mother went to that hospital, what she wanted most was a mother to cook her dinner and wash and iron her clothes. She always tells the story about how my grandfather used to take her out of school so she could wash clothes for everybody and she was only 9. I think that really bothered her, so she makes sure that we always have good food to eat and wear pressed, starched clothing. This is the way she shows us how much she loves us, not by that *mushy* stuff like kisses and hugs.

Sometimes when I look in my mother's face, I feel really sorry for her because she had no mother. I think not having a mother is probably the worst thing in the world. I always want to see her smile because then her eyes don't look so sad, and I do try my best to make her proud, to help her when I can, and to make her laugh. When it works, I feel so much happiness, but when it doesn't, I feel it's my fault, that if she didn't have to marry my father because of me, she'd be happy. And you never know with her. She can become really unhappy over anything. She says, "I'm depressed," and then she goes to her room and won't talk to anybody, sometimes for days. Even if people come over she likes, she won't come downstairs. My father, on the other hand, can be screaming from the top of his lungs, but if someone comes over, he starts smiling and is nice to them. Not my mother though. This does bother me sometimes because I know the visitors don't understand and I think they might feel she doesn't care about them, but that's not the reason, because sometimes her own father comes over when she's in a mood and she stays in her room. My Aunt Boot doesn't like this at all. I'm not sure what she doesn't like about it because she tells my grandmother in Italian, but I can see she's mad. What bothers me is that nothing can get my mother out of her mood. So what I'm trying to do is watch her carefully because I figure that if I can nip her unhappiness in the bud, it won't go so far as to confine her to her bed, where she refuses to talk or eat. I'm not very good at it yet, but every day when I'm walking home from school, I think about whether she's okay or in her room, and sometimes I'm afraid to know. I think when she gets in that mood, she wants to die, and that scares me. I don't think I can love her more than I do, but even that is not enough to make her happy. I know she's not too happy with my father, even though he doesn't hit her and stopped being a whoremaster. I think my mother had a very difficult childhood, and I think my father didn't. I think that maybe what you go through as a child makes a big difference in who you become. I know that mine has been a lot easier than my mother's. My mother does say that she was my grandfather's favorite and when she'd get really bad earaches, he'd put oil in her ears and let her sit on his lap. Sort of like my grandmother does for me.

I really love my mother's father because he's always smiling. There are people that you know love you because you can see it right on their face. That's how I feel about my grandfather. I'll never forget how he brought me all those comic books when I was 7. But I never liked his macaroni because he used to make long, thick spaghetti and the gravy was never as good as my grand-mother's. Sometimes, when we lived on St. John Street, my mother would take me and my brother and sister to my grandfather's, and she would say she was leaving my father. But as soon as we got there, my father would show up and take us back home. One time my mother told Vince and me to go hide in back of the washing machine in my grandfather's shed. When my father came, he was furious and was shouting that he didn't care if she left him, but she would never take his kids away. When he found us, he took us home and made us sit on the couch, and we weren't allowed to move or talk until she came home. I remember I used to wonder why he did that because he looked so mad and paid us no mind. I would sit there really scared, wondering if he would hit her when she came home and afraid, at the same time, she wouldn't. She always did come home, though, because she's our mother and nobody will love us like her. Although that was only six years ago, I can't remember whether that was one of the nights he hit her. I wonder why I can't remember that? Every time she would do this, I would question why because it never seemed to solve anything. My mother says that she fell in love with my father at first sight. He was in charge of running a dance, and she thought he was so handsome that she knew he was *the one* just by looking at him. He was eight years older than my mother. He was 25 when I was born, but it seems to me that my mother is the mature one.

It's hard for me to understand why she does get in these moods now when she didn't when things were so bad. Maybe she did, and I didn't notice because I was too young. She keeps on saying how she loves the store and how nice it is not to have to worry about money, but yet sometimes I think she still wants to die.

When my father is really mad at her, he tells her she's crazy just like her mother. I want to scream at him when he does this because everyone knows that you should never say that to my mother, but I can't scream at him. I'm afraid of him. I'm not afraid of my mother though. I'm only afraid she'll kill herself or wind up in one of those hospitals like my grandmother.

April 5th, 1959

My mother's mother was allowed to leave the hospital today and came for a visit. It's the first time I ever saw her, and she looks just like my mother. She has really white skin and wears her hair in a bun like my other grandmother. Other than that, she's nothing like my other grandmother. I was a little bit scared of her because she was real quiet and she sat up so straight in the chair. My mother introduced me to her and she said, "How do you do." She was real formal and I didn't know whether I should hug her or not. I was afraid she might not like it, like my mother. So I just smiled at her and said, "Hello, Grandmom." What bothered me the most was that she never smiled, not once, the whole day.

After she left, my mother and I talked about it and my mother said that she thinks my grandmother is being abused in that hospital, and then she started to cry. I didn't know what to say or do. I just hoped my grandmother wouldn't come again if it was going to make my mother so sad. It hurts me in the pit of my stomach when she's like this because I feel so helpless. Then I felt guilty about feeling that because I couldn't get my grandmother's face out of my mind. I don't think I ever will because it was my mother's face, but sadder, so much sadder.

I went to church the next day and I prayed as hard as I have ever prayed that my mother wouldn't go out of her mind like my grandmother, and I prayed that no one would ever abuse my grandmother again. And then I cried because life was so hard and there was nothing I could do about it.

May 1st, 1959

I was accepted into Camden Catholic High School, so was Mary Lou. Carla is going to St. Joe's. Some of my friends were accepted, and others weren't, so I felt happy and sad both at the same time. Now that I've been accepted, I still have a chance at the scholarship. That's a relief.

June 14th, 1959

We are graduating today and graduation ceremonies are being held in the church. We rented white caps and gowns. My parents are coming and my grandmother. My grandmother is all dressed up. She's even wearing a hat.

I'm very nervous because my father just bought a new toy for himself, an eight millimeter movie camera, and he has decided to film our graduation from the choir loft. This makes me think he is sure I'm going to win the scholarship. I'm not so sure though, and I'm not just saying that to be modest.

Monsignor Michael hands out all the diplomas, then he announces that the four year scholarships to Camden Catholic High School were being awarded to five students for academic excellence, and my name is called first. The church had been real quiet so all I heard was my grandmother gasp in surprise. This made me feel both bad and good at the same time. I have to go up to the altar but I don't cry. I'm happy and relieved. After all the prizes are handed out, the two eighth grade classes, consisting of 70 students, march out of church.

For the first time in my life, my father kissed me on the lips. I know because his mustache tickled and I always wondered if it would. His eyes were so proud and shining and he was so happy that it made me happy. My mother's and grandmother's eyes were filled up with tears, and all my friends congratulated me and I felt on top of the world. I don't think I had ever been so happy in my life. I doubt I'll ever be that happy again.

When we got home, all the family was there and they had a cake, and everybody was hugging me. My cousin was proud too, I could tell, even though she didn't hug me. I wish I could win things every day. I wish everyone would be proud of me like this all the time. I think for a brief moment, they have forgotten I am a skinny *stewnod* in the awkward stage. And it's nice.

June 30th, 1959

Although my cousin says I have no common sense and for the most part she is right, I do know that I will not be able to win prizes all the time. Sometimes I'm going to lose and sometimes I'll just be ordinary. I wish my parents were proud of me just for who I am and not for what I do, then life would be so much easier. My friends' parents don't seem to mind that they don't win scholarships, and seem to be proud of them and love them anyway. I wish sometimes I knew the secret my parents know about me that no one else seems to know. If I knew why they can't love me unless I do something spectacular, I might be able to change what's wrong with me.

I was looking through some of the poems I've written and ran across this one:

> I wish I could be nicer,
> And perfect in every way.
> I wish I made fewer faces,
> And listened to what my parents say.
>
> I wish I could read every
> Book anyone would write.
> I wish I danced every dance,
> And even learned to fight.
>
> But no one can be perfect,
> Not in each and every way.
> Not even for an hour,
> Let alone an entire day.

Although I was 10 when I wrote this poem, I still feel the same way now that I'm 13. Sister says only God is perfect. I wish she would tell my parents.

My father seems to be concerned about my shining at everything. I have to be the smartest and never make a mistake. My mother seems to be concerned that I'm never selfish. It is really important to her that I think about other people first. She doesn't think I should be concerned about my feelings at all. She always says my problem is I've had it too easy and that I don't have any problems. But it's so hard to think about everybody else all the time because sometimes what hurts one person is the best thing for another, and it can get really confusing. I can't make her understand that I do care for other people. I'm really sorry that Vince is retarded and that my sister has a harder time in school. I feel badly when my friends don't have any money to go to the movies or can't learn to dance. I really don't always think about myself, but the way she tells it, I'm never supposed to think about myself at all, and I feel bad that sometimes I do. My mother says that if the family is having troubles, I shouldn't be happy. But that would mean I could never be happy because one of them always has a problem. If my sister gets an A in school, my little brother falls. If my little brother doesn't get hurt, Vince is sick. It never seems to end. That's why I think I always wanted to be an only child. That way I could feel happy, without feeling guilty, whenever I wanted. Basically I'm a happy person. I like to laugh and when I laugh, I laugh so hard that tears run down my face and my whole body shakes. My cousin always says I get on her nerves because I laugh so much, but it feels really good to do that. It beats crying. Now before I can feel happy, I have to make certain my mother is not depressed, my father is not angry, my brother, Vince, is not sick, my sister is happy and my baby brother is safe. By the time I think about all that, I forget what it was I was happy about in the first place.

Most of the people in this family seem a little miserable to me. My Uncle Joe is always mad at somebody. My mother says he left home when he was 13 and lived in New York all by himself and that's why he's so miserable. My Uncle Jack smiles a lot, but he can't sit still for one minute. He always seems to be running around going nowhere. My Aunt Lissa sleeps all the time and is only happy when she's drinking. My father is always in a bad mood. My mother says it's because he doesn't want any responsibility and doesn't like to work. My mother is sad most of the time because of the hard life she had. And my Aunt Bootie seems to be the unhappiest of all. She's always telling my grandmother that because of her, she doesn't have a life. I don't like when she says this to my grandmother, but my grandmother can pick up for herself and does. My brother, Vince, never looks like he's happy although my mother always tells me he is happy in his own little world. My sister's real quiet, so I can't tell. And my baby brother, who's 4, is just plain goofy.

The only ones who seem happy to me are my Aunt Stell and my cousin Rosalie. When I'm at their house, we laugh all the time. It's mostly about me, but I don't care. And my grandmother always seems happy. I start out being happy every day and am happy in school and when I'm with my friends. But my happiness often leaves when I come home, and even on those days I'm still happy when I'm home for a while, something is usually wrong with somebody and I have to pretend I'm not.

But when they're all in a good mood at the same time, we have the most fun. Everybody laughs, sings and dances. They're really funny—fun people when they want to be.

July 1st, 1959

My grandmother is going down the shore soon. Since I'm a star at the moment, I ask my parents if I can stay with her for a few days, and they say it's okay. I'm going down the last week of August and I'm going to have my own room. I think this is the best. I'm also going down with Mary Lou and her parents for a week in July, and my parents are allowing me to have a graduation party in the new building in September because it's empty and we'll be able to dance. It's really big and the floor is linoleum. I can't wait. I wonder if I would have been allowed to have a party if I hadn't won the scholarship and decide not to think about it because I don't want to ruin how happy I am.

July 6th, 1959

I'm going down the shore with Mary Lou and her family, and my mother says she and my father are going to come down on Sunday to visit. My parents really like Mary Lou's family. That makes it nice, because if they didn't, I wouldn't be allowed to go. I've only stayed at the shore overnight with my aunt and uncle when I was younger, and I'm really excited. They show the new movies down there much sooner than at the Savar or Stanley. I think we're going to see *The Nun's Story* and *The Diary of Anne Frank*. I like Audrey Hepburn. Mary Lou's mother says I look like her. I'm not sure if I really do or she says that because we're both skinny. We'll get to go to the beach every day if it doesn't rain, and if it does, we can go the penny arcade. There is absolutely nothing I dislike about the shore. Mary Lou's mother is very nice to me, and her mother and father never yell at each other and are not moody like my family. My Aunt Bootie starts making fun of me and tells me to be sure I don't stay out in the water too long and turn blue. She always says that when I was little, I never knew when to come out of the water and when they finally made me, I was wrinkled like a prune, shivering and blue. She thinks this is really funny. I remember those days too. What I liked about them was that when I was shivering and blue, they would wrap me in a towel and hug me until I was warm. My Aunt Bootie used to make veal cutlet sandwiches and had a big thermos filled with soda, and we'd buy ice cream from the man on the beach. We went to Margate then and she'd always rent a raft and after the beach, we'd go into Lucy, which is a big elephant with steps and rooms. We used to have such a good time, my cousin, Rosalie, my brother and me. I had forgotten about turning blue and shivering because my memories were only of that blanket, veal cutlet, the raft, and Lucy. I think it's nice that you can choose those things you want to remember and forget the other stuff.

July 8th, 1959

Mary Lou and I are down in Atlantic City and having the best time. We went to this teenage dance and two boys came up to us and told us they were French and said, "Parlez vous Francais?" We figured out that they were asking us if we spoke French. We wanted to say yes because they were really cute, but there are certain things you cannot lie about, even if you are willing to commit the sin, and one of them is whether or not you speak a certain language. We're really flying high though because those boys spoke to us. I'm flying even higher than her because I don't have any breasts yet, although my mother did break down and buy me a training bra. Winning that scholarship is bringing benefits that never stop.

July 10th, 1959

My mother and father came down with friends of theirs and stopped in to see us. Since I became a teenager, my father has set down certain rules of behavior. No tight pants, no tight sweaters (like I would wear them anyway), no talking to boys, and *no* lipstick until I'm 16, which is more than two years away.

All my friends are allowed to wear light lipstick but me. But I do it anyway and then I rub it off my lips before I go home.

When my mother and father left, Mary Lou and I were going to the boardwalk so I put on some lipstick and felt very grown up. We were walking up the boards leading to the boardwalk and my parents were walking down at the same time, so there was no way I could get rid of that lipstick. My father looked at me like he was really mad and said, "Get yourself to the nearest water fountain and stick your head in." Then he just walked away.

I called my mother before I went home because I was afraid, and she said that she had to hear him all the way home but she calmed him down. I was so relieved and I knew I could never love my mother more than I did at that moment. I felt sorry that she had to hear it all the way home for, after all, it wasn't her fault. But she sounded fine so I didn't think he was too mad.

I know that I'm going to have to be more careful about disobeying him. But I have to wear lipstick sometimes because everybody else does and I don't want to look like a baby.

July 14th, 1959

In September I'll have to work in the store every day after school and on Saturdays and Sundays. I'm not too happy about this but my father says, "No work—no eat." I really don't have a choice, but I'm not going to let that ruin my summer. Mary Lou and I are going to get to go to *Bandstand* as soon as we're 14. This has been the best part of my life. My family is still thrilled that I won that scholarship and whenever they introduce me now to anyone, they say, "This is Milissa, she just won a four year scholarship to Camden Catholic." They say it so fast like it's part of my name.

We just ordered our new uniforms for Camden Catholic and they are green jumpers with white blouses. I had a choice of cotton or nylon blouses, but my mother insisted on cotton so she can starch them. I'd rather have the nylon ones because she has a tendency to go crazy with that starch, but she's paying for them so I have no say.

<u>*August 14th, 1959*</u>

I'm down at the shore with my grandmother and I never knew she could be so strict. I'm not allowed to go anywhere by myself. Today this really old man, who's staying at the hotel, is being really nice to me and, of course, I'm being nice back. When we're at dinner my grandmother wants to know what he said so I tell her he asked me if I wanted to see his room. She told me I shouldn't go into anyone's room like I was 8 years old. I thought it was stupid anyway because all the rooms are the same and I had no reason to see his. Later we were sitting on the porch and my grandmother started talking really loud to that old man. She asked him in broken English whether he wanted to show *her* his room. I felt sorry for that old man because his face got all red and I felt like a big rat. He didn't do anything wrong. I couldn't understand why she was so mad. She seemed mad at me too because that night she locked me in my room from the outside, and she told me not to talk to anyone unless she was there. I'll probably never understand adults. The poor man just wanted to show me his room. The way my grandmother was acting, you would think he wanted to kill me. So now I'm locked in my room every night until she opens the door in the morning. I'm sure glad she gets up early because the bathroom is down the hall and last night I almost peed my pants.

<u>*August 31st, 1959*</u>

We're going to the shore to pick up my grandmother. My Aunt Boot says I can go because I think she wants my help in lugging all my grandmother's clothes because her husband, my Uncle Tony, has a bad heart and he does nothing at all. He doesn't even work.

When we get there, my grandmother is really happy to see us. I'm glad that old man isn't around because I still feel bad that I got him in trouble. I don't even know why, but what I do know is that he'll never ask anybody up to see his room again while my grandmother is around.

While my grandmother and aunt are paying the bill and saying their goodbyes, I take a walk to the boardwalk to see the ocean. As I sit on the bench, I could almost feel and taste the sand as I had for so many years. There's a certain scent of salt air and there's always a breeze. Now that I'm older, I hate what the salt air does to my hair, but I didn't care back then. When my aunt would tell us we were going to the shore, I was so happy I'd laugh and jump up right in the air.

In September I'll be starting high school and I'm both happy and sad about that. I'm also nervous about it. Not all my friends will be going to Camden Catholic, and I'll miss them. And the classes are going to be much bigger than grammar school. I won't know too many people at first, and people don't believe it but I'm shy. I'm not shy with people I know, but I'm not able to just walk up to somebody and feel comfortable right off. It takes me time. Sometimes during this past summer, I'd start worrying that maybe no one would talk to me or like me, and that maybe none of my friends will be in my classes. Based on the entrance exam we took, I'm in the college preparatory course, and not everyone is in it. And besides, there are several levels. I'm not in the top level. This was a disappointment to me. I'm probably not going to be one of the smartest there. I will have Latin and Algebra, which I've never had. But I don't worry about it too much. I try not to worry too much about the future because as the song goes, "What Will Be, Will Be." I don't seem ever to hold any thoughts for too long. I don't exactly know why, but I don't. My mind is always jumping around. One of my friends from grammar school, Sonia, who is not going to Camden Catholic, is a child of divorce. That is what she calls herself. And although I like her a lot, she is always talking about it. I figure if you talk about something, you must be thinking about it. Well, anyway, she talks about it all the time. We all felt bad for her because her father would have to come around school to see her. No one I know is divorced, so it must be a big deal. Sonia says her sister hates her father, but she doesn't. He buys her all kinds of things and seems like a very nice man. Her mother is nice too. But even if my parents were to get divorced, I don't think I'm capable of thinking about it too long. That's just the way I am.

Even though Sister Regis told my mother I'm exceptionally focused, I can only focus on anything for a little while and then I need to focus on something else. My mother says that's because I get bored too easily, and she says that she doesn't envy me because I'm going to have to spend my whole life entertaining myself. But I do focus long enough and I think that's the most important thing.

Sometimes when I'm taking a test, I am totally unaware that anyone else is in the room, even myself. All that exists is that test. Maybe I tire myself out because I go too deeply when I am thinking about something.

I don't know what I want to be when I grow up. Part of me would still like to be an actress and get to express things I can't in real life, but my mother says this is probably just a pipe dream. But I do know this, I will always love to read. I liked it from the first. When I was 7 and found out what a library was and where it was, I went, by myself, and got a card and took it home for my mother to sign. That opened up different worlds to me. Some people think reading is stupid and that it's better to be doing things. But the way I see it we all get just one life. We can only do certain things in that life, but reading allows me to know what it feels like to do lots of other things.

I also know that I'll always love music and I'll always dance, always. Of that I have no doubt. And the only other thing I'm completely sure of is that I will always love the ocean. When I look at it, it makes me calm. There would be many days when I would lie on the beach and look up at the sky wondering if heaven was right behind the clouds and what it looked like, and then my eyes would look at the ocean and I knew that there was no way heaven could be more beautiful. I loved the seagulls and the salt air and the change the ocean undergoes. One minute it's calm, and the next, ferocious waves pound as if the ocean were mad. No matter how long you look at a mountain, that mountain doesn't change, but the ocean always changes, even when it's calm. Sometimes it looks gray and sometimes it's a shiny blue. I think I'm like the ocean, always changing colors and moods. I think people look at the ocean on a calm, beautiful summer day and think, "Isn't that water calm?" Isn't that ocean nice?" But they don't understand the ocean because they don't seem to know that it is something very different underneath. I'm just like that and whenever I come and sit before it, as I am doing now, I will feel like I'm home, just as I'm feeling now.

And although I know that nobody owns the ocean, I always think it's mine, just like I think what's inside of me is mine because I'm the only one who really understands. I don't think you know something by just looking at it; and although my father may think he owns me, he'll never own me because he doesn't understand what's inside, and my mother doesn't either. Although I try to be obedient and agreeable, no one can really know or understand what I think or feel because these things are mine alone, just like the ocean.

September 5th, 1959

We had my graduation party and I was allowed to invite boys. We danced and it was really great. I think when you're happy it's easier to be nice, because I even invited Mikey and Goody-Two-Shoes and was happy to see them when they came. And that is something. A good time was had by all. Isn't that a neat phrase? I read it in a book. We had lots of food to eat and played the newest records. Everybody was laughing and having a good time, even my father. I even saw my Aunt Boot smile once or twice. I never realized what a beautiful smile she has, dimples and all, because she doesn't smile much, if ever.

My friends all called me the next day saying they had such a good time. Carla said it was the best party she ever went to. I felt really special at my party, and I think it's nice to feel special. I'd like always to feel special, but realistically, how many scholarships can you win?

September 8th, 1959

Today is the first day of high school. Camden Catholic is located about a mile from my home. We can either take the bus or walk, depending upon the time and weather. I live the closest so everybody comes to my house. Mary Lou and I have only a few classes together though. The school is so large and there are hundreds of students entering as freshmen. I find it extremely intimidating, but it's exciting too. I miss grammar school where I was friendly with everyone, but as I am maturing, I understand what my cousin meant about things not always being black and white. It seems I often hold two different feelings about things and people at the same time, like school is intimidating and exciting, my classes in Latin and Algebra are interesting and hard, the kids are friendly and distant. I remember that whenever I read books when I was younger, I used to wonder if people really had names like Ellen and Scott. Our Lady of Mount Carmel school was predominantly Italian and most of the kids had Italian-sounding names. Camden Catholic is Irish and so I've met an Ellen, a Geraldine, a Sean, and a Maureen. I get a little uncomfortable because when I used to talk to my old friends, we enjoyed the shorthand of familiar homes and customs. Now if I tell Ellen we had gravy on Sunday, she doesn't know that I mean tomato sauce. Culturally, it is quite a shock. I think when you are surrounded by the same ethnic group, you tend to think that everybody in the world is just like your family. Well, at least they're all Catholic.

Since I'm shy, I figure I better smile a lot. This way, even if I can't be totally comfortable with everybody at first, at least they'll know I'm not being unfriendly. It's easy to make friends though, because you have the teachers, classes, and homework in common. And though at first I felt like an alien, being with the same kids all day, every day, I'm starting to feel I'm becoming a part of it. We have our own lockers and a cafeteria where they sell food. We even have a gym and an auditorium. When I was in grammar school, everything was held in church because we didn't have a gym or auditorium. We did have a cafeteria, but it didn't sell food. Most of the kids in my classes are very smart so it's hard for me to speak up in class because I don't want all these strange faces looking at me and thinking I'm stupid. Here being dark is different because many of the kids have blonde hair and blue eyes. Some even have red hair and green eyes. I think we may look exotic to each other. Everybody seems to know about South Camden. I'm not quite sure why, but think maybe because it has movies, good shops and restaurants; and they, for the most part, live in small towns like Collingswood and Audubon. I've never been to either of those places. It seems, though, I have the same conversation every day and it goes like this:

Where do you live? What grammar school did you go to? Do you like Sister Jose? Are you going to the dance Friday? Do you come to school by bus? Do you know...?

Half the time I don't even remember the answers. I'm not too good at small talk because it doesn't interest me much.

October 12th, 1959

Mary Lou and I are going to *Bandstand* today. This is such an unexpected surprise because my father is becoming very strict, but the benefits of that scholarship continue. I know what they say about Italian fathers, but none of my friends' fathers are like mine. It is as if his only priority is making certain I remain a "good girl." I haven't done anything which would make him distrust me, but he acts as if I did. I don't think Mary Lou is aware of what a big thing this is. I know that my mother and her mother had to work on him for weeks. I heard my mother say, "What kind of trouble can she possibly get into? You know what time she's leaving, you'll see her there on TV, and you know how long it will take her to get home. God, she's only 14. She isn't even fully developed yet." I could have lived without that last part, but it was a small price to pay for being allowed to go.

Bandstand is a very popular show. People all over the United States watch it, but I don't think it has any bigger fans than Mary Lou and me. We live it and we breathe it. We've been let out at school at lunch because of the teachers' conference, and when we get there, the line is a little long, but I think we have arrived early enough to get in. We don't talk to each other because we're too busy looking for the regulars, Justine, Bob, Arlene, and

Kenny. I'm a little surprised about how much makeup everyone has on. I don't have any on. Mary Lou has a little lipstick, but I don't dare put any on today because the Gestapo (my mother's name for my father) will be watching and I'm not sure whether it will show up on TV. I'm probably going to look like a drowned out rat, but I don't care. I'm just glad I'm here.

We get in and it's much smaller than it looks on TV. It has a tier of wooden benches and we just stand there looking around. I feel like a farmer must feel when he goes to the big city for the first time because we're younger than most of the kids, have little, or in my case, no makeup on, and I have fried eggs for breasts. They're starting the show and here we sit and no one asks us to dance, so we decide to do the Calypso together and try to maneuver ourselves in front of the camera so our families and friends will know we got in. Before we know it, it's over. Dick Clark looks the same as he does on TV except he has makeup on too. Sometimes I have looked forward to something so much that when it actually occurred, it was disappointing. *Bandstand* was exactly how I thought it would be, even better. Milissa Elisa Maroni has been to *Bandstand* and in my world, that's really something.

November 6th, 1959

I've made many new friends in school. School is kind of fun. Every Friday night, there's a dance in the gym. Camden Catholic is known for its dances. Boys ask girls to dance and all. At every dance, they have a ladies' choice, but unless I'm standing next to somebody who I just danced with, I won't ask anybody because I'm afraid he'll say no.

I started to work in the store now when I get home from school until it closes at 7 p.m., and on Saturdays and Sundays. My father never allows me to go to any football games and I feel left out of things, but sometimes my mother works on him and I'll be able to go, but usually only if it's a Sunday home game. He really wants me in that store because if my mother has to run the register, she can't cut the meat and he has to do it. For the same reason, I can't join any clubs either because they meet after school hours.

It seems the kids are forming cliques and I don't fit in anywhere. Everybody's friendly and all, but I don't feel a part of anything or attached to any particular group. I do go to the dances though, and love them. A girl from the neighborhood, Bern, and I have become friendlier this year. We were always in the same grade in grammar school, but she was always in the other class so we really never hung out together. But we really get along well and she comes to the dances every week with me. She's blonde and popular. She doesn't go to Camden Catholic, she goes to Our Lady of Mount Carmel, which has a two year business school course for girls only. My cousin goes there too. In two years, they'll be able to go to work in an office which is a big deal around my neighborhood. People always say with admiration, "She works in City Hall," or, "She works for lawyers." Like it's equivalent to winning the Nobel Prize. That's because most of the people who are my parents' age didn't even finish grammar school and work in factories. I think when you are hired to work in an office, you can wear really nice clothes and people know that you're smart. My mother says she can't understand why I'm not really interested, like most girls my age, in clothes, shoes, and jewelry. For some reason those things don't interest me. I mean I do need and like nice clothes for the dances and all, but they are not that important for the most part. I don't know why, they're just not.

We're going to have a Freshman Frolic at the end of the year and we're allowed to have dates. I hope I'll be asked and allowed to go. With my father, I never know. Also, Camden Catholic is known for their senior plays. This year it's going to be *Bells Are Ringing*. I can't wait to go, I've never been to a live play before except those old Christmas pageants every year in grammar school, most of which I was in, usually playing a shepherd or one of the Wise Men. I don't know why I was never chosen for the Blessed Mother, but it never happened. But this play is going to be just like the ones on Broadway, with rehearsals, dancers, singers, and even a live orchestra. And you are not assigned parts, you have to try out, just like you do for the real plays. Everybody is allowed to try out, but the seniors usually get the good parts.

I did join the Glee Club. Sister Maria determined I'm an alto, but I think it's too low for me and I don't really like it because I never get to sing the melody, just the harmony. When we sing all together, we do sound great. As in most things these days, there is good and bad. The good part is that I am doing something, belonging somewhere; but the bad part is that there are about 60 of us and there is no socializing because whenever we're together, it's for a rehearsal. The other clubs have more socializing and even take field trips. So I am a part of things, and yet I'm not.

I wonder if life is always going to be like this, black and white at the same time. I don't care if everything has two colors as long as those colors aren't gray and beige, which to me are dull and duller.

December 3rd, 1959

I made a couple of new friends and we have lunch together every day, and I'm starting to feel about them like I did about my old friends. I hate gym though. I hate everything about it. I hate having to shower in front of everybody and being expected to perform impossible tasks. I found out that you could use your period as an excuse every once in a while. The other day in gym, we had this pommel horse that we had to swing over and then saddle. Well, I had gum in my mouth and I was so excited trying to perform that feat that the gum popped right out. Chewing in school is a no-no, chewing in gym is a detention. Our gym teacher is not a nun. She's tall and skinny and acts like a boy. Every time I can't do something, she embarrasses me and says, "Any boob can do it." I want to say, "Not this boob," but don't because she's very free with those detention slips.

I just try everything I know to get out of it. One time we were playing volley ball and someone's fingernail went into my wrist. It barely bled and it didn't even hurt, but I asked to be sent to the nurse and our gym teacher couldn't say no. Now, she wants us to shimmy up a rope extending from the ceiling. I figure she's going out of her mind, but there go the Ellens and Maureens doing it. Well, I'll tell you, there is no way I can do that. Luckily the bell rings before I have to humiliate myself. For the first time, I recognize that I possess psychic powers because I know I'm going to have cramps, a cold, or a pulled muscle right before the next class. You have to pass gym though. For the first time in my life, I wish I had a heart murmur, like my sister, because then I wouldn't have to take it at all.

Some of it is fun. I love volley ball unless I'm being mutilated, and there are certain calisthenics I can do that I enjoy. But most of the things are humanly impossible or shall I say, impossible for this human.

It seems the Ellens and Maureens of the school are more athletic than the Milissas and Angelas. I think it's because, having been brought up in the city, other than playing baseball once a year, or jump rope, we never engaged in sports. I think the suburbanites have. My friend Angela from the neighborhood is worse than me though. Every time she goes to do something, she falls. She's always falling down the steps too. Everybody laughs, but not at her, if you know what I mean.

A good day to be sick is definitely gym day. What I do is attend gym a few weeks in a row and then devise a plan to get out of the next one. While I'm figuring that out, I'm really happy.

We also have to attend Mass right before lunch in the auditorium. For some reason, my class always has to sit up front, and by the time we get to the cafeteria, the line is unbelievably long. Lunch is the shortest hour of the day without having to spend half of it in line.

January 1960

I've started to work on my mother to see if my father will allow me to go to the Freshman Frolic if I'm asked. Some kids are going as a group, but I'd rather have a date. But the problem is I'm not allowed to date. This has not been an issue before, but the Frolic is in May and I don't want someone asking me and my having to say, "I have to ask my father." Then I'll get a reputation for being a baby. I think you can get reputations easily in high school, and I think once you get them, they're hard to change. My mother's been a big help in these things because I think that, even though she never went to high school, she knows you can't be left out of things, although she still says, "If your friends were all jumping off the bridge, would you?" I hate when she says this, but I can't say anything because I need an ally in the war I'm having with my father. I want to grow up and he wants me to remain a child, but only in fun things. He'd like me to work as if I were an adult.

April 3rd, 1960

The Gestapo said I can go to the Freshman Frolic with a date. Now all I need is the date. Some of the kids in my class are already going steady. I think I'd like to go steady because then you don't have to worry about dates or being cool or people liking you. I think when a guy likes or loves you enough to want to go steady with you, that gives you a certain allure. There are lots of cute boys in my class that I'm attracted to. It's funny though, when I see any male classmates from grammar school, I can't think of them romantically. They will probably always be silly, stupid little boys to me. Not that they would want it any different, I'm just saying that's how I feel, that's all.

It's fun being an adult. Everyone talks about dates and boys and makeup. I don't know much about any of those things, but it's fun to hear other people my age talking about them. At this week's Friday night dance, this boy Ritchie asked me to dance. He's really cute and has lots of freckles and black hair. I never knew anybody who had freckles, so it's interesting to me. Lots of kids in this school have freckles and they hate it, but I kind of like it because it's different. Anyway, Ritchie asked me to the Freshman Frolic and I accepted. Ritchie is only about two inches taller than me and I'm only 5'3", so I think one of the reasons he asked me is because I'm short and many of the girls tower over him. But that's okay with me. After all, there are many girls shorter than me or just as tall as me too, so it's not insulting or anything.

Now I can get a dress. I can only wear a one inch heel though because I don't want to be taller than Ritchie. This is a date and not a date. It's hard to explain, so why try?

April 4th, 1960

My mother and I went shopping for a dress for the Freshman Frolic and I bought a pretty pink flowing dressy dress. I also bought a crinoline slip and a padded bra. My mother says I'm too young to wear padded bras, and she always says small breasts are beautiful, yet her bras are padded to cantaloupe size while her breasts are the size of small oranges or large tangerines.

I don't ever want to be one of those people who delude themselves and don't see the truth about themselves because they get on my nerves big time. Another thing that gets on my nerves is a phony. I just finished reading *Catcher in the Rye*, and I agree with everything Holden Caulfield says, but especially when he criticizes all the phonies. The way I figure it, if you are pretending to be someone else to make someone like you, it isn't *you* they really like, so why bother? I liked Holden Caulfield very much. I think he had a good heart and he was just so broken up over the death of his brother, that he lost his way. Puberty is really hard, and I think that might have been part of his problem because he was still a virgin and all. I did think he was extremely immature for 16 though, but I think it takes boys longer to mature than girls. My mother says she's still waiting for my father to mature and he was just 40. My father was born on April Fool's Day and my mother was born on Valentine's Day, and I wonder if that will make me a fool for love. Getting back to *Catcher in the Rye*, Holden looks cynically at things like I do, but the way he expresses himself is really funny.

I have this voice in my head that says these cynical things and I can't help it. When I was in the seventh grade and had Sister John Boniface for a teacher, whenever she got on my nerves, in my head I'd call her Bony Face, things like that.

I don't even know how to confess it either. I've thought of saying that I have a sinful sense of humor, but the priest would probably think I told dirty jokes. Then I thought maybe I was being judgmental, but I'm not really. I think I just look sideways at things. Sometimes I even make myself laugh.

I finally figured out what impure thoughts actually are, and realized that I confessed to thousands of sins I never committed.

Easter Sunday, 1960

My school burned down and it's a catastrophe. Now we're going to have split sessions until they rebuild. We'll finish out our freshman and sophomore years going from 12:30 to 5 p.m., which cuts down on my hours of work. But in junior year, my classes will begin at 7:30 a.m. and finish at 12:30 p.m. This is a double whammy because I'll have to get up really early and work all afternoon. I already hate junior year, but I'll be like Scarlett O'Hara and think about that tomorrow. *Gone With the Wind* will always and forever be my favorite book.

May 16th, 1960

The Freshman Frolic was fun. I don't have much else to say about it. It was more than I expected, but also less.

May 22nd, 1960

Mary Lou and I went to see *Bells Are Ringing*. I don't think either of us had any idea how much we would love live theater, but we did. That's all we talk about now. Every time we see the stars of the show in the halls, we gawk at them and then tell each other what they were doing and who they were with. My cousin thinks I'm extremely weird so I tell her that I can't help that I have fallen in love with the *theater*, which I pronounce like a British actor. She hates it when I act like this, that's why I do it. I try to talk her into going to see it with me, but she doesn't want to watch a bunch of children act, she says. She can pull it off too. She's only 15-1/2, but she looks like she's 18. She wears her hair in an upsweep, which is quite sophisticated, and she has large breasts. Mine have grown too, but not much. My mother has determined I'll be small like her. She says when I'm older I'll be happy about that. I hate to insult my mother, but somehow I don't see that ever happening.

What really amazes me about adults is how they can lie to themselves to make themselves feel better and really believe it. There's this lady around the neighborhood who weighs about 180 pounds and is about 5 feet tall. The other day she told me that when you get to be 30 years old, you have to eat less to maintain your figure, that your metabolism slows down. I think her metabolism must have died and forgot to tell her. Also, women always tell you that they had a beautiful figure when they were younger before they had kids. I remember them when they were younger and they look just the same to me. Then there's this woman who's about 40, and she told me that when she was my age she was considered a real beauty. Although I didn't know her then, it's really hard to believe she was ever beautiful because she has one of those big Italian beaks and her eyes can look at each other. I don't judge people by how they look, really I don't. But I can't stand it when people lie to themselves and if they do lie to themselves, I think they should do it quietly because, quite frankly, I feel their lies are insulting to my intelligence.

Me, I have small breasts. I'm slender (not skinny). I have nice skin and big brown eyes. But I hate my nose. It's not big, it's just shaped oddly. Everyone says it goes with my face, and they say geniuses are hard to find. I have nice lips and a forehead that goes on for about two days. What I hate is that my face is thin. Everybody in my family has these nice round, full faces, but me. When I'm sick and pale, my eyes look twice their size and I look like I should be posing for a poster that says, "Feed the children."

I'm very young looking, not womanly at all. I think if I'm ever allowed to wear makeup, I may be pretty. But proably by the time that happens, any beauty I may possess will have faded. All in all, though, I'm not too bad looking.

June 30th, 1960

School is out. I did get on the honor roll. I love Latin because you can see where so many of our words began. I like high school, but I don't love it. And I wanted to love it, I really did.

July 8th, 1960

My grandmother is going down the shore again and my cousin and I are going down for four nights. I told my cousin that my grandmother locked me in my room the year before, and she said that was not going to happen. I don't think so either because, after all, I'll be 15 and she'll be 16 this year.

My cousin and I always have a good time together. We have the same sense of humor, like to laugh, and can be quite silly at times. We were walking down the street the other night and I was doing my imitation of Charlie Chaplin's walk and we were both laughing hysterically when a policeman stopped us because he thought we were drunk. We weren't though, just silly.

We're down the shore and we don't sit with my grandmother on the beach because we're not children any longer. So here I am lying on the blanket, all calm and happy in my own little world my family calls "Missyland" when this really cute guy asks me my name. And I can't remember it. It wasn't even that I was nervous. I was just somewhere else, a place where my real life doesn't exist, a place I visit often. This guy thought I was being snobby. I wasn't, I just really couldn't remember my name for a few minutes. He probably didn't get a good look at my breasts or he would have known I have nothing to be snobby about. I don't like snobs. My mother calls them "people who think who they are." We're taught in school we should use as few words as necessary to communicate, but I'm not allowed to correct my parents. Even if I were allowed, I wouldn't because people who do that are really snobs and

I don't like them. My father says "irregardless" all the time. I'm not going to tell him it isn't a word. I never correct anybody. The way I look at it, I have my own problems, having no breasts being merely one of them. Another is that I drastically need lipstick and need to wait another year to wear it. Everybody is already wearing eye liner, rouge, mascara, and powder. While they look glamorous, I look like Casper the Friendly Ghost going to grammar school. One good thing is that no one is allowed to wear makeup in school so, there, I don't stand out like a *white* flag. I have learned to pinch my cheeks real hard to get some color and it makes me look healthier. I also bite my lips, but I have to be careful doing this because one time when this really cute guy, Mike, was approaching, I bit my lips so hard that I made them bleed. I'm sure I looked real glamorous with blood running down my chin.

August 15th, 1960

I had to work in the store all summer. My job description is cashier, but I also have to cut lunch meat, grate cheese, pack the shelves, and help people carry their groceries home. Too bad I'm not in a union. There must be child labor laws that apply since I'm working about 50 hours a week. I don't work every minute though, so when I'm between customers I get to read all these wonderful books. At the beginning of the summer I read some classics because I was still in a school mode, and then I read a romance book and biographies. From when I first started reading, biographies have always been my favorites because I feel like I have company when I'm reading them and I try to determine if I'm like the person. Sometimes I am and the author explains what certain traits mean, and I don't feel so different.

August 21st, 1960

My favorite day is Sunday because the store is only open until 12 p.m. and I usually go to Mass so I don't have to work a lot of hours. When I walk in the house, after church, my Aunt Boot is cooking gravy and it is my favorite smell in the world. I know that I'll always remember that smell with pleasure no matter how old I get.

September 3rd, 1960

Mary Lou had to tell me she was planning a surprise 15th birthday party for me at her new house. She moved this summer. It's not that far, but you do have to take a bus, which we do. She had to tell me because it was touch and go whether my father would allow me to even go to a party where boys were invited. I guess he thinks I might get pregnant at Mary Lou's house with her mother and father there. And in front of all the kids. His strictness isolates me and I hate it. About one month before, he finally says yes and it sure was one great party. We danced and snuggled. I even got a real kiss, not just a Post Office one, and I'm glad I didn't know it was coming because I had this fear that my lips would land on a boy's nose. But when Jim kissed me, our lips met and I liked it. I liked it a lot.

September 20th, 1960

I'm a sophomore now and it feels much more comfortable than last year. Carla told me this boy from the neighborhood, Bobby, likes me. Quite frankly, I really didn't believe her but it turned out to be true. He's cute and he's a senior at Camden Catholic this year. There is nothing more impressive than dating an upperclassman. Since I'm not allowed to date though, it's not quite so impressive.

October 4th, 1960

Someone asked me out on my first real date. His name is John and he's in my homeroom. It's going to be a double date and I asked my mother to ask my father because when I ask him anything, he just says no real quick. Since it's a double date, I'm allowed to go. We're going to see the movie *Where the Boys Are* at the Savar and then we're going to Calico Kitchen for a hamburger. John's father is driving us.

John didn't touch me at all. He didn't kiss me or even hold my hand. That he didn't made me feel really good because I knew he didn't ask me out to "see what he could get" like my father says all the time. He was a perfect gentleman. Since his father drove us, I was home by 10:45 p.m. so I didn't get in any trouble. Now I am wondering if I'm allowed to date, but I don't want to push it with the Gestapo. I think small steps need to be taken here. I liked having a date though, and I'll be able to talk about it in school on Monday like all the other girls do.

November 3rd, 1960

I think the most horrible thing in the world is to feel things that are so awful that you can't tell anyone. I'm always being told how lucky I am. School is easy, I'm fairly popular, my parents will buy me anything I want, I can eat anything I want and never gain weight. Sometimes I feel that I am lucky, but sometimes I feel I'm not lucky at all. I often feel that my brother, Vince, is the lucky one, and just feeling that makes me feel ungrateful and like a despicable human being. But I do. I think he's lucky because everyone loves him just for himself. They expect very little from him, while I feel that I'm always being tested and judged, and that I always have to win something to be accepted and loved.

When I was little, I thought my mother had too many kids and that's why she didn't act like other parents. She never worries about me. When I come home from a dance, she's already asleep. I asked her once why she didn't worry and she said because she thought God would never let anything happen to her children. I thought this meant that only God knew how much she loved us and He would never hurt her that way. But she worries about Vince all the time.

I sometimes think if there were a fire, he would be the only one she'd save. I used to think it was because he was always sick and needed her. But shouldn't she know that all of us need her? She has this very special closeness to Vince and it seems that, after that, she doesn't have anything left for anybody else. When I feel like this, I hate myself, but no matter how awful I think my feelings are, they won't stop.

One time when I was about 9, my father drove Vince and me to the doctor because my mother was always worried something was wrong with him. As we were going out the door, she told me to have the doctor look at the rash on my arm. My father waited in the car and I went into the office with my brother. My brother was fine and I had the German measles. My mother was mad that I was sick, like it was an imposition on her, and my fault. Any time I've ever gotten hurt, she smacks me because I'm bothering her. If I ever try to discuss anything with her, like problems I have, or insecurities I feel, she tells me to look at my brother. I stopped discussing anything except unimportant things with her a long time ago, mainly because her attitude to my problems was more painful than the problems themselves.

Whenever my brother cries, she's there. But whenever I cry, I just go to my room alone because I decided that my parents don't make me feel any better. If I have a problem, I deal with it the best I can.

I get tired of always feeling guilty because I'm normal, and I get tired of feeling that my brother is sick because I'm normal, and I'm tired of trying to handle problems alone and always feeling like I can't. And I'm also tired of feeling that I have to constantly be perfect. I'm tired of feeling that I'm invisible if I'm not winning a prize. And I'm tired of feeling so alone, so useless, and so unnecessary.

But what I get tired of most is just feeling these things. I think I'll probably get punished for my feelings and I can't tell anybody about them. I wish Vince would have been normal, for him, but for me too.

December 4th, 1960

My sister is 9 now and she acts like she hates me. I think she thinks I get all the attention, but what she doesn't realize is most of it is negative. For every spelling bee or scholarship I have won, there have been a thousand things I have done wrong. Sometimes I feel like I'm 50 instead of 15.

My little brother is 6 now and he's just plain bad. My father never hit any of us, but he hits him. My mother worries when Larry gets hit and stops my father, and she worries about my sister too sometimes, but she never worries about me because she thinks everything is easy for me. But it's not easy, it's never been easy. I just gave up talking about it.

I love my mother more than anybody in the world. Sometimes I feel like I'm her husband because she discusses all her problems with me instead of my father. It's probably because, for the most part, my father is her problem. It breaks my heart that she has to work so hard and that she never had a mother. I try to do everything I can to help her, to take some of the burdens off her because sometimes I think she will not be able to take any more. When I look in her eyes, I see a sadness that absolutely breaks my heart. She looks like she has had so much pain in her life, and then I feel even more guilty for thinking she should help me with my stupid, teenage problems. But I think it anyway. I feel neglected anyway.

Sometimes I think having a brain is the greatest gift God gave me, but sometimes I think it's a curse. Because I could handle some things alone, my mother thinks I can handle everything alone and I really couldn't. I really can't.

And when I have to, I get really afraid inside and it makes me feel weak because I'm so afraid. I think I'm afraid all the time and not even always sure why. It's like some vague, unidentifiable fear.

I always think the next thing my parents expect of me, or the next problem I have to handle alone, will be my Waterloo. Somehow I manage without falling flat on my face, but instead of giving me confidence, I just become more afraid because I know God is going to punish me for being so selfish and needing so much, and resenting my brother, Vince, and thinking my parents don't love me, and wanting one person to care if I'm happy instead of always having to make sure everybody else is.

December 15th, 1960

I'm going steady, but it has to be a secret because my father hates him. His name is Bobby and he gave me a ring that has two hearts on it. We can't go out on dates because my father won't allow it, so we see each other at the dance or around the neighborhood. The fact that my father doesn't allow it makes it even more exciting to me. We haven't kissed yet, but I can't wait. Because Bobby is a senior, I get to meet all his friends and going out with a senior is a big deal around this school. I think he's going to ask me to his senior prom, which would be the most spectacular thing in the world, if I'm allowed to go. Maybe I will be, my mother says, because it's not a regular date and because Bobby's mother shops in our store. We have our own song and it's "In the Still of the Night," and no matter who we're talking to at the dance, when this song plays, we leave and look for each other and dance. I think I love Bobby, but my mother says I have no idea what love is. During the dance this Friday, he asked me to take a walk around the school yard. We were holding hands and they started to play our song and he stopped and we kissed. It was the most romantic thing that ever happened to me. Bobby is very jealous if I talk to any other guys, and I'm glad because it means he really loves me.

We've been trying to figure out how we can go on a real date. My friend, Bern, has agreed that she and I will tell my father we are going to the movies. We'll leave my house together and walk for a while before we meet Bobby, and then she'll walk ahead of us alone and we'll all go to the movies together, where she'll sit somewhere else to allow us some privacy. I'm not too comfortable with this idea, but my discomfort is surpassed by my excitement, and it's starting to sound like a good plan.

January 4th, 1961

Bobby and I did go out on a date and it was wonderful. First we held hands in the movies and then he put his arm around my shoulders. He is really strong and he makes me feel protected, and I like the idea of belonging to somebody. On the way home he asked me to the prom. I have to let him know if I'll be allowed to go, so I'll start working on my mother as soon as I get in.

We are having a Sophomore Hop, but since I'm going steady I won't be able to go with a date, except for Bobby, and I can't do that. A bunch of kids are going without dates and I'll probably do that too because everyone will know I'm alone only because I'm going steady. There are rules in high school, and one of the rules is that you never want anybody to think you're unpopular. Everybody seems to judge you on who you are dating. Somehow I don't like it, but it is a rule and you must follow the rules if you want to be popular or have the guts not to, and I don't. If you go out with a popular guy, everyone assumes you're cool, even if you're not. Cheerleaders are the most popular girls at school. I didn't even try out for the cheerleading squad because I didn't think I'd make it and I wouldn't be able to attend the games anyway. I somehow think it's better not to try out than to try out and not make it. Because if you don't try out, the kids can think you're not interested, but if you do try out and don't make it, they just will think you're a misfit, a loser. There are many things that everyone does I can't seem to. For example, the fact that I have to work and can't go to the games is enough of an explanation as to why I didn't try out, but I always have to be honest with myself and I know deep inside that I would have loved to be a cheerleader, but I didn't think I'd make it. I notice that people really are capable of telling themselves lies or not facing up to the truth about themselves. I think they're a lot happier doing this and I wish I could. Sometimes I try to make excuses for myself and I'll be successful for about an hour, and then the truth seeps in and no matter how much I want it to leave, it doesn't. The truth about yourself is sometimes hard to take. As far as I can see, it has only one redeeming quality and that is, if it is the truth, it will be the same truth 50 years from now and you never have to try to remember what lie you told yourself at any given time. And the truth about all of this is that I wish I could tell myself lies to make myself feel better because it wouldn't hurt anybody. If I could, I would, but I can't. And that's the truth.

May 7th, 1961

The prom is two weeks away and my father has finally made up his mind that I can go. It's a formal affair and I have to get a long gown, and Bobby's going to buy me a corsage but he can't order it until he knows the color of my gown. He's going to look so handsome in a tux and we're going to double date with his best friend, Frank, and Frank's girlfriend who I met and like very much. It's funny, you would think I would feel out of place with seniors, being two years younger, but I feel quite comfortable. I think it's because I'm mature for my age. I'm very excited. I can hardly wait. I have to be home by 12 midnight, which is really quite early, but it beats not being allowed to go at all. The prom is going to be held at a huge ballroom, and afterwards we're going to see a show in Philadelphia. Getting home by midnight is going to be cutting it close, but the worst my father can do is punish me, and the punishment will be worth it. Bob's friends are going down the shore the next day, but I told him there's no way my father will allow it. He's so understanding about everything because he says he loves me. I think this is actually the first time anyone has ever said those words to me. They don't say things like that in my family. My mother will say all mothers love their children. One time I asked her right out. I think I just wanted to hear the words, and her answer was, "What do you think?" I don't know what makes these particular words so hard to say, but I think everybody should say them to the people they love or maybe they just will never really know.

May 28th, 1961

I never had so much fun in my entire life as I did at Bobby's prom. The ballroom was decorated so beautifully and I wore this gorgeous pink gown. My parents took my picture about 50 times in it. I had my hair in an upsweep and even wore a tiara. For the first time, I looked like a woman and I felt like a woman too. It was so nice to be with Bobby and not have to look over my shoulder for my father. I don't even know why my father dislikes Bobby so much. He's very polite and my father knows his mother. My mother says it's because Bobby's like him. My father says someday I'll appreciate it and understand why he's so strict. I doubt that. It does feel good that he waits up until I get home and seems to worry about me when I'm out. But I think he's more worried that I'm going to disgrace his name. He says that all the time, "If you disgrace my name, I'll disown you." I wish sometimes he'd just worry that I might get hurt. I think I'd understand that because that would mean he loved me and couldn't bear the thought of losing me. But all his strictness proves to me is that he doesn't want anyone to think he was a lousy father and raised a whore.

I got home from the prom about 12:15 a.m. and my father started yelling at us as soon as he opened the door because he said midnight was midnight, and it was 12:15. Those 15 minutes cost me two weeks of dances, but it was worth it.

June 17th, 1961

I liked the split sessions because I didn't have to get up real early and only had to work in the store one hour. But sophomore year will be finished soon. In my junior year, school will start at 7:30 a.m. and I'll be home by 1 p.m. and have to work for five to six hours. Bobby has graduated and I won't see him any more in school. Maybe, though, I'll be able to join a club since they were used to me working only an hour this year. I'm not going to bring it up until the end of summer. I don't want to use up all my favors too soon.

July 7th, 1961

Mary Lou and I are spending a week at my Aunt Lissa's. She has an in-ground pool at her home in Moorestown. I think my aunt is going to let Bobby and Joey, his friend, come over to swim for one day too. She's pretty cool, my aunt. I think she knows how to have a good time and enjoys other people having a good time too. The only problem is that she sleeps all the time; and when she's sleeping, it's like she's in a coma. I remember sometimes my cousin and I would go overnight to the shore with her. In the mornings, we had to sit around the room until she got up, then we had to run and get her juice, and then we had to wait until she got dressed. By that time, it was mid-afternoon and the sun was almost going in. She is fun when she's awake though. Another good thing about her is that she hates to do anything alone so when she needs to go shopping, she'll take me with her and she always buys me something. She has lots of money. Once when we were down the shore having dinner, she asked me what I wanted and I said lobster. She started to laugh and said that I had champagne tastes and beer pockets. She's right about that. But she bought me the lobster anyway and I loved it. She's always saying these neat things like, if she's waking you up she'll say, "Rise and shine," or "Good morning glory." She's not like anybody else I've ever met. My mother says that I could live to be 100 and I'll never meet anyone like her. She's the one who saved my life when I had that convulsion as an infant.

I think she drinks too much though, but no one else seems to notice so I'm probably wrong. When we would leave the beach, my cousin and I would have to wait until she stopped in a bar for a drink before going back to the hotel, and it was still light outside. My cousin and I didn't tell anybody though.

I have to warn Mary Lou about my aunt sleeping a lot and expecting us to get down on our hands and knees to pick up lint. But I won't mention the drinking because that's not nice and besides, Mary Lou probably won't even notice. Besides the pool, which would be enough in itself, my aunt has a recreation room with a stereo and a floor made for dancing. I know because I danced many a dance there. Mary Lou has met my Aunt Lissa and likes her because she really makes us laugh. I just hope she doesn't drink too much in front of her, as it would be highly embarrassing. We're really looking forward to it. Mary Lou knows how to swim because her father taught her. I have to ask her where because there are no places to swim in the city. My mother fears water, and whenever I'm near it and she's around, I have to get out because she says she's afraid I'll drown. I should get mad and all, but I don't, because it feels good that she's worried. Mary Lou says she'll teach me how to swim. I wonder, if she can though, because now I *am* a little afraid.

July 10th, 1961

I just found out about Hidden Lake, where we can take a bus, and all the kids are going on Sunday, even Bobby, though my father doesn't know it. It takes about an hour to get there but it is really going to be fun. I always have fun with my friends. It seems to me adults have forgotten how to play, and they only seem to be happy when they're drinking. I wonder why? A few of us will just go down the street and get a pizza at Pete's Saloon, which also has a restaurant, and we'll laugh and have such a good time. We don't have to drink or even do anything particularly special to have a ball.

The other night I was sitting on my friend, Jen's, steps and a couple of guys came up and began talking to us. We were having such a good time that I didn't see my father in the car driving my mother to Bingo. He stopped the car in the middle of the street, rolled down the window, and yelled for me to get into the house immediately. I was never so embarrassed in my entire life. He usually does his reprimanding, hollering and criticizing in the house, not in front of my friends. I had to listen to him for an hour about how trampy I look sitting on a step talking to boys, and how no daughter of his was going to disgrace him in front of the whole neighborhood. And then he said I couldn't go to the dance on Friday. When I was small, whenever I did something he didn't like, he stopped me from going to my dance class, and now it's the Friday night dance. You'd think he had something against dancing, but he just takes away whatever he knows I like the most. I think that's very smart of him, even though I hate it. I'm glad I'm going to my aunt's soon. At least, my father won't spy on me.

July 17th, 1961

Mary Lou and I came to my Aunt Lissa's yesterday. Bobby and Joe are expected tomorrow and we're very excited. My aunt's been on her best behavior. She makes us laugh all the time. She's a really good cook too, and at night she makes us ice cream sundaes and we play word games. Mary Lou is quite the swimmer. She's trying to teach me. She holds me up in the middle, shows me how to kick my legs and move my arms, and then when she lets go, I deflate in the water. We think it's because I'm afraid. I can swim under water though, but for obvious reasons, not too long. Mary Lou is very patient. I keep telling her to forget it, I'll learn another time.

We've picked up a lot of lint in two days. I can't understand why my aunt just doesn't pass the sweeper. And she's constantly running us up and down the stairs about 20 times a day, but it's a small price to pay because we're having a really good time.

July 18th, 1961

Bobby and Joe arrive late morning, and I have a very romantic time with Bobby. I think Joe has a crush on Mary Lou, but she just likes him as a friend, so she says.

My aunt's in and out with drinks and food; but, other than that, it feels very adult. She won't tell my father either because, like I said before, she's really cool.

I hate to see them go, but they do in the early evening, and Mary Lou and I go downstairs to the recreation room because we're teaching ourselves how to do the waltz. We think we're pretty good too. It was a great day. We're both tanned and healthy looking, and I'm really going to hate having to go home.

August 15th, 1961

Italians are really big on respect. I call a lot of people uncle and aunt who aren't really, just close friends of the family or distant relatives, like a fourth cousin or something. I realize this is just part of the culture. When I was a child, this was often confusing to me, but it isn't any more. It's just one of those things Italians do.

The other night, my father's first cousin died and everyone went to the viewing. For years, I called it an "awake," not a "wake," because that's how my family used to say it. I used to think it was called an awake because the person was not awake. Just one of those things you accept without thought, like passing the sweeper. That's what we call vacuuming, and it does make sense, if you think about it, because you do pass the sweeper over the rug. When I said this to Mary Lou at my Aunt Lissa's, she started to laugh, and I found out that non-Italians say they are going to run the sweeper, not pass it. The same thing with gravy. Non-Italians say tomato sauce. To them, gravy means a brown gravy that you put on roast beef. But when you grow up with a certain name for something, wrong or not, it's hard not to call it that. It's the same with aunts and uncles. Although they're not and you know it, in a way they are. I know that's confusing, but it's just what it is.

Well, anyway, it was decided that I would stay home with the kids because my parents were afraid everyone would know no one was home and rob the store. It was also decided that my Uncle Don, who's a close friend of my father, would stay with us. Since he wasn't a blood uncle, he didn't have to go to the wake like the rest of them. My parents were expected home about 10:30 or 11:00, and the kids usually go to bed by 8, so it seemed like a good deal to me because I'd get to stay up in peace and quiet and watch what I wanted on TV.

I knew my Uncle Don wouldn't act like them because he has always been nice to me. I don't usually think in terms of being someone's favorite, but I don't think there is any doubt in anyone's mind that I am his. He has always been very proud that I do so well at school.

I often wished he was my father because he was always complimenting me and smiling at me. Once, when I was 6, he even bought me a real cowgirl outfit, and, another time, he took my brother, Vince, and me to the 5 and 10 and told us we had five minutes to buy anything we wanted. I never knew I could move that fast, but I could, and I did. Every time I think of that day, I feel again the excitement and the magic of it. My Uncle Don was always interested in what I was learning, who my friends were, and things like that. He acted like a real uncle, even like a father sometimes. My father noticed it too, but he said that Uncle Don could act so nice all the time because he wasn't responsible for my discipline. I guess in a way he was right. My father is right about many things. My quarrel with him has never been that he's wrong in theory, just in practice.

It was about 6:30 at night when everybody left, all of them dressed in black. Sometimes when an Italian woman loses her husband, she wears black the rest of her life. My Aunt Bootie says that this shows respect. Once when I was little, about 6, I was taken to a burial, and the wife tried to jump into the ground. That's something I'll never forget. They stopped her before she did it, but really! Italians are big on funerals and cemeteries. My Aunt Bootie carries on at viewings and burials all the time. She actually screeches and wrings her hands. She's really quite scary. I said to Rosalie once that we could hire her out as a professional mourner.

After they left and the kids went to bed about 8:30, Uncle Don came in as planned. I remember I was watching *Imitation of Life* which had started about 7:30, and was really enjoying it, but I didn't like that black girl trying to pass for white and being ashamed of her mother. Her mother was so good to her. She couldn't help it she was black. Uncle Don was watching it with me and since I had no idea what it was about, I wasn't prepared for the ending when the daughter began screaming and running toward her mother's coffin. Now I've always been able to cry at the drop of a hat, but this was so sad I was close to sobbing, and I was really embarrassed in front of Uncle Don. Whenever I start to cry watching TV with my father, I go upstairs when it's sad, because he always looks at me and laughs when I cry. But I just cried downstairs that night because Uncle Don isn't like my father.

Instead of laughing at me, he sat on the sofa next to me and put his arm around my shoulder. I didn't know what to do because nobody had ever done that before. Crying is a solo act around here. So I just sat there and then he lifted my face to his and kissed me right on the lips. I jumped up so fast and was so scared I knocked my soda all over the rug. I went into the kitchen to get a wet rag and he said that nothing was going to happen, that what he did wasn't wrong because he wasn't blood. He also said that I made him do it because I always said that I wanted to marry a man just like him. I didn't say anything because I was too scared. I thought he might rape me because when he kissed me, I smelled liquor on his breath.

It was about 9:15 and I never wanted to see my parents as much as I did. I was sort of in a trance. Uncle Don tried to make small talk. I may have even answered him, but I don't remember. I just remember looking at the clock on top of the TV and trying to will those hands to move faster. He was right too. I did say I wanted to marry somebody like him, but I didn't mean *him*. I wanted somebody who was nice to me all the time, who admired me, and who didn't yell and make me feel badly. He said I flirted with him. If I did, I didn't know I was doing it. He kept talking about how it wouldn't be good to upset my parents and his wife and kids. And I just sat there, in a daze, full of fear and a deep sadness.

I decided I wouldn't tell anyone because the only thing it would accomplish was to cause trouble. Suppose my father killed him. My father was capable of that. Then I would be responsible for it all, his wife would be a widow and his kids would be left without a father, and he was promising that it would never happen again. And I knew it wouldn't because I would never be alone with him again.

My parents came home and I went up to my room, never so happy to see it and my sister. My mother asked me if anything had happened. She said I looked funny. I just answered, "No, nothing happened." She said if something had happened, she would find out about it. But she never mentioned it again, and I told no one except my cousin, Rosalie, who I swore to secrecy on her mother's life. My cousin is really good with secrets, but I knew I'd be 100% sure she wouldn't tell if her mother's life was involved. She said she thought I was right not telling anyone. "After all," she said, "he didn't rape you."

For weeks I was in a funk, trying to figure out why that happened, trying to think back to see if I had flirted with him. The saddest part of it all was that I felt so betrayed because he had been so special to me, and now he was just going to become a bad memory. I vowed to be very careful in the future with boys, and I promised myself I wouldn't flirt and say things I shouldn't, and I also decided to break up with Bobby. Not because of what happened with my uncle, but because it just was too painful having to hear my father go on and on about how much he couldn't stand him, and feeling like I was being spied on every minute of every day. It just was too much for me. I gave him back his ring, and he took it. Maybe my father was right about him after all. He wrote me this beautiful love letter, which I'll keep forever, because it's the first one I ever received and it might be the last.

Besides, I am going to be a junior this year and he has already graduated. I want to be able to date other boys. I don't think I ever want to get married anyway. Everyone always tells me I will, but I really don't think so. Why should I? All married people seem so miserable and never have any fun. Some of the women who come in the store are only 22 or 23 years old, yet they look 50 to me. Their eyes are so dull and they have only two dollars to spend and they can't buy what they really want. They're holding crying babies on their hips and look so tired, so beaten down, like their lives are over and they know it and accept it. They never get to go anywhere or do anything. All they do is cook, clean, and take care of babies. I don't want to do that with my life. Maybe I'm talking myself out of it because, deep down, for some reason, I fear intimacy, but even when I look around at my parents, my aunts and uncles, none of them seem too happy. Everyone says in order for a woman to be happy, she must have a husband and children. But all these women have those things and they don't seem happy to me at all. I don't mean happiness like in carefree fun, but the kind of happiness that you can see in people's eyes when they talk. I don't want to be like them with their dead eyes. I want to travel and see the world. I want to be able to choose what my life will be and not take somebody else's life as my own. But if I do marry, first I have to straighten myself out, to figure out what's wrong with me, because the way I am now, I don't think anybody could ever love me, not really.

Besides, since that thing happened with Uncle Don, I have to be careful who I trust, because it really hurts when you think one way about a person and then find out they're not like that at all. People can fool you, and the fact that they fooled you doesn't hurt half as much as knowing they never really cared about you in the first place.

I'll just have to be more careful and not trust people so easily. Like my mother used to say, as smart as I am, I'm that dumb too.

I know what a coward I am because all Uncle Don did was kiss me, and yet I am acting like I was raped. I feel like that though.

September 4th, 1961

I'm very confused about what is the right and wrong way to feel. This has been a problem for me since I was very little. One time when I was about 7, my cousin and I were taken to a viewing for my godfather, Johnny. At first, I was afraid because I had never seen a dead body until then, but after a while though, I got used to it. I remember my cousin and I were sitting in the middle row, talking and laughing, not a lot and not loud, and my mother came up to us and said that I didn't have any respect for the dead and that I had no feelings for anybody but myself. I didn't even know what I was supposed to feel because I hardly knew him. I had only seen him about five times in my whole life. I remember I felt bad because I had done something wrong, but I also remember feeling that I didn't know what it was.

Ever since then, it seems whatever I feel, I should be feeling the opposite, or more or less. If I feel worried or sad, I'm told it's silly and I shouldn't feel that way. If what bothers other people doesn't really bother me, I am told I'm cold and don't care about anybody or anything. For a long time, I had no idea what I was supposed to be feeling, so I tried hiding all my feelings, but my mother said something must be really wrong with me because I showed no emotion. Then I figured I'd react to everything, and I was told I was thin-skinned, a crybaby, and too sensitive for my own good. When I feel something now, I always check with somebody to make certain my feelings are appropriate.

I often ask Mary Lou, "If so and so did such and such to you, would your feelings get hurt?" If she says yes, then I allow my feelings; but if she says no, then I try to stop them. Even if somebody else might think it's silly, as long as one person agrees with me, I feel okay.

I'm better at thinking than feeling. Thinking wrong is not as bad as feeling wrong because you can change the way you think, but you can't change the way you feel. I often try to put myself in another's place when they hurt. I can do it really well now. I think I can actually feel what they're feeling. The problem is that I feel sad more often than I ever have. I don't think my mother's right in saying I don't care about anyone because I do, and I think that constantly being aware of and sad about another's pain is ruining my life. I'm not mature enough to decide what pains of theirs to take on and which pains to ignore, so I just take it all on. That way I can't get into too much trouble with my mother.

The kicker was yesterday when I was telling my mother something about somebody at school, and she said that I shouldn't concern myself with other people's problems. And then she said that my problem was that I didn't have enough of my own problems to keep my mind occupied.

I do think the way I feel is terribly wrong. I just have never known how to feel correctly. And, by that, I mean like other people; and, by that, I mean like my mother. It isn't even the difference between right and wrong for confessional purposes. It's more about being normal.

My cousin says it's okay to feel whatever you feel, but that's easy for her to say. I remember once she made an outrageous statement, and all my Aunt Stell said to her was, "Rosalie, why do you think that way?" No name calling, no judgment. I think Mary Lou always has the right feelings and never needs to be told she's wrong.

If I listen to my mother, I am never to have feelings about myself, but always feel sorry for other people, but not all people, just family. I am to show emotion, but not too much, and am to show it only when she's in the mood. I'm not permitted to laugh too much when she's in a foul mood, or even to cry too deeply, because she'll usually say, "I don't want to see it. Go to your room."

Now I'm not even sure what I'm feeling and whether the feelings I do have are mine. No wonder I'd like to be an actress, because then I'd have a script and a director.

September 16th, 1961

We went to the Latin Casino for my 16th birthday to see Nat King Cole, who my father insisted he knew. We did go backstage and he told Mr. Cole it was my birthday, and Mr. Cole was very gracious, shook my hand, and wished me happy birthday. I doubt whether my father knew him. He's always trying to act like a big shot. He told me once that he knew Frank Sinatra and Dean Martin, and that they both came to his after hours club. He did have a club, though. I remember it because it had a slot machine which he allowed me to play when I was about 5. My father has the ability to make life special if he wants to. I remember when we lived on St. John Street, he would take my cousin and me to Clementon Park and he'd let us go on all the rides. My mother would be screaming at him not to take us, which I could never understand, but it probably had something to do with our not having enough money to eat. One time when he had the club, he bought me several little chicks at Easter, about four of them. Three of them died immediately, but the fourth one was lost, so he said. I remember I searched for hours everywhere, but never could find that chick. Now that I'm older, I think that chick died too, but my father didn't want me to feel sad so he told me it was lost. I love him for caring that I was sad and trying to protect me. He doesn't do that too often. He doesn't seem too interested in my being sad these days. He doesn't know I broke up with Bobby because he never knew we were going steady. But he has probably noticed Bob doesn't come in the store or hang around the outside, so he's probably figured it out. My father's no dummy, just a little odd. For instance, I think part of him likes that boys are interested in me, but he doesn't like it if they're too interested. I don't think he'd like it at all if no one asked me out, because then he'd probably think I was a "dog," which he always calls unattractive women, and he would be ashamed of me.

I think a part of him likes that I'm smart, but another part of him doesn't want me to feel too good about it. He always tells everyone that I have brains I haven't used yet, but then he tells me that I'm not as smart as I think. He also tells me I should become a professional and not have to depend on anyone. He's different from other fathers that way. Most of my friends' parents think they should get a secretarial job and then get married.

My father treats me like I'm a boy. I think it has something to do with me being the oldest and Vince being sick.

September 20th, 1961

I'm now a junior and I hate it already. One reason is that we have to be in school by 7:30 a.m. for the split session. The second reason is that I have geometry and chemistry lab, neither of which is easy for me. Abstract principles are very difficult for me to comprehend. Geometry is worse than chemistry with all those squares, rectangles, arcs, and degrees. I'll never use this knowledge in life, but I must take these courses because they are required. And the last reason, if not the least, is that Miss Goody-Two-Shoes is in my homeroom and up to her old tricks. She really hasn't changed much except now her breasts are bigger than her mouth. She still stays after classes and talks to the nuns; but she's better than she was in grammar school, which I think she has totally forgotten, because she treats me like her long-lost friend.

I talk to her because I'm polite, but once I don't trust somebody, I never trust her or him again. Like Don, who used to be my uncle. I barely speak to him now. Nobody seems to notice, but he does. I'm extremely uncomfortable when he's around, but not as uncomfortable as he is, I bet. I have to chuckle, though, because my father, who thinks he knows every evil that ever lurked in any male psyche, hasn't a clue. He's always putting down all my dates, and here is one of his best friends, worse than any of them. But I haven't said anything and I never will because all it will do is cause a lot of trouble and it won't change what's happened. It won't change what I feel still.

October 1st, 1961

I'm dating Kenny Tracy, who used to date Mary Lou, and he asked me to the Junior Prom. I'm only a little excited because once you've been to a prom, the second time doesn't hold the same allure. Kenny's blond, and he's popular. We've gone to the movies and he's fun, but he really isn't my type. My type seems to be tough guys. They're more interesting to me. While my friends seem to get into hot and heavy relationships, I look for things that are wrong with my dates so I can stop myself from getting involved. I think something is really wrong with me, but I have no idea what.

Of course, the fact that I'm not interested seems to make them more interested in me. I think boys like a challenge but I feel sorry for them, in a way, because they really don't know how much I don't want to be involved. I'm nice to them and friendly enough, but that's it. I guess I'm a late bloomer. I hope so anyway.

Bern and I go out all the time on double dates and we have lots of fun. After a date, we usually go to Cooper River where we park and watch the "submarine races." That's an *in joke*. We make out there. Making out for us is not the same as it was in my parents' time. All we do is kiss and hug. I'm sure some people do more, but that's all we do.

One time Bern and I were on a double date and I had a black bulky sweater on with a heavily padded strapless bra. I must have been moving around a little, when I realized my bra was down to my waist. So I said to Bern, "Let's go to the ladies' room." When we got out of the car and I showed her where my bra was, we almost peed ourselves laughing so hard. What bothered me is that my date never even noticed.

One time we were really bored and decided to walk to Broadway and get on the first bus that came. It let us off on a dark, deserted street called Cattel Avenue, and we had no idea where we were or what we should do. She was really afraid so I didn't have to be; and I would make these noises to scare her even more. She really is a good sport though. Finally a bus came and we got home. Where was my father when I needed him?

My father's car can often be seen around the school when the dance lets out checking up on me. I heard my mother tell him that if I was going to get pregnant, I could do the deed at intermission or right during the dance. I think he does it to remind me that he may be anywhere at any time, so I should always be on my best behavior. He acts just like the nuns and priests at the dances do when they come into the dance, whenever they want, sometimes midway through and sometimes at the end, to make certain we're not dancing too closely. As they say, when they separate us, "Let us leave room for the Holy Ghost." The Holy Ghost must not have been too happy the other night when a boy I was dancing with got an erection. We weren't even dancing that close. After, he wanted my phone number, but I didn't give it to him because his lack of control scared me. I have a lot of control. I'm sure the boys I date think I have too much, but I'm scared since that happened with my Uncle Don. If he could lose control like that, having known me since I was a baby and being like a father to me, how can I expect 16 or 17 year olds to be able to control themselves? I don't want to get pregnant because it would be a disgrace, my father would kill me, and everybody would say I'm just like my mother, and besides, I'm too young to have kids. It's ironic that a part of me wants to be like everyone else, yet the other part wants to be different. I figure that I may not ever be an interesting or mysterious person because I haven't had enough pain in my life. It seems all the characters I most like in books have led much more interesting, painful lives and, as a result, are possessed of a passionate, mysterious nature. So sometime last year, I pretended I was different than I really was, but it dawned on me that if people liked me when I was pretending, then they weren't really liking me, so I saw no point to it and stopped. I would someday like to be a passionate woman, a character, an enigma, an eccentric. I just love the sound of the word *enigma*.

This new guy I met, Rich, said I was an enigma and he also said I had depth. He is as handsome as a movie star, and I think he really likes me. He hasn't asked me out yet, but the grapevine says he's going to. He went to public school and he's two years older than me, so he has graduated already. He has a good job and is going to college at night, and is really a nice guy. He seems a little *too* nice for me though, but I'll wait to see. He looks like Richard Beymer in *West Side Story*. I loved *West Side Story* and anything else Natalie Wood is in. She's my favorite actress. People say I look like her, but she's much prettier than I am. They just say it because we're the same type, small and thin with big eyes. I'd love to look like her, especially in the breast area, and I'm quite flattered when people say it, but I really don't. There goes that truth ingredient again. Sometimes though if I'm nervous about giving a speech or walking into a party, I pretend I am her and everything becomes much easier.

Despite my lack of talent in both geometry and chemistry, I manage to get B's, but it did take a lot more effort than I'm used to expending. When I handed my father my report card, I was proud because I had to work so hard for those Bs. All he said, as he quickly glanced at it, was "Get those Bs up." And then he handed it back and walked away. Effort doesn't count with him, only results count.

My friends always tell me that their parents are pleased if they just do their best. I imagine that makes everything a lot easier. I always do my best every day, but it's often not enough for my parents unless it results in an A or a prize. I always feel that I have to go beyond what's comfortable for me, and I always agonize over whether my grades will reflect that. To do my best would be like recess.

The nuns can be really cruel at times. My chemistry lab class is held in a different building from my next class, which is Spanish. When I get out of chemistry lab, I really have to high-tail it in order to make it to Spanish. One windy day, I was about two minutes late. By way of explanation, I told Sister that I was coming from the lab, assuming she would attribute my tardiness to the fact that I had to change buildings. She said, looking at my windblown hair, "Did the lab blow up?" Everyone laughed, of course. It's beyond me why women who dedicate their lives to God find it necessary to embarrass people and then get such pleasure from it. It was a good line, though.

Recently I was laughing in another class and the nun just stopped the class and said, "Milissa, I want you to be happy but not *that* happy." I worry so much about controlling my anger and my tears and my big mouth that I've never tried to control my laughter. I'm not going to either. Maybe all these perfect people should learn to control their critical natures and their meanness.

I'm going to the Junior Prom with Kenny, and I'm going to wear the same gown I wore to Bobby's Senior Prom. My parents would probably buy me a new one if I insisted, but it seems like such a waste since my class hasn't seen the one I have. I'm always told I should be more practical and exhibit more common sense; but when I am, no one even notices. When we bought that gown, my mother and I discussed how it could be cut down, but we both knew that would never happen. Besides, this prom is not as important to me as the first one was. I'm like that. That's another one of my flaws. Once I've done something, the next time it doesn't hold my interest as much, if at all. Whenever I ask my mother who her favorite child is, she always says there's something special about the first, because everything is new for parents too. I think she's just being nice, though, because I always pick a good time to ask her. Everyone knows Vince is her favorite. I don't blame her or anything. I'd probably be the same if I had a sick child. I think she tells us all a different story when we ask. She probably says to my baby brother, "There's something about the baby." And to my sister, "Everyone said you looked like a doll when you were a baby, that makes you my favorite." Probably Vince doesn't even ask her because he doesn't have to.

I know my sister thinks I'm the favorite, but if I am, I'd hate to think what she is feeling and how she is treated. I think it might look that way to her because my life is exciting compared to hers, because of our ages, but eyes on you don't always look with admiration. She can't seem to understand that; and besides, she gets away with a lot more things than I ever did. She made a huge mistake the other day in the store and my father said, "Everyone makes mistakes." And I said, "Since when?" And he just sneered at me and walked away. Some favorite I am.

February 3rd, 1962

My mother takes pep pills, which are red capsules, and she gets them from a doctor. She seems to have a lot of pep, but I heard my father tell her she should stop because they're not good for her heart. She said he should be the one taking them and maybe then he'd get off his ass and do some work.

She's been taking them for a while and I'm starting to worry because she's taking them more and more often, and I think they're changing her personality. She's always bragging about herself and how she works better and faster than anyone, and how beautiful she is, and how this guy or that guy is interested in her. She was never like that before. Sometimes I feel like I'm her mother. I thought parents were supposed to worry about their children taking drugs, not the other way around. I don't think she sleeps too much either, and when she gets in her mood, it's worse than it was before. Her moods always scared me; but for some reason, they scare me even more now.

March 4th, 1962

Some kids are taking the SATs, but I'm not. I can take them next year if I want to. My father says, unless I go to Rutgers in Camden and live home, I can't go to college at all. I'm saying, "Okay, then I won't go at all." My mother says I'm only spiting myself. That's probably true, but if I go to college, I'll feel on the outside, just like I did in high school, if I live at home. I won't be able to be a part of anything again. He'll always want me in the store. Besides, I'm getting tired of school. I mentioned to my mother that I should quit, but she said that wasn't a good idea. Since she usually doesn't give me any advice, I figured this must be important and decided to stay. But it's going to be different in senior year because what's the use of studying so hard if I'm not going to college and my grades are never good enough anyway.

May 16th, 1962

The prom was fun.

July 7th, 1962

Our Lady of Mount Carmel has an annual carnival that I've been going to since I was a child. It's even more fun now than it used to be because lots of boys go, and we go on the Ferris wheel and dance. They sell all my favorite foods, such as cotton candy, popcorn, and apple sticks. It usually runs for one week during the summer, and then my friends and I go every night.

I'll be 17 in September and my cousin will be 18 at the end of the year. She's quite sophisticated and pretty these days, with her blonde hair and green eyes. We're planning our trip to the shore this year and I think, since we're older, it's going to be even more fun. Just like the carnival is.

July 18th, 1962

I'm now dating Ritchie Cragio. I like the way he compliments me for things I'm not, but would like to be. After he read some of my poems, he said I have a great amount of depth. He also thinks I'm interesting and mysterious. I do like him a lot. The only problem I have is that we do the exact same thing every week. It's kind of boring to somebody like me, who constantly craves variety. We go the movies, then we go to Cooper River. He doesn't even take me to get something to eat, so I told him about it. The next couple of times we went to a restaurant, but now he's back to the same old thing. I absolutely detest sameness. It just is so boring. My mother says that most people do the same things all the time. I don't know why I'm like this, but I am. It's not even a pretend thing to make myself appear more interesting to other people.

I never, ever, like to do the same thing. If we go to a dance one night, then I want to do something different the next night, like go to a movie or bowling, or to even stay home. It doesn't even have to be terribly exciting in itself, as long as it's different. When I read, I always read different kinds of books. I may read a romance novel one week and a classic the next. My favorite book is still *Gone With the Wind*, but since then I've read so many more that are really good. I read *Marjorie Morningstar* and loved it. I couldn't believe it was written by a man because he seemed to really understand the feelings of young women. Sometimes, if I like an author, I'll read all of his books. Usually though, I don't enjoy them as much as I did the first. I also read poetry. Mostly everyone thinks this is weird, but I like poetry. I particularly like Shakespeare's sonnets, especially the one that ends, "If this be error and upon me proved, I never writ nor no man ever loved." Is that not the most beautiful language ever written?

I think love should be overwhelming. It should be larger than you are, like in *Anna Karenina* and *Gone With the Wind*. I think I'm a romantic, and I think unless it's perfect, I won't settle. I don't want some humdrum gray life which "knows not victory or defeat." I want a life of plays, music, books, travel and romance. I don't know why. I don't know anybody who has a life like that or wants one either. I don't even know how you go about getting it. But, somehow, it just feels right. It's like when you see a certain fashion and you know it will fit you, and you also know that you will always love it, even if it is no longer stylish and even if no one else likes it. Somehow, you just know it's right for you. I hope I find someone to love and that the love I feel will be so great that I'll forget to look for his flaws and to protect myself. I know loves like that must exist.

Everyone thinks I'm a little nuts on this subject. My friend, Angela, falls in and out of love every week, and each time she's sure "he's the one." I'm not like that. I'm just not.

Mary Lou has met someone who goes to a different Catholic school, and I think she's serious about him. His name is Ron and he seems very nice. I think they may get married after high school. I'm beginning to feel more odd as each of my friends fall in love. I hope I don't have some deep psychological problems which render me unable to love. I don't think I do. There's no reason for them.

August 17th, 1962

My cousin and I are down in Atlantic City with my grandmother, and we are both experimenting with smoking cigarettes. My grandmother and her lady friends were sitting on the beach, and we sat far behind them, sneaking a smoke. Later, my cousin questioned whether I thought my grandmother saw the smoke, which I never even thought of. I guess we're not as adult as we'd like to be. Everyone gets all dressed up at night in Atlantic City and walks the boardwalk in heels. This is sometimes problematic because your heel can get caught in the boards. They do sell these rubber heel covers and they work, but I'm always losing mine. My cousin says some things never change.

We have decided to go to a fancy restaurant for dinner and there is one on Pacific Avenue we have our eye on. It's called Chumsky's, and it's Jewish. We both get dressed up and go. I look at the menu, which is not too large, and find that there are not too many foods I recognize, and I'm afraid to order anything I'm not familiar with because I can't eat something if I don't like the looks of it. This, too, has not changed. But there is veal cutlet, so we both order that and it comes with the house vegetables of peas and potatoes. It is bland for my taste, but it's okay, I guess. But when the waiter comes to take my dish away, remaining on this pristine tablecloth are about four peas. I look at them, my cousin looks at them, and then we look at each other and start to laugh. So much for sophistication. But it was a different experience to be eating in a fancy restaurant all by ourselves, one we will probably not duplicate soon.

We decide it will be really cool to stay up all night like adults, and we do. Staying at the hotel is this hippie-type guy who's expounding on God knows what, and we get the giggles. I always get the giggles when I'm sleepy, and this is sleepier than I've ever been. I can barely keep my eyes open. I think staying up all night is greatly over-rated, and I don't think I'll do that again soon either, maybe never.

My cousin, Rosalie, is out of school and working, and she has a really good job with the railroad. She's like an adult with her own money. Me, I'm still in school. I'll be going into my senior year soon in the newly built Camden Catholic School in Cherry Hill. We'll be transported by bus, which we have to get on Broadway at 7:30 a.m., and have a full course load, including gym, yuck. It will be nice to be the first graduating class from the new school. Even so, I'm not looking forward to it. I'm just so tired of school, so tired of tests and grades and rules; but my mother says I should graduate, so I will. I want to have more fun this year. I'm still working every day in the store, and I still can't join clubs or go to games. But I can go to basketball games because they're held at night.

High school is a lot different for me than grammar school, where I was a star. I'm only mediocre here, which I don't like because it makes me feel invisible. I'm not sure why, but it does.

I have worn the same uniform for three years (I have had it dry cleaned) because I'm still the same height and weight; and because, contrary to popular opinion, I'm not sloppy and I do take care of my things. Now, in the new school, we have a choice of the same jumper or we can get a pleated skirt, green and white, with a blazer. I could probably get one if I wanted, but it really doesn't matter to me because I only have one more year. My parents are very easy with money. All I have to do is ask them for something and they'll buy it. My friends like coming to my house because I have a stereo and a tape recorder into which we can sing and then play it back. My father bought the tape recorder so he could add muffled sounds to the blurry movies he takes. I also have a Ouija board which everyone wants to use, and a bookshelf with all kinds of paperbacks. My friends are always surprised when they come over and they ask why I didn't tell them I got this or that, but that would be like bragging.

My father is the only driver in the family and he has two cars and a truck. He just bought himself a Cadillac and has kept the Plymouth he had. I sit behind that Plymouth all the time and pretend I'm driving it because I can't wait to get my license. I can get a learner's permit when I'm 17, and intend to go on my birthday in September.

We have two guys helping us in the store, Matthew and Joe, and they both refer to me as *the queen*. They'll walk in and ask, "Where's the queen?" or "What's the queen doing?" My mother thinks they both have crushes on me, but you wouldn't know it. They're always teasing me, but she says that's one of the signs.

In our bathroom, there is a trap door which is eye level with the tub. Matt told me the other day that my brother, Larry, told him that if Matt gave him a dollar, he'd tell him what I look like nude. Matt said he told him that he'd give him a dollar if he didn't. That kind of thing. My brother is a royal pain in the butt. I'll be taking a bubble bath and be feeling really comfortable and relaxed and look up and see these eyes peering at me through the trap door. When I catch him, he starts laughing like a demon, and then I have to scream for my mother and he runs away. Because he's so bad, my brother has learned to run very fast. I think he could run in a marathon if he wanted. My parents have taken him to a psychiatrist, but the doctor said he's just spoiled and there's nothing wrong with him. You can't prove it by me though. There seems to be something very wrong with him. He steals all the time. He has found my brother, Vince's, cache; and as soon as my brother puts money into it, Larry takes it out. Vince does notice once in a while, but Larry keeps saying it wasn't him.

I keep my purse in my bedroom closet. The other day, I was missing $20, and my brother had a new bike. Now you don't have to be Einstein to figure this one out, but I decided not to accuse him directly. So I waited until he brought the bike into the house and said, "What a lovely bike I have." And he just got this huge grin on his face no denial could erase.

I don't care much about money. My mother says it's because I have everything I want, and I think she's probably right. My friend, Angela, can't believe that I'll tell my mother I don't need money when she asks. It's not even that I'm trying to be honest. I really just don't care about it. I probably will care about it some day, because adults seem to think it's very important, but I don't now. My friend, Jean, calls me a rich bitch, and I don't know why. We're not rich, but I guess it might seem that way with three cars, a store, and my mother has a beautiful diamond ring and a mink coat. I don't want people liking or disliking me because of money. I'd rather they like me for myself. When I was little and we had no money, I didn't feel poor, except that one time the nun made a spectacle of me in front of the whole class because my uniform was too short, and I don't feel rich now. I guess my opinion of myself doesn't depend on the status of my parents' financial situation, which has absolutely nothing to do with me. And besides, if people just like me because they think I'm rich, they really don't like *me*. And what if all the money is lost, will I then cease to exist? I just think it's better if people like me for exactly who I am, because I'll always be that.

August 20th, 1962

My parents have decided to put my brother, Larry, into Stratford Military Academy because he has no discipline, is not living up to his potential, and refuses to go to school. I think he may either be a genius or an idiot. I've read about kids who become bored in school because they are so ahead of the work being taught. I entertain this thought fleetingly. I'm just trying to give him the benefit of the doubt. They bought his uniform in which he looked very handsome. He's starting in September.

September 4th, 1962

I started my senior year today. It's nice being a senior and knowing you have only one more year. I've given up on winning prizes. There are just too many kids, many smarter than me. I'm still dating Ritchie, but I go out with others because we're not going steady or anything. Everybody seems to be preparing for college, marriage or a job, but me. I don't really care if I'm different; in fact, I like it. I don't try to be different, but I don't try to be like everyone else either. I think I just like to be the best me I can be. The problem with that is everyone else thinks I should be different, or better, or less of something, or more of something else. I'm not certain why because I always let people be who they are. The way I look at it is they have a right to be; and then depending on who they are, I also have a right to be friends with them or not, to like them or not, to love them or not. It seems that I have been surrounded all my life by people who want to change me. I think they want me a certain way so that I'll do what they want. My opinion is that if I'm not a criminal, or hurting anyone, or interfering with anyone's life, they just should leave me alone. But they never do. Rosalie says I should tell them off when they say hurtful things, but I don't because I think they're entitled to their opinions. And, besides, I always think I'm reading it wrong or overreacting to it. Because, in a way, I still think I don't feel or think like other people. I'll probably work in the store after high school since I have no skills and I won't be going to college. I'd still like to be an actress because I'd like to be able to express things without embarrassment, ridicule, or punishment.

I notice that people always want to know if I'm thinking about marriage. I don't know exactly why they care so much about what I do. They always say they just want me to be happy. They don't even know me really, so how could they know what will make me happy? It's not that I'm a phony, I just don't confide in too many people about things. I don't try to be different, or talk differently, or do things differently outwardly. I just keep all my differences to myself. What I show is *a part of me, but only a part*. It's ironic though how from just the little I show, everybody thinks I'm like them, when, I'm like no one really. Ritchie says I'm a chameleon, and I think that's true enough. Basically I present the part to each person that will be understood and accepted by them; but just as you couldn't identify a stew by eating only one potato, none of them have any idea who I am because of the parts of me I don't share. I seem real normal but I'm not.

September 16th, 1962

I got my driving permit today.

September 18th, 1962

Matt and Joe are teaching me how to drive. My father says he can't because he'll wind up killing me. The other day, Matt was outside the Plymouth, setting up some stupid barriers, and Joe told me to hit the brakes. I was nervous and I accidentally hit the gas, and Joe made a dive to the floor and hit the brakes with his hand. Matt thinks he saved his life.

September 20th, 1962

Matt and Joe took me in my father's Plymouth and made me go around this circular driveway three times until I hit a bush, and then we left, and fast. They're now saying they'll only teach me in empty lots or driveways. That could be a problem when I have to take the road test.

October 5th, 1962

Today is Friday and I was in English class when a friend, Ellen, turned to me and whispered my name. I turned my head toward her and did not even have an opportunity to respond when our teacher, Sister Wilfred, told me to stand up. I didn't stand right away because I wasn't sure she meant me because I hadn't done anything. But by her tone and the direction of her glance, I finally did stand and had to stand for the entire class. She'd teach for about 10 minutes, then stop and say, "Look at that hussy. She doesn't even have the decency to blush." Why would I blush? Then she would teach for another 15 minutes, stop and say that I was brazen. She kept this up the entire class and my legs and back were getting really tired, but I learned new ways to tune people out. I think this incident helped me to raise my "tune-out" abilities to an art form.

After class was over, Ellen felt badly because she knew I had done nothing but turn my head, and she wanted to go and explain this to Sister. I told her not to though, because Sister is about 99 years old and either won't believe her or will forget the explanation in under five minutes. Besides, it's Friday; and by our next class on Monday, Sister will have no memory of the incident at all, or me, for that matter.

Rumor has it that Sister Wilfred fell down an elevator shaft many years ago. I don't know if she acts the way she does because this is true or because she's 99. I don't even know if she's 99, but she looks it.

For weeks now, Sam Weatherly has been tying bells to his shoelaces. While Sister is teaching, he shakes his foot and they ring. He did it about 15 times and each time, Sister sent someone to the door to see who was there. One day, he did it about three times within a half hour period. Of course, we were all falling out of our seats laughing. This, she doesn't notice.

Well on Monday, she must have had a lucid moment because when Sam rang the bells and she sent someone to the door and no one was there, she decided to walk up and down the aisles to see who had bells. When she saw them tied to Sam's shoes, he stood up, blushed, and told Sister that he had absolutely no idea how those bells got there. And she believed him because, as she said, "He's such a nice boy."

If someone had told me this story, I wouldn't believe it, but it happened. I was there.

After my public humiliation, I went to the Friday night dance and my notoriety had apparently preceded me. No one knew what I had done, and when I told them, everyone was hysterical laughing. It's better to make people laugh, the way I look at it. So all night, every dance partner made jokes about my being a hussy, brazen, and how I failed to blush. It was a really funny story, but my back still hurt a little. It's easier to dance non-stop for an hour than to stand absolutely still, I've discovered.

I am a little fearful though because I don't know whether Sister Wilfred will remember the incident long enough to give me a demerit. If you get three demerits, you get automatic detention, and I already have one. Someone made me laugh in homeroom, and Sister Jose sent me to the lab, which was next door, until I "learned to behave." As I was sitting there, I really started to laugh because I could hear my cousin, Rosalie, saying that I'd probably be there for the entire year if appropriate behavior was the criteria for my return.

It does seem I'm getting in a lot of trouble this year. As a result, Sister Jose has made me hall monitor. I guess she thinks that if she gives me the responsibility of making sure everyone acts right, I'll act right in the process. If there are people who are misbehaving and I don't get them to stop or tell on them, by the time Sister returns, *I* get the demerit. I hate it. I'm not a rat, but I find it awfully hard to keep everybody in line. This is a job for Miss Goody-Two-Shoes, not me. I'm not a leader nor am I a follower. And if you have to be one or the other, I guess I'm in trouble.

October 14th, 1962

The most stylish hairdo this year is the flip. Everyone wears it, but it looks different on everybody depending on the length, color and texture of the hair. My hair has a natural wave, is thin-textured, but abundant, and does not fall naturally into a flip. I have to sleep with rollers every night and when I comb it out, it looks pretty good, but starts to deflate as soon as I leave the house.

I've begun to use warm beer on it to thicken the texture, which my father thinks is funny. It doesn't smell like beer once it's on your hair, and does give it some body. Now, it deflates at lunch.

My father has been critical of my hair for as long as I've been fixing it myself, maybe even before then, I don't remember. Every time he looks at me, he asks if I'm going to do something with my hair. This is quite disheartening when I've just spent a half hour on it.

I look at everybody at school and other than the curly heads, all of them seem to have these perfect flips which sway each time they turn their heads. Except me, that is.

Some of the girls even bleach their hair and say that it makes it thicker and more manageable. But I could never have lighter hair because my eyes and brows are too dark, and I don't want darker hair because then I'd look like all those older Italian ladies around the neighborhood who cover their gray. Their hair winds up looking like a helmet of unnatural color. So I'm stuck with this baby fine, dark brown, unruly mess whose flip flops more often than not. Another reason to feel different is to look different.

October 18th, 1962

For as long as I can remember, when my mother and father fought, she's told him how much she hated him. She keeps on throwing things up to him that he did. Once he apparently said that none of his children were as good looking as he, or that my brother, Vince, couldn't be his since he was disabled.

I heard a new story today. Apparently when my mother was about eight months pregnant with my sister, Catherine, my father beat her up and my sister turned and was a breech birth. I can't imagine that he could be that mean, but my sister was a breech birth and she does have weak ankles, which my mother blames on him.

She also told me that one time when Catherine was about three months old, my father came home drunk. It is when we lived in the other house. And they began fighting and the baby was crying, so he opened the window and threatened to throw her out unless my mother stopped. She must have stopped though, because Catherine's still around.

I don't remember those things. Sometimes I wish my mother wouldn't tell me them. There's nothing to be done about something that happened a long time ago. All it does is make me fear and dislike my father even more than I already do.

Sometimes I think that we learn how to behave when we're very, very young, and we feel things for which we have no explanation. I think that may be why I was always afraid growing up that he would hit her again, or that he really didn't love us, or that she would go away to the mental hospital.

I think I knew very young that my mother didn't have much time and didn't want to be bothered. She always tells this story, which she thinks is really funny, that when we used to go to my grandfather's, when I was about 3, and I would get tired, I would lay my head on the sofa and fall asleep standing up. When she used to tell this story, when I was younger, I thought how cute that was, but now I question, as I see other children climbing up on their mothers' laps, why I didn't do that. I also don't know why she didn't understand that I was tired and take me home to sleep, or why I didn't feel comfortable enough to even express it. And all the nightmares I used to have when I was small, I never went into her room, nor did she come into mine. And yet I remember my friends telling me that any time they woke up, their parents would go into their room and comfort them, or I even see it around the neighborhood with the little children. It's something I've never done though.

My mother says that I'm really stupid because I let people hurt me all the time, and she may be right. When I was about 3 years old and I would go to my grandparents', there would be about four people all sitting in chairs, who were relatives of my mother, and they would ask me to sing and dance. I remember thinking I was pretty good. After I did it though, they would give me the raspberry and I would start to cry. But then they would say they were only kidding and ask me to do it again, and I would. And they would give me the raspberry again, and then I would cry again. I often wonder whether I ever refused to do it or if the raspberries went on and on. I don't know why they liked to see me cry. I guess they thought it was funny.

November 1st, 1962

Italians are very superstitious, and my mother especially. They believe the usual superstitions about walking under ladders and black cats, but there are some that I think may be generic. Now that I've been friends with non-Italians, I often have to check whether what I think is based on nationality, or whether it is universal. For instance, my mother believes that if a bird makes doo on your car or person, that is lucky. How that's lucky, I can't quite understand. Also, if you drop a comb, you have to step on it for good luck. On Christmas Eve, we always have dinners consisting of seven fishes because that's considered lucky; and if you receive a Christmas card with the Three Wise Men on it, you're supposed to hang it above your door and make three wishes on the back which they believe will be granted within the next year. My family also believes that a fly in your home in the fall means prosperity for the coming year. When I was little, my mother used to tell me I was going to be very lucky in my life because I had hairy legs, and I believed her. Whenever you express a hope or wish, you're supposed to "knock on wood" so as not to jeopardize its fortuitous conclusion. And whenever you compliment somebody, you're supposed to say "God bless" so that they won't get the *maloiks*. The *maloiks* are headaches which occur as a result of someone else's envy. There are people around the neighborhood who actually pray over your head when you have the *maloiks*. They basically say three Hail Marys and three Our Fathers. If they yawn during the Hail Mary, then a female gave you the *maloiks*. And if they yawn during the Our Father, then a male did it. Annunziata, an old woman living on Cherry Street, does the *maloiks* for my mother almost every day. I'm the one that has to take my mother's bobby pins and sit while Annunziata mumbles all these prayers. My mother swears that the headache goes away though.

Also, if two people say the same thing at the same exact moment, you are to hook up pinky fingers and make a wish. We're also supposed to wish on the first star in the evening and any new place we enter. If you find any coins on the pavement or around the house, then you're supposed to pick it up and if it's heads up, then it means that you'll be lucky. This also applies to bobby pins. I remember once my aunt was cleaning our house and she was real happy because she found a bobby pin and then she found another one and another one. And then she thought she wasn't so lucky after all because she had to bend down each time and pick it up.

The way I look at it, most of these superstitions are attempts to make yourself feel better when something bad happens. I think this is good, in itself, and for this reason I often go along. I love being Italian. It feels very natural to me.

December 5th, 1962

I got my third demerit today because Sister Jose said I had eye makeup on, which I did and I didn't. I had mascara on last night, and some must have remained on my eyelashes, which are dark to begin with. Sister marched me into the ladies' room and stood by me until I washed off all "remnants of the devil." Somebody should tell her mascara doesn't come off with water, and that marching is for the armed services.

I have detention tomorrow. They give you a day's notice because there are no late buses, and someone has to come and pick you up. So I have to tell my father and when I do, he refuses. He says I got myself into trouble so I'll have to get myself out. So I call Johnny Locho, who drives and sometimes takes me to school in the mornings when I miss the bus, and he says he'll pick me up. Detention is a gathering of many delinquents in one room for an hour with no discernible aim. It is so stupid, words cannot describe it. Of course, my punishment at home is I'm not permitted to go to the Friday night dance for two weeks. One time last year, when my father was in a worse mood than usual, I answered him back and he said I couldn't go out for a year, and he never retracted it. At first, my mother told me I should ask him to reconsider, but I wouldn't do that because that would be like begging, and I don't beg. Well, although I didn't beg, I did lie and sneak out until he forgot about the punishment. A year is a long time. I do have this thing with my father now. I'm just so tired of his orders, threats, and ultimatums.

I'm 17 years old and I'm tired of being treated like a child. Quite frankly, I do wish him dead on occasion because I think his whole purpose in life is to ruin mine, and I'm sick of him. As far as I'm concerned, he, single-handedly, ruined my high school years by forbidding me to go to games, join clubs, and attend parties. I felt like an outsider for the whole four years, and the worst part of that is that I've never given him any reason to mistrust me. It's not my fault my mother got pregnant at 17. I think that, in addition to his mistrust and fear that I'll disgrace his name, his laziness plays a big part in his strictness because if he punishes me or does not allow me to engage in extracurricular activities, I'll be able to work longer hours in the store and he won't have to. I can understand why my mother was so fearful, when I was little, that I'd be selfish like him. He is the most selfish person I've ever met. A part of me is tired of school, but a part of me would like to go to college just to spite him. But I don't want to feel like a misfit for another four years.

Someday I'll return to school because it is a very natural place for me. It really is where I've experienced my greatest joy, not just because of the prizes won, but also because of the challenges met and the knowledge gained. I will always be a student in one way or another because that is who I really am. Other than being an actress, there really is no other profession that interests me enough, and I'm a little uncomfortable making a decision, at 17, about what I want to do with the rest of my life.

My problem is not disinterest, but interest in too many things. I really should have been born wealthy because I have a dilletante-ish nature and I would rather dabble than delve deeply into anything. I can see the difference between my sister and me in this regard. We both have an interest in astrology. I'll read about the various signs and houses and know enough to understand what it's about, but she plots charts, talks about degrees, configurations, and retrogrades. Nothing really interests me enough to exclusively devote all my time and effort. I hope I change because I'll never be successful at anything the way I'm going. In this way, I am like my father. I have taught myself to finish what I start; and instinctively, I know how much I need to delve into something to pass a test. But once my interest is satiated, I'm done with it. I don't think we can change our basic natures, but I think I need to have more discipline. I don't because most subjects came too easily and I never had to expend too much effort. I don't think it's that I'm so smart as much as I am a quick study and have a highly retentive memory. My mother's right about having to constantly entertain myself.

I go through things quickly, like the time I decided to read the dictionary. That lasted all of two months. But at least I still have the old faithfuls of reading, writing, dancing, music and theater. The only reason I'm slightly interested in working in the store is so I can read all day and not have to get up at 6 a.m. I think I'm a little lazy too, like my father.

December 10th, 1962

Today is my sister's birthday, and she is 11. She's having a group full of her school friends over when my father starts screaming out my name. I run to his side and he blames me for having broken the tape recorder because he's recording and is hearing nothing. I patiently point out to him that the reason he wasn't hearing anything was that he had not rewound it. I think he might have scared all the 11 year olds though, because they were all looking at me with really large eyes.

Following my sister's party, it was discovered that all my father's expensive fish in the aquarium in our living room were dead. He said nothing to my sister. This is getting curiouser and curiouser.

December 19th, 1962

My mother is always complaining that my sister and I don't help around the house, so when she went to Bingo, I decided to iron some clothes that were in the laundry basket. I like to iron, especially handkerchiefs, because they're easy. After I ironed and folded the clothes, I put everything back in the basket.

The next day, I saw my sister had the same idea, which I found insulting since I had already ironed them. So I was being a little smart mouthed with her, and my mother came in from the store. When she found out what was going on, she started to laugh and called everybody in from the store. Apparently, the clothes were dirty.

My sister's still mad at me from last week. She keeps borrowing my tops and stretching them out because she put on some weight. She's been going to Weight Watchers and is really miserable now because she's always hungry. So she took one of my new white turtlenecks, wore it, and left it hanging on the knob in the bathroom after I had told her specifically I didn't want her wearing it. So I was hollering at her and she looked at me with murder in her eyes, and said, with venom dripping, "*Go to hell.*" And I said, without hesitation or thought, "I've been there and they said to send the fat one down." She jumped up like a ferocious tiger, ready to pounce, and I ran into the bathroom and just managed to get the door locked before she reached it. She went back down the hallway and charged that door like a bull, and I was fearing for my life. Even though she's only 11, she's extremely strong. Fortunately for me, my mother heard her charging and came upstairs. I wouldn't come out until my mother assured me that she had her under control. The week before, my sister had punched me so hard in the back that I thought I'd pass out. When I went into the store to tell my parents, they both started to laugh. I guess it is funny because I'm 17 and she's only 11. But she carries quite a wallop.

Even after my mother told me my sister was calm, I waited another 10 minutes to come out. My cousin has told me, through the years, that if I'm going to continue to have such a smart mouth, I'd better get some brawn to back it up. I'm starting to think she's right. I hope my sister starts eating soon because, if not, I may never live to see my 18th birthday.

January 3rd, 1963

Matt took me to Motor Vehicles for my driving test, and he whispered before we took off, that I should stop at every corner, whether there was a stop sign or not, and look both ways. I heard him, but I forgot. And I failed. He said he's never, ever teaching anybody else to drive. I think he should have used the words "try to teach," somewhere in that sentence because I've never even been on a road except for that stupid test. Everybody thought it was funny, because the man from Motor Vehicles did not even let me try to park, I was so bad. And that's what they were so worried about, the parallel parking. I think I'm going to have to go to driving school. But I think I'll wait a while.

January 14th, 1963

I asked Ritchie to my Senior Prom early because I heard Mikey was asking me and I don't want to go with him. Although he deserves for me to hurt his feelings, after all the times he laughed at me when we were kids, I don't really want to, but I don't want to go to the prom with him either.

My good friend, Ellen, doesn't have a date yet, so Ritchie is going to introduce her to his friend, Frank. It would be fun to double date.

February 10th, 1963

Ellen met Frank and they hit it off, and he's going to take her to the prom. I've decided to get a white gown because, as I tell anybody who will listen, I'm not getting married so this will be the only time I get to wear white. They laugh when I say this, but I mean it. It's not like I'm against marriage, I just don't think it's for me. I think I'll ask Ritchie for a black orchid corsage. He should love that.

March 4th, 1963

I have been trying to behave myself this term because last term, my marks entitled me to be on the Honor Roll, but because of my demerits and ultimate detention, I received a D in conduct and was kept off. My father looked at my report card, ignored all the good grades, handed it back and said, "If you don't know how to act by now, you never will. No dance for two weeks."

So far, I've been pretty good. We listened to the cast album of the *Sound of Music* in class and I just loved it. But somebody said something that made me laugh, and Sister stopped the class to comment. But I didn't get any demerits.

We started a retreat at school and Father O'Brien spoke and told us that when we kiss, it should take no longer than it takes to say, "good night," or it's a sin. He also said that if you think about doing things, it's as bad as if you did them. I think Catholicism makes you crazy. Think about it logically, how can a passing thought of engaging in intercourse be the same degree of sin as actually doing it? It just makes no sense. And if we only let a boy kiss us for the second it takes to say good night, none of us would ever have another date. I make sure that my petting is always under control because, since Uncle Don, I don't trust men too much and I do *not* want to get pregnant. My dates probably think I'm frigid, and I may be, I'm not sure. I never let myself go, never, in any way, not even when I sneak a little liquor.

Speaking of control, or loss thereof, my mother seems to be taking more of those pep pills and I worry about it all the time. Somebody said they could affect her liver.

May 1st, 1963

I just found out that Ginny, one of the girls in my homeroom, is pregnant. Apparently the nuns are allowing her to graduate. She's going to get married right after school is out, and the baby will be born in the fall.

I'm pretty friendly with her but she didn't tell me. Apparently she hasn't told anyone. I did notice that she was gaining some weight, but not that much because she still wore her uniform. I'm glad they're letting her graduate instead of throwing her out. She is a really nice girl and has been dating her boyfriend for at least a year. Other than him, I don't even remember her dating anyone else. My mother says, "The good girls are the ones who get caught because they don't know what to do."

I wasn't certain whether I should say something to her or not, then decided not to because that way, if anybody asked me any questions in school, I can honestly say I don't know anything. Besides, I figured if she wanted to talk about it, she would have. I feel bad for her though, because she'll only be 18 and a mother.

She probably knows I'm naïve about sex, which I am, because I remember that about three months ago, she had a black and blue mark on her face and I asked her how she got it. By the way she answered me, I knew it was a passion mark. I just thought that you got them on your neck. I had one once. Luckily, it was winter and I could wear turtlenecks, because if I couldn't and my father saw it, he probably would have killed me. My friend, Angie, had one too; and when her father asked her how she got it, she told him she fell down the stairs and he believed her!

My girlfriends and I never talk about sex. I think everybody I know is still a virgin, but then I thought Ginny was too.

Last week, this married couple down the street was having this horrible argument out in the street which drew a crowd. I was sitting on the step minding my own business and they were really going at it. She kept calling him a cunt lapper and I had never heard those words before. That night, at dinner, my mother's brother, Uncle Bush, was over and we were all eating and I asked what it was. My poor uncle got really red in the face and started choking, so I figured it must be something really bad. My mother said we'd discuss it later, but we never did. That's why none of us know anything. Unless someone tells you these things, how are you supposed to know? After my uncle almost choked to death, I thought it best not to mention it again. I really didn't care anyway, I was just making conversation.

May 4th, 1963

My brother's been thrown out of Stratford. He flooded the bathroom. He's like my father in that ultimately he always gets his own way, so he's back, having learned nothing.

May 14th, 1963

We had our Senior Prom. Ritchie and I doubled with Ellen and Frank and it was really fun except that we had a car accident. No one was injured, except my head hit the ceiling of the car. There wasn't any blood or anything, so we just kept going.

I felt sorry for Frank though because he was driving his father's brand new car. It wasn't even his fault. I hope his family's not like mine. Around my house, you can get into trouble whether it's your fault or not. I still have to be home by midnight and everyone's going to the shore tomorrow, but I can't. My father says he's worried we'll get in an accident, which is funny in light of the fact that we already did.

My father actually interrogates my dates when they come to pick me up. They're all afraid of him. He asks them questions for about 15 minutes without as much as a smile on his face. That's why I'm always home by 12.

One guy I dated came over, and while my father was going through his 20 questions, we both happened to look at his socks, which were purple, and then at each other. I knew my father wanted to laugh, but he didn't. But I had to hear about it for about two months. He'd say, "Are you going out with Purple Socks tonight?" My father thinks he's a comedian, and sometimes he *is* funny. But not as often as he thinks.

May 20th, 1963

We had a scandal at school. One of the junior boys punched a nun. He was immediately expelled because, so we were told at assembly, there is no reason, no excuse that will be tolerated for this type of behavior. I didn't know the junior, but I know that nun, and the only thing that surprised me is that it's the first time it happened to her.

It's hard for me to understand how some nuns can be so mean. We're taught that they have dedicated their lives to God and they're brides of Jesus, yet they don't act anything like Jesus. I wonder if they are familiar with the part of the Bible which says, "Suffer the little children to come unto me, for such is the Kingdom of Heaven."

Even though most of them are fine, and some of them even exceptionally kind, it seems the bad ones are the ones everybody thinks about. That junior has become a rebel-hero at school, and I find that very sad.

May 26th, 1963

Everybody went out on Sunday, and my sister and brother were hungry so, being in my new domestic mode, I decided to make them Lipton chicken noodle soup. I saw this big green blob which, in my wisdom, I decided was foul and threw it out. Apparently that was the actual soup. It's been the subject of too many discussions since. I think I'm giving my mother enough material to do stand-up comedy. She's been telling everybody who comes in the store about the soup and my ironing dirty clothes. She's even throwing in things from my childhood like when I was about 10 and she told me to get a head of lettuce and I brought in cabbage, or how I used to say "husker" instead of "huckster." She's even bringing up that pie plate story that happened about 10 years ago.

They are funny stories and I do laugh along with everyone because I don't care about domestic things, and I don't care if I'm ever good at them. And I've learned to laugh at myself. I have to admit that I often do some dumb things, which I'm happy to say are quite amusing.

June 1st, 1963

We had to fill out a form for our graduation at the end of the month which required our middle names. Since I wasn't given a middle name at birth, I left it blank, and Sister gave me the form back and said, "No middle name. No graduation." She then said I should put my confirmation name down, so there it was again, Milissa Elisa Maroni.

When you're baptized, you have to have a Catholic name. That's why my name is spelled Milissa with the "i", and not Melissa with an "e". Of course, my parents could have spelled it with an "e" by giving me a Catholic middle name, but it seems my mother didn't have time for that. My mother bought me this beautiful Bible when I was about 7. It is the type of Bible in which you're supposed to record information concerning your Catholic life. But my sister, Catherine the destroyer, wrote our names in it, and listed herself first. Even though it's obvious that the names should be recorded by age, and even though it's my Bible, she did it anyway. This is the reason we don't get along. She has been destroying my property for as long as I can re-member. I didn't even make a fuss, because to do so would be futile in that there was no way to erase the information already recorded in ink.

I think this type of behavior has been instrumental in my lack of concern about *things*. Why get attached to them when they're here today, gone tomorrow (sometimes today). I'm still convinced that I'll be 80 years old and will not have one material possession because either my mother, brother, or my sister will have destroyed it.

My friends all have report cards, dolls, toys, and mementos from when they were really little. My mother isn't sentimental at all, so I have absolutely nothing. Not even a sample of my hand-writing, which I would like to see so I could know what all the fuss was about. They leave you alone about handwriting in high school as long as they can read it.

I've been reading a book on handwriting analysis and it says that you can tell certain characteristics by handwriting. I was shocked to discover that handwriting is very personal and that each person has his or her own, like fingerprints. It explains why I couldn't write the way the nuns wanted, but what I can't understand is why everyone else could.

June 21st, 1963

I graduated today as a member of the first graduating class of Camden Catholic High School. I waited in trepidation for my name to be called. There had already been some snickering when one kid's middle name was Valentine, but when my name was read, the bishop must have thought it was a typographical error and just read Milissa Maroni. How lucky can you get?

July 5th, 1963

Other than going to the shore with my grandmother, there was nothing special about the summer except that being around the house all the time has brought to my attention how deeply my mother has changed. It's like she's going through a teenage rebellion or maybe a mid-life crisis, I'm not sure. She's only 35 and I think she might be getting tired of being married. I just hope she's not tired of being a mother.

She gave me one of her pep pills and I couldn't sleep for two days, talked all the time, and couldn't eat. And I think she takes a lot more than one every day. I swore I'd never take another one because I didn't like how they made me feel. My mother says my father doesn't like them either.

My father is getting bored with the business and is talking about us running the grocery store while he runs a bar off of Westfield Avenue in Camden. No one wants him to do it, but I think he'll do it anyway because he always does exactly what he wants whether people support it or not. In a way, I guess that's admirable, but he hurts too many people. My mother keeps saying she'll leave if he does it, and he tells her there are three doors so she'd better pick one. My mother's right though. They have a good business at which they're making money, and she can't understand why he always needs to have change. She really doesn't understand because she likes sameness. Even though I understand why, being like him, I think he has to learn to take her feelings into consideration. After all, he is a married man with four children. He's starting to go out again too, so my mother thinks he has a girlfriend. They fight a lot, but he doesn't hit her now. Thank God.

September 7th, 1963

I went to a dance in Oaklyn, and when I came home my mother was sitting outside on a folding chair. When I got close to her, I could see she had a gun in her lap with which she said she was going to kill my father. I got her to come into the house. Not long after, he came home too. She aimed the gun at him and I stepped in the middle of them to stop her. She didn't shoot anybody, but my father may owe me his life. My sister said that it was at that moment, when I placed myself between my mother, that gun and my father, that she knew for sure how truly stupid I was. I told her that I knew my mother wouldn't have shot me, and she asked me whether I ever considered the gun could have gone off accidentally. I hadn't. Perhaps she's right. That was stupid.

September 17th, 1963

I'm finally 18. My sister really hates my guts and I'm not quite certain why. I think it's because she thinks I get all the attention. She keeps on saying that she wished Mary Lou was her sister because one time, when she went to Mary Lou's house with me and admired all of her dolls, Mary Lou said that she could take anyone that she wanted. She was quite impressed with that and keeps on throwing it in my face. I hesitate to remind her that

I have no dolls to give anyone. But I don't think that's the real reason. I think there's a lot of tension around here and I think we're all feeling it.

There doesn't seem any way to talk my father out of pursuing his newest toy, and I can see that my mother's becoming more and more frustrated and unhappy.

October 1st, 1963

My mother tried to kill herself today. She had to go to Cooper Hospital. She was extremely depressed and felt that she had nothing to live for. I slept with her the entire night for fear that she would get up and try it again before she went to the hospital for psychiatric treatment. Now I know how mothers feel when lying next to their newborns.

October 4th, 1963

I went to see my mother at Cooper Hospital today and she was painting The Last Supper by numbers. She hardly talked, and I could see that she was extremely depressed. The doctor says that if she doesn't respond to the medicine and psychotherapy, she's going to have to have electric shock treatments. She doesn't know it yet.

October 10th, 1963

They gave my mother an electric shock treatment today, and when I went to see her, her temples were burned. I wanted to burst out crying, but I couldn't. She was in a daze. She knew who I was but I just felt that she wasn't completely there. This would be bad enough, but knowing that her own mother went out of her mind makes it doubly hard.

October 20th, 1963

My mother's home from the hospital and she's really different since she had those shock treatments. My father, true to form, is showing absolutely no sensitivity to her.

November 6th, 1963

Although my mother is adamantly opposed to my father buying the bar, and even though she had a nervous breakdown and almost killed herself, he's still intent on doing what he wants. He is merely waiting for the financing at this point.

December 4th, 1963

My father bought his bar and is spending a lot of money to fix it up, and my mother's furious. It's going to be called the Black Orchid and he's going to open it in April 1964. My mother keeps on saying she's going to leave, and he doesn't seem to care. I can understand her frustration. She works very hard and has the full responsibility of the house and children, and he is acting like a single man with no responsibilities.

She's much changed since her shock treatments. There's a cold stillness to her that was not there before. It really worries me.

April 3rd, 1964

My father opened his bar and he doesn't work in the store any more. He sleeps all day and goes to the bar every night. He usually comes home drunk and they're always fighting. My mother accuses him of having a girlfriend and he denies it. My mother is starting to go out at night too. She gets all dressed up and leaves about 9 p.m. and comes home 3 or 4 o'clock in the morning. It's odd, when I was little, she used to tell me everything. And now that I'm older, it's like I'm her enemy. I don't like her going out at all, and she knows it. I think she's dating some-one because she whispers all the time to her friend, Frannie.

It isn't that I care about my father's feelings. It's just that I don't want to think about my mother going out on dates with other men. She told her brother I'm jealous because she's attractive to men. It really isn't that though. I feel betrayed like I did with my Uncle Don.

All my life I have placed my mother on a pedestal. In any arguments she had with my father, I always took her side because I felt sorry for her, because she had had such a hard life and I tried to help her carry her burdens. I felt sometimes like I was her best friend, her husband, and her mother all in one. It feels like she's doing this to me too, not just to my father. She doesn't even tell us she's going out and when she does, she doesn't tell us where or what time she'll be home. If there's an emergency, we have no way to reach her until she gets in. It seems to me that there has been a dramatic reversal of roles.

I think those damn pills are changing her personality entirely and I don't like it. I can't say anything either. I've tried, but now we don't speak to each other. You'd think it would be hard not to speak to each other, working side by side all day, but it isn't. I hate that I withdraw from people, just like my mother, when I'm angry or hurt, but I can't help it.

I feel as if I'm in her way, especially because I'm 18 years old. I think she's looking for a boyfriend and doesn't like the idea of *me* any more. She's always bragging in the store about how sexy men find her. I don't want men to find her sexy. She's my mother, for God's sake.

Another thing that scares me is that if my father comes home when she's out, he'll kill her. He has called her on the phone and I just tell him she's asleep; but if he comes home, there's no hiding the truth.

I think my grandmother knows she's going out too, and it's really embarrassing. I don't think my mother realizes that no matter how bad my father is, he is still my grandmother's son and she is always going to pick up for him.

I don't approve of what she's doing and I can't help how I feel. All I heard my entire life was how hard her life had been and was and how she never did anything wrong, and how she was a virgin when she conceived me. She was like the Blessed Mother or a saint to me, and now she is this stranger I don't know, and she doesn't seem to be thinking through what she's doing or care if she hurts anybody.

April 20th, 1964

My sister told me that my mother introduced her to her boyfriend in a bowling alley and that he's really ugly. She said my mother told her not to tell anyone so she only told me, and I was extremely upset. It's hard not to have any control over your life. Everything they are doing is going to have repercussions for all of us. I never want to be in the position again where my life is being determined by the actions of people who don't seem to care.

It's also definite that my father has a girlfriend. She runs the bar for him. My father's good fortune in life is that he always gets people to do his work.

May 15th, 1964

My mother found a receipt for a bedroom set in my father's pants and it wasn't bought for us. It's been hell around here. I'm afraid because I sense that something is going to break. And people wonder why I don't want to get married. I don't think anyone is considering what effect this is having on all of us. I feel like I have no parents. All the parents I know constantly worry about their children and try to protect them from the ugliness of life. My parents present it to us daily and expect us to have no adverse opinions. I know I have problems, but I'm never going to take any victims because of them.

Sometimes I feel like I'm an orphan and that I have no one to turn to. There's a saying I read once, "Oh, Lord, your ocean is so large and my boat is so small." That's how I feel as I wait momentarily for the finale hoping, at least, it doesn't end in someone's death. I feel rejected and betrayed and that my whole life has been nothing but a mistake, that I'm a mistake. I pray all the time that everything will be all right, but I don't think it will be. Sometimes I don't think it will ever be again. I think I've always been afraid and I think I always will be.

May 17th, 1964

Today I sat in the store and swore to myself that no one would ever do this to me again, that no one would ever trap me in his web and make me feel that I had no way to exit. Whenever I have made promises to myself in the past with this kind of emotion and resolve, I have kept them. And I know I'll keep this one too. For as long as I live, I'll never let myself get in the position where my life depends on anyone else, because I don't think you can depend on other people. They're usually only interested in their own pain and vindictiveness, and they never seem to think about what effect their actions will have on others, or maybe they do think about it, but don't really care. It doesn't matter though, the effect is the same.

June 6th, 1964

My mother left today. I came downstairs about 9 a.m. and my Aunt Boot told me she never came home last night. I asked if she left a note and was told that she hadn't. Apparently she is mad because of that bedroom set. I just started to cry. My tears came from a place so deep that I was afraid they would never stop and I was afraid they would because when they did, I knew I'd have to look at it and I didn't want to look at it ever.

After I cried for about an hour, they told me to go into the store and I asked my aunt what I was supposed to tell people. She said to tell them that my mother went away for a few days. I really could have been an actress because everybody believed everything was okay, even though my eyes were swollen and red from crying.

My father and Aunt Boot are talking and making no effort at shielding any of us from the truth. And the truth, according to them, is that my mother is nothing but a whore and they don't understand how she could have left because even whores don't leave their children. My father is saying he has no intention of begging her to come home, and my aunt is screaming that he can't expect her to take on all their responsibilities.

July 18th, 1964

The days have now become weeks and she isn't home, and he doesn't ask her to return, and my aunt does take on all the responsibility. But she's carrying on a lot about it and my father is tired of hearing her, so he leaves too. He is now living with his girlfriend and says, "It's easier for me to stay there." For whom, I think?

My aunt is not too happy about all of this and is making no effort to conceal her rage. As far as she is concerned, we are not her responsibility, and she's right. But she runs the store and makes our meals anyway. Every morning, she wakes my brother, Larry, up for school by calling my mother every foul name known in the English language, and she strings them together in such an original fashion that she creates images one would rather not see. "You mother is a fucking whore. I hope they find her dead with a prick up her."

When she's waiting on customers, they talk about the type of woman who would leave her children. They speak of us as if we are inanimate objects which have been placed on the wrong shelf. No one speaks to me of it, and they act as if it is nothing. But it is something. Mothers should never leave their children, never, not under any circumstances.

August 15th, 1964

I really can't take it. I'm a nervous wreck all the time. My aunt's always screaming and singing that song, "The Party's Over," with demonic glee as she tells us why we can't have certain things from the store. "You're spoiled brats," she says. "Your parents spent money like drunken sailors on leave, and now you're going to have to learn the value of things."

She acts as if it is our fault. I do think it might be my fault, but what did my brothers and sister do? I can't stand to look in their faces, so raw is their pain. Vince doesn't understand everything, but understands enough to be so very sad. My brother, Larry, is acting out at every opportunity, and my sister, soon to be 13, is devastated, as if puberty wasn't bad enough. I don't know what to tell them or how to comfort them, so I just try to be kind. It seems my grandmother and I are the only ones who are.

August 30th, 1964

My sister came home all agitated today because her friend's mother asked how my mother was doing, with a sneer, like she was laughing at her. My sister wanted to know what she's supposed to say to people. I tell her to say that she's doing fine and make sure that she looks at the people straight in the eye when she answers. "You didn't do anything wrong. You don't have anything to be ashamed of. Don't let them see your hurt." I can only tell her to act the way I am acting. I don't know if it's the right way or if there is a right way, but it is the only way I know.

September 15th, 1964

My mother sent me a birthday card today and she signed it "Love Always. A mother's love never dies." How could she sign it that way? I find it hard to believe that you could love someone and make them suffer like this. It's even harder for me to understand because she knows what it feels like, her mother having to go to the hospital when she was my sister's age. That's all we heard about our whole lives, that losing a mother was the worst pain in the world. If she knows, how could she have done it? How can she continue to stay away?

January 18th, 1965

I went to see Dr. Glass, our family doctor, today and asked him if he would give me nerve pills, and he wouldn't because he says I'm too young to start taking medicine. But everything I eat comes up. I hate to get up in the morning. I feel as I would imagine a prisoner of war must feel, every day fearing what new pains will be inflicted, sure of nothing but the fact that there will be pain. I cry all the time.

I've thought it through and I do think it's my fault because, before my mother left, when she was dating, I wasn't talking to her. But even if that isn't the reason, I feel like I failed her. It seems that from childhood I tried to keep my mother happy, to take some of the burdens off her, and now I feel it wasn't enough. Now I feel *I* wasn't enough.

I'm petrified to have to go out in the world, because if my parents could hurt me like this, I can't imagine what strangers will do.

My aunt locks the door between the store and the house every night when she goes home, because she doesn't want us getting any snacks. I have the key to the front door, but my Uncle Tony stands guard and every time I use it, he tells my aunt, and there's hell to pay the next day. It just isn't worth it, so I go buy snacks on Broadway and keep them in my room for us.

November 8th, 1964

My brother, Larry, wants a soda from the store, and I tell him no. He gets a rubber band, stands on the stairs, and is shooting straight pins at me. They are going into my arms and my legs, and every time I try to get the rubber band from him, he threatens to shoot the pins in my eyes; and he's a little nuts, so I fear he will do it. Eventually he stops and is lying on the floor watching TV. I call Catherine over and tell her to hold him down, which she does, and I straddle him and start to pound. I never thought I was capable of such anger, and afterwards I feel really badly because he's had enough hurt, but I had bottled up all that frustration and fear during his siege on the stairs and really couldn't help it.

December 25th, 1964

I hate the song "I'll Be Home for Christmas," and I'll hate it until the day I die. I was shopping the other day when it started to play, and I had to walk out of the store because I just couldn't hold back my tears. The words are just the way I feel about my mother.

As if Christmas without my mother isn't bad enough, the heater breaks and my aunt says she's not getting it fixed because she has no money. My poor sister has bronchitis and no one seems to care. Maybe we'll all just die, and then we won't be a problem to anyone. My father bought us watches and he expected us to be grateful, but I wasn't grateful at all. My mother sent some things over too. Sometimes when something is overwhelming to me, I have this ability to talk myself through it, and that's what I did this Christmas.

January 14th, 1965

I can't imagine how anyone will ever love you if your parents don't. Whenever I call my father because *his son* is out of control, he says, "What do you want from me?" and hangs up and goes about his business. He doesn't come over, he never even calls later to check. I want him to act like a father, that's what I want from him.

People are sympathetic to my mother because they say they don't know how she took it, my father is such a cold-hearted bastard. I want to tell them that while he may be a bastard, we're not, and she left us too, but I don't. Family business must always stay within the home, I've been taught. Besides, I'm too ashamed.

February 13th, 1965

My sister and I are going to see my mother. I told her she mustn't tell her that my father left too. My sister wants to because she thinks our mother might come home, but I think it will only start trouble. I'm afraid my mother will kill herself or, if she confronts my father about it, he'll kill her.

The way I see it is that too much time has passed for her to just come home now because she wants to. She's going to have to get permission from the "man who calls himself my father." He comes to visit every other day for about an hour or until my aunt starts in on him and gets on his nerves. It must be nice to have somewhere to run, some haven, someone to whom you can turn. The only ones who seem to understand or care about what we're going through are my Aunt Estelle and my cousin Rosalie. They get mad about what's going on around here and I know they feel sorry for the kids. In theory, everyone seems to think it's such a terrible thing, a mother leaving her children; but, in actuality, we are expected to act as if it is the most natural thing in the world to be abandoned by your parents. When my mother left, it felt like the devastation caused by an earthquake when everything is turned upside down; and when my father left, it felt like the dreaded aftershock which sometimes causes even greater damage. Sometimes I think her leaving was worse because we were still numb when he left; and sometimes I think his leaving was worse because we were already in such pain and he had to know what it would do to us, but he just did it anyway.

February 28th, 1965

I don't think my mother really has a clue as to what's going on around our house. When my sister and I went to see her, she spent the whole time blaming my Aunt Boot for assuming my father's responsibilities which she thinks hasn't helped the situation at all. My Aunt Boot and my father are constantly blaming my mother and while they are all blaming each other, not one of them has taken one moment to explain to us why we shouldn't feel unloved, rejected, and abandoned. Not one moment. Not one act of kindness.

March 3rd, 1965

My father wants to give my sister and me his girlfriend's old bedroom set which was replaced by the new one which broke up our home. I refuse it and everybody screams and yells, but I don't want it. I tell my father I'd rather sleep on the floor than in that bed. My aunt is screaming and carrying on like a crazy lady, but I won't take it, and I tell her if she wants it so badly, she should take it herself.

Easter Sunday, 1965

My mother fixes up this huge Easter basket for us which sends my aunt on a rampage about how my mother left and is not worried whether her children are eating, going to school, or safe. All she's worried about is an Easter basket. My aunt's right, but it is a wonderful Easter basket.

October 4th, 1965

My sister still thinks we should tell my mother that my father left, but I still disagree. It's amazing that she's listening to me on this. She usually pays me little mind. I think we must feel, all of us, as soldiers feel or, like comrades, fighting the same enemy. We need each other. We don't hug or anything like that because that's not our history, but we need to know that some things are still the same, that some people remain, and that this God awful pain is shared.

December 10th, 1965

I will always hate fish sticks because Fridays have become fight days around here. My father usually comes around dinner time, and when my aunt starts in on him about the money and the responsibility, I'm usually chewing on a fish stick. Catholics are not permitted to eat meat on Fridays, and I can't refuse to eat those fish sticks either because that provokes my aunt even more.

I worked all day last Saturday in the store and asked her for a piece of steak. She gave me this slimy green piece of meat which I refused to eat. Histrionics followed. The wind-up was that she refused to give me anything to eat. Luckily, my Aunt

Lissa was over and ordered pizza. Sometimes things have a way of working out.

It's getting so that if I desire something, I'd rather pay for it than hear her carry on. I gave my grandmother a dollar two weeks ago and told her I wanted to buy some ravioli, and she told me just to take them from the store because it was my store, but I said I'd rather pay for them so I wouldn't have to hear my aunt.

My grandmother doesn't like that my aunt denies us food. Before my aunt goes home at night, she sets the heater way down (she finally did get it fixed). My grandmother stays with us for a couple of hours; and before she goes home, she sets the heat back up. Whenever I felt anonymous in my life, I used to daydream about performing some heroic act so people would notice me. But I've learned that sometimes heroes are simply people who do the right thing every day with love. My grandmother is a hero.

September 16th, 1966

My father bought me a 1966 Dodge Polara for my 21st birthday and it's beautiful. It's orchid with a black top and white interior. I knew he was getting me a car. I did finally get my license. I went to Millie's Driving School.

Before I got it though, he had my Uncle Jack bring over a yellow Chevy something or other. It was so small, I thought I was on a scooter. My uncle kept on saying it was a creampuff and I was getting angrier and angrier. After all, I deserved better having worked for peanuts since I've been out of high school, not to mention assuming his parental responsibilities.

When my uncle and I pull up in front of the store, there is my Polara sitting with an orchid on the steering wheel. I don't think I ever saw a prettier car. It's fully equipped, but then my father always does buy the best. My father can best be explained by a line in *Cyrano de Bergerac*, "Ah, but what a gesture." He is good at the surprises, buying the best, or any act that can be completed in a short amount of time so as not to tax his interest level. But the everyday, mundane, responsible tasks are not to his liking, and my father never does anything that is not to his liking, and he never considers any needs but his own.

October 1st, 1966

Months have now turned into years and she's still gone. I showed her my car and she liked it. She said she hopes my father pays for it. That's another thing about my father, once his attention is no longer held, he just walks away like he did with the business, like he did with us. He bought me the car on credit in my name. He is awfully interested in my having good credit. My suspicions tell me that it is not an unselfish desire though, because he just purchased a pizza oven on my credit without my knowledge or consent. It doesn't matter though, because I wouldn't have had a choice.

November 4th, 1966

My brother, Larry, is now 10 and he is really out of control. He doesn't understand why he has to go to school if he's bored. Sometimes the nuns actually come over and get him in the morning. They probably feel sorry because my mother's gone. He's always in trouble with them though. Last week, he climbed on the roof of the school and proceeded to shoot arrows at the nuns. They never figured out who it was because he can run faster than anyone I know. The only reason I knew it was him is because he thought it was really funny. I think something is really wrong with him, despite what the doctors have said, because he just doesn't seem right to me.

Yesterday he was riding his bike and broke his front tooth. It made me cry, the loss being so permanent, and his teeth having been so perfect. All this blood was gushing out of his mouth. All I told him to do was to put ice on it. I would like to comfort them but I don't know what to say. I think deep down I think there are no words of comfort, and I don't think I know how to comfort.

January 4th, 1967

I don't usually tell anyone my mother and father left because I'm extremely embarrassed and I know they'll wonder what's wrong with us that both our parents left. But the people around the neighborhood know and they talk about it as if it is the most normal thing in the world, but I don't think it's normal. No mother I've ever known has ever left her children, not even in the books I've read, and I've read thousands of books. Mothers are supposed to protect their children, even give up their lives for them. They're not supposed to walk away. In one way though, I'm glad people don't think it's anything that important because I never want anyone to pity us. It's just so hard for me to understand why no one seems to understand the depth of our suffering, how insecure it makes you feel, how lonely, how sad.

I think they're just some words to them, "Her mother left," whose import doesn't register because no one has a frame of reference for it. There are certain pains which are universal and which everybody should understand, like grief, loneliness and rejection, so they should know that abandonment would cause these emotions. I don't expect them to know my feelings of inadequacy and failure because they'd have to know my role in this family, and no one ever knew that. For a long time, I didn't know it.

Sometimes I think I'm not going to make it, and sometimes I don't even care.

February 1st, 1967

It really got to me today, and I told my father that I hated him and I was leaving too. I don't remember what started the argument, but I do remember what ended it. He said, "Only rats desert the sinking ship," as he walked out the door to go to his home.

March 5th, 1967

Throughout this ordeal, I have wanted to leave. But I couldn't. As I'm getting older, I realize often there is more than one reason why we do things, the black and white issue again. Even though I wanted to, I couldn't leave because I was scared to live by myself, I was afraid that I couldn't earn enough money to support myself; but, mostly, because I couldn't do that to my siblings. Knowing how it feels to be left, how could I possibly ever leave?

March 18th, 1967

My aunt wants my sister to quit high school and work in the store, and my sister screams at her that she hates her guts and there is no way she is quitting school. My sister's tough, and tough is good around here. Tough is necessary.

My grandmother's always talking to my father in Italian. Unfortunately, I can't follow it all, but he doesn't get mad, just quiet and pensive. I think she's picking up for us, telling how he shouldn't have left and how he should let our mother come back, that children need their mother. I know enough Italian to get the gist. He hangs his head, but he doesn't do anything, he doesn't change anything. If he is ashamed of himself, and he should be, then he should make it right, because what people think and what they feel is not as important as what they do.

My siblings are innocent in all of this, and I doubt there will ever come a day in my life, no matter how old we all are, that I will not see them as wounded children. And, no matter how mad I may ever get at them, I will remember this time and forgive them, for it is criminal what my parents have done out of weakness, insensitivity, and selfishness. My mother keeps saying she didn't mean to hurt us, and every time she says it, I wonder if shooting anyone accidentally renders them less dead.

I know my father is no good, but we are good. I know my father doesn't really love her, but we love her. And I know that she didn't expect it to go on this long, but she should have known my father would never have begged her to come back. After all, she was married to him for 20 years.

She should have known that if my aunt hadn't taken over, he would have just expected me to. Every day I worry about something happening to my aunt because she's always clutching her chest and screaming. I wouldn't know how to do this. And as bad as my aunt is to us at times, at least she stayed. For this I will be forever grateful. I think we know she loves us despite her ranting and raving.

I went to a movie with Anne, a girl from the neighborhood, last week and she became very upset because we were one-half hour late getting home. I tried to calm her down because I thought she was overreacting, and she turned to me and said, "Just because you don't have anyone home worrying about you..." I didn't hear the rest. I had heard enough. When I got home, I cried myself to sleep, mainly because what she had said was true. The next day I told my aunt and her eyes filled with tears, and she said that that was a horrible thing to say. It's always been like this. The Maronis could brutalize you beyond endurance, but no one else was ever allowed to hurt you. She screams, she deprives, she hates the responsibility, but she takes care of us, and that's more than anyone else is doing.

March 23rd, 1967

My grandmother was very upset that I told my father I hated him, and I apologize to her because she's my hero. But I do hate him. I won't always, but I do now. One thing I know is that I will never go to another movie with Anne, and I will never forgive her. Another thing I know is you have to be very careful in whom you confide because people can be really mean.

Palm Sunday, 1967

I went to see my mother today. I had been praying to St. Jude, the apostle of the impossible, who is known to work miracles in cases despaired of. And, today, for some reason, I feel everything is going to be fine.

Good Friday, 1967

My uncle called. Apparently my mother fell asleep in bed with a lit cigarette and her mattress caught on fire. She had been drinking. I went to the emergency room at Cooper Hospital and my uncle had a real attitude, as if all this is my fault. He probably thinks I should leave my father's house and tend to my mother's needs. Fortunately, my mother didn't get burned. She just suffered smoke inhalation. Now all the good feelings I felt on Palm Sunday are dissipating. I don't think anything's ever going to be better.

May 16th, 1967

I think my mother and father are talking because there's a lot of whispering going on around here. It seems to be good.

Why is it they're all so willing to share bad news, but the good is said in unshared whispers? I don't ask anybody though, because I can't afford to get my hopes up, only to have them dashed again.

It's odd that I have written poetry my entire life, and yet, throughout this two year ordeal, I haven't written one thing about it. I just think it's too painful. Part of me is hurt, another part understands, and another part will never understand. But I'll always be different because of this. It has changed me somewhere very deep inside, but I don't know exactly how.

Sometimes I worry that my mother will find out that my father left too, and sometimes it's hard to believe that she hasn't. She only lives about two miles away, and my Uncle Bush, her brother, comes to see us all the time. He's the only one in her family who likes my father. I wonder if he tells her what's going on, and I also wonder whether she asks. And I can't believe Larry never told her. He doesn't listen to me at all.

She doesn't act as if she knows though. I would think she'd be furious and insist on coming home, but that hasn't happened. She is drinking a lot and probably still taking those stupid pills, so maybe she blocks it out, or maybe she really doesn't know.

I still try to protect her though. Her sad eyes get me every time. She's living like a queen compared to us, and yet I feel sorry for her. I guess I'll always feel sorry for her because in many ways, she's like a wounded child too, and there are many things with which she can't cope. I know that. I've always known that.

Until I die, I will love my mother, for ours is a special bond. I fell in love with her when she used to sing "Baby Face" to me. Her eyes weren't so sad then, but looked shining with love. And once I love somebody, I don't think I can stop.

June 18th, 1967

And then she came home. She was uncertain of her welcome, so my Aunt Lissa went out to the car and escorted her in. She went to my grandmother, fell on her knees, and asked my grandmother to forgive her, she was sorry. Everyone cried. It was over, that which would never really be over. I looked at the faces of my siblings, Vince, now 20 years old, Cathy, now 16, and Larry, now 13. All of them so relieved their pain was over. I was happy they still possessed the innocence to believe that.

We talked for a long time, and she was angry that we had not told her my father had left, or how badly we had been treated by my Aunt Boot. She "would have done something had she known," she said. I told her it was my idea to keep it a secret because I was afraid she would be too hurt and do something foolish. Even though she said we should have told her, somewhere deep inside, I knew that not telling her had been the right decision.

January 4th, 1968

Things were different for a while. Things returned to normal, so we thought.

We didn't forgive her because there was nothing to forgive. She did what she had to do. "I didn't do it to you or because of you," she said. "I didn't mean to hurt you." I knew I would never be the same because the pain had been too great on too many levels for far too long.

But I couldn't hate my mother. She was my mother. I vowed I would never sign my cards _Love Always_ because I no longer believed love is forever. She always said a mother's love was the greatest love. I still believe that, but the belief petrified me for if the greatest love could reject, desert, and abandon, what would those lesser forms of love do?

July 1st, 1968

We ran the store for over a year, but large supermarkets made its continuance unprofitable, so she closed the store, fought with my Aunt Boot, and threw her out of our house, and my grandmother went too because it was her daughter. My mother pleaded with my grandmother to stay, but she wouldn't. She went across the street and never came to our house again. I used to visit her every day.

No one put me in the middle, not the woman who was supposed to love me above all others, nor the woman who had.

October 6th, 1968

I then went to work as a secretary in a law firm. When I had been employed about six months, my mother said she was getting an apartment in the fall of 1969, and it only had two bedrooms. There were other words I heard like "it was about time I was on my own." "We couldn't live there any more." Words that echoed in my ears like some distant truth I didn't want to face, but had to.

December 17th, 1968

My sister and I discussed getting an apartment together.

February 19th, 1969

My sister told me today she has decided to go to college, and she will be living with my mother.

September 16th, 1969

My grandmother died today on my 24th birthday. Her heart had been failing for a long time. My cousin and I had been at the hospital all day. Someone had bought me a birthday cake, so we went to my house to have a piece. As soon as we arrived home, the phone rang telling us my grandmother had died. We had only been gone for about 15 minutes.

I wanted her not to die on my birthday. I prayed all day that she wouldn't, but she died at 10:30 p.m. She almost made it, this woman I could hug, this woman who accepted me unconditionally, this woman who returned my love with a quiet devotion and depth. I was really depressed following her death. Within a five year period, I'd lost my mother, my father, and my grandmother, who had been my mother and father. I knew that if my parents had been different, I would not have had to endure so much pain, but I also knew that if my grandmother had been different, I would not have endured.

I would be alone soon and I dreaded it, but I had no choice. I wonder if I ever had any real choices. Although I was afraid, part of me welcomed being alone, if only for the honesty of it.

September 16, 1970

I survived the year. I've been so lonely. The silence is so deafening that I cannot bear it. I do everything humanly possible not to have to go to my apartment. It's so small. I fixed it up nicely, but I hate it. I am expanding my horizons. I started college, and I'm doing really well. It serves the purpose of keeping me occupied. I'm always looking for things to do, places to go. I want to make friends and lose myself in others because I do not know how to do this.

My role in the family was always so well defined. It always seemed that I was taking care of my mother and Vince and Catherine and Larry. Now, there is no one. Only me. I do not have a clue who I am. So long have I pretended to be different from what I was that I don't know what's real or what's pretense.

October 13, 1970

Today is Mary Lou's 25th birthday. We're still friends. She has two sons. She seems happy. She's still Mary Lou, but I am no longer Milissa. Sometimes, I'd just like to close my eyes and never wake up. I don't know why either. There is nothing terrible about my life. I like my job. The people are like family to me. I'm getting promoted. They are very complimentary about my work. I love my boss. He's a lawyer, and only a few years older than I. He is just a wonderful boss. I made some new friends here and at school. I date a lot. No one special. I travel. But I'm intensely lonely. And it makes me very anxious. I'm afraid a lot.

November 3, 1970

I am taking a psychology course and I have determined that I have "free-floating anxiety." I probably should talk to a psychologist, but I can't afford that. I am learning to "gird my loins," and pretending to be different from what I am. I should be good at it—I've done it most of my life. I asked my father for some help. I told him I was depressed. He said "What do you want from me?" Some things really don't change. All I know is I feel different—alienated—alone.

December 1, 1970

I go to my mother's every Sunday for dinner. She and my sister are getting closer. I feel really left out. I miss my grandmother so much. I asked a priest how she could have died on my birthday. I wanted to know what I had done so wrong to her. I never wanted to hurt her. She was, and is, my hero. He didn't know. I thought priests were suppose to know everything. I don't go to Mass anymore. A few weeks ago, I went out to a party and came home really late. I went to my mother's for dinner and thought I'd go to the 6 o'clock Mass. Given that I was tired and slightly hung over, I thought it was quite a sacrifice. The sermon was about original sin. And the priest said that we are all sinners and all evil—no matter how much we try. So I decided not to try anymore. What's the point. Quite frankly, I'm really tired of hearing I'm not good enough. No one has to say it to me anymore. I got it. The tape is always playing in my mind. I'd still like to know what is really wrong with me. Why I was never good enough.

I have to make certain people don't really know me. I am hiding my vulnerabilities from them. Some people call me "aloof" or "stuck-up." My mother says I always had an "air" about me. Someone said to me the other day after we had been speaking that she had been hesitant to speak to me because I seemed, ready for this, so "self-contained." I took it as a compliment. It means the ruse is working.

I have to do this because too many people trample on my vulnerabilities. I want to be invincible, or at least, seem so. To seem so is enough for now. I am afraid if I don't do this they will destroy me.

ROSEMARY BURGO

AND THEN……

My father, Lawrence Maroni had several additional businesses until his sudden death in February, 1982. While driving home from my Aunt Boot's house, he crashed into a wall. It was never determined whether he had a heart attack and consequently the accident or the accident and then a heart attack. He was survived by his estranged wife and four children.

My mother, Marie Maroni, remarried long after my father's death. She finally lived a life of leisure. She kept a lovely home and had peace and laughter in her waning days. She rarely suffered from the depression which had haunted her youth. She loved the casino, her children and grandchild (hopefully not in that order). My last memory of her "up and about" was Christmas 1994. She had Christmas dinner and we laughed. I gave her a music box of a mother and daughter, which played "Who Can I Turn To?" It made her cry. In the beginning of 1995, she was suffering from the "flu." It turned out to be lung cancer. She went to the hospital on the first Thursday of Lent and died on Good Friday. A week after she entered the hospital, she went into a coma so she never heard her diagnosis. This was a blessing.

My brother Vince, lived with my mother until her death. Subsequent to her death, he had a colostomy and spent three months in a nursing home. He lived with my mother's husband for a couple of years after her death, then me. He hated living with me. He wanted to be on his own. I dealt with the Division of Developmental Disabilities attempting to get him supervised housing and he went to live with a private family. He came to feel part of the family—like an older brother and developed skills he had never needed. On September 11, 2005, he had a stroke which left him unable to walk, confining him to a wheel chair. He lived in a nursing home until his death on October 12, 2006.

My sister Catherine married in 1977 and had one child who was born in 1980, my parent's only grandchild. She remains married.

My brother Larry is still alive and unmarried.

My cousin Rosalie married in 1996 and remains married.

My Aunt Boot developed Alzheimer's disease and passed away on March 12, 1996. Her nieces and nephews survived her.

My Aunt Stella, after a lengthy sickness, passed away on October 19, 2004. Her daughter Rosalie survives her.

All of my father's siblings have passed. My mother has two sisters and two brothers who are still alive.

My friend, Mary Lou, married a few years out of school. She has two sons, three granddaughters and one grandson. She remains married.

My friend Carla married a few years out of high school. She had two sons. In March 2002 she passed away from uterine cancer.

POSTSCRIPT

And now in retrospect, it is so understandable. All of it. The why of it. The when of it. It didn't happen one day, it happened over a period of time when I took the "best" of me and buried her. I went on to be highly educated. I did live a life of culture. I did live my dream. The only problem was that I was an imposter. I fell in love a few times. I knew those great loves I had dreamed of as a child. It was an exciting life filled with interesting people.

And then it began, the moments "in between" commitments "in between" vacations "in between" relationships, those moments when I felt something was missing—a sadness. Those moments grew into days and months and years and I could no longer conceal the pain from myself.

And then my mother died. It was sudden. She had the flu, or so we thought. But she wasn't getting better. We had a wonderful relationship. I adored my mother. I took care of her, and she took care of me. I would never be the same following her death. She died on Good Friday. She was in a coma, and I sang to her. I rubbed her arms and I kissed her. I never did that when she was up and about because she wasn't comfortable with physical affection . She opened her eyes one day and mouthed the words "I love you."

When my mother died, I felt as if someone had kicked me in the stomach. I actually bent over from the unseen blow. And I became a different person, everyone said. But the truth is I finally became me. The journey was very long and extremely painful. Anger followed tears to be followed by more anger and more tears. But, finally, at the journey's end, I found a peace and strength which, not withstanding my successes, had eluded me.

When I was finally strong enough, I had Missy tell our story. She told it well. She told it fairly. She told it courageously. I found myself forgiving and understanding, or, should it be, understanding and forgiving.

It's very simple really. They all did their best. It wasn't always right or enough, but it was their best. And they loved me. Of that I have no doubt.

And the irony—the real postscript—is that when I finally allowed my inner child to emerge—it was she, who I had buried so deeply, who had the courage to journey back and show me the way home.

JOURNEY FORWARD

Unable to accept the unacceptable.
She sought control over the tiny corner she inhabited.
They could silence her voice but not her head
They could access her good, but not her best.

They could say black was white and she'd nod,
Ostensibly in accord
As her mind strove to remember.
It was a time of fleeting pains and longer joys
When, despite their words, she knew she was special,
The doubts creeping in silently, slowly,
As they continually bade her to forget.

I am, she shouted,
Each time she failed to eat their desires
And her writing spilled over the pages of conformity.
I am, she whispered,
To all those who would listen,
To a God she knew loved her
As she was.

She fought the battles chosen for her,
Her only weapon being the purity, simplicity and joyousness of
that place
She vowed they would never touch.

As with a precious jewel, she buried it so deeply
That none had access.
But through the years she felt an unease
Like a lost memory
Begging to be remembered,
A missing part growing each year
Until it demanded freedom
Too large to be held unheard.

And spilling out, she wrote
The story of bondage and freedom,
Of love and indifference,
Of joy and pain,
Of that place, none had touched.
The jewel unearthed, the voice heard, the tear shed.
I am, she whispered, I am
With their screams finally being silenced
By the whispers of her truth.

AUTHOR BIOGRAPHY

Rosemary Burgo is a second generation Italian-American who was born and raised in South Jersey. She earned a BA degree in English Literature from Rutgers University and a JD degree from Rutgers Law. She is admitted to practice law in New Jersey, Pennsylvania and the United States Supreme Court. She currently holds a New Jersey license in Real Estate. She is a published poet and has served as an Adjunct Professor of English at Burlington County College.

1391179

Made in the USA